PITT LATIN AMERICAN SERIES

JUAN PERÓN AND THE RESHAPING OF ARGENTINA

Juan Domingo Perón in June 1974, three weeks before his death. (Courtesy Juan Carlos D'Abate)

Frederick C. Turner and José Enrique Miguens
EDITORS

JUAN PERÓN
AND THE
RESHAPING
OF
ARGENTINA

UNIVERSITY OF PITTSBURGH PRESS

Published by the University of Pittsburgh Press, Pittsburgh, Pa. 15260
Copyright © 1983, University of Pittsburgh Press
All rights reserved
Feffer and Simons, Inc., London
Manufactured in the United States of America

Library of Congress Cataloging in Publication Data

Main entry under title:

Juan Perón and the reshaping of Argentina

   (Pitt Latin American series)
   Includes index.
   Contents: The cycle of Peronism / Frederick C. Turner—Evita and Peronism, 1946-1955
/ Marysa Navarro—The return of Peronism / Wayne S. Smith— [etc.]
   1. Argentina—Politics and government—1955-   —Addresses, essays, lectures. 2. Perón,
Juan Domingo, 1895–1974—Addresses, essays, lectures. 3. Peronism—Addresses, essays, lec-
tures. I. Turner, Frederick C. II. Miguens, José Enrique. III. Series.
F2849.2.J8   982'.064   82-4870
ISBN 0-8229-3464-7   AACR2

for
Frederick
José Ignacio
Kit
Liz
Marcela
María
who all lived in Perón's Argentina

Contents

Preface

This book, and the friendship that lies behind it, began in 1972 and 1973, when grants from the National Science Foundation and the National Endowment for the Humanities allowed Frederick Turner to carry out research for a year in Argentina, where he worked closely with José Miguens. In turn, a Fulbright fellowship in 1976 brought Miguens to teach at the University of Connecticut, where the plan for this book took definite form. It had long seemed to both editors that the activities of Juan Perón and the movement that he led have been repeatedly misinterpreted and misunderstood, not only by Argentine partisans but even more by foreign scholars, who have tended to treat Peronism in terms of the models, concerns, and national interests of their own countries rather than in terms of its actual roles within Argentina. A book written by specialists in different aspects of Peronism, one combining insights from both Argentine and foreign academics, one where the various contributors would actively read and comment upon each other's essays, seemed to be in order, and the present volume is the result.

Among the authors of the ten chapters in this study, four were born in Argentina, four are native North Americans, one is Brazilian, and one was born in Spain. The group includes sociologists, political scientists, and historians, as well as a career diplomat and a Peronist politician. Their perspectives are diverse. When each author was asked to write and contribute an original essay to this volume, no rigid conformity was imposed; authors were selected simply on the basis of the depth of the research that they were known to be carrying out on their topics. Yet, now that the chapters have been assembled, it is clear that a continuity does indeed run through them. While they are frequently critical of particular policies or orientations of Perón and his followers, the authors are strongly convinced of the importance of Peronism, not only within the history of Argentina but also for the light the movement can shed on social processes and political decisions in other parts of the world as well.

The book has taken on an added significance in light of the 1982 war over the Islas Malvinas, which the British call the Falkland Islands. With the U.S. government supporting the British position on these islands in the

South Atlantic, and with the loss of life associated with the British bombing of airfields on the islands, the sinking of the Argentine cruiser *General Belgrano* outside the two-hundred-mile war zone, and the bloody land battles on the eastern island, Argentine public sentiment has naturally veered sharply against the United States. While the public policies of Argentina and the United States are currently at odds, while Argentine patriotism has been aroused and Argentine public opinion has grown highly critical of the United States for siding with the enemy after the casualties of war have become heavy, it is nevertheless reassuring to be going to press with a book jointly conceived and written by Argentine and North American scholars over the past six years. Social scientists can help decision makers to appreciate the complexities of political processes, social movements, and historical causation, and they may do so most effectively when the academics of different nations share their insights and conclusions together. Now, during the Malvinas crisis, it is easy for scholars (like the Anglo-Argentines living in Argentina) to feel frustrated and embittered, impotent in the face of events which seem to be controlled, to the extent that anyone can control them, by others. Yet, in the long run, scholarship can crucially inform the context in which social and political decisions are made. The collaboration among intellectuals of different nationalities that lies behind this book will outlast the conflict that covered the headlines of the world press during the year in which the book was being prepared.

The debts of the volume are large. It would never have become possible without substantial, serendipitous financial assistance from the National Science Foundation, the National Endowment for the Humanities, the Fulbright Commission, and the University of Connecticut Research Foundation. Among the colleagues who have read over the drafts of the manuscripts or greatly encouraged the joint efforts that brought them into being are Pedro David, Robert Potash, James Buchanan, Ronald Hellman, Hugh Clark, and Betty Seaver. To Francisco Di Blasi, who translated three of the essays from Spanish into English, a special note of thanks is in order. Carlos Miranda and Carlos Marcelo D'Abate worked hard in acquiring the illustrations.

While each author takes responsibility for the errors or omissions in his or her essay, the editors bear the burden not only for their own contributions but also for the volume as a whole.

JUAN PERÓN AND THE RESHAPING OF ARGENTINA

FREDERICK C. TURNER

The Cycle of Peronism

Juan Perón was far more than the most important leader of Argentina in the twentieth century. In many ways, he was a prototypical figure of this century. His ideals were far grander than his lasting achievements; he sincerely wanted to improve the welfare of the least privileged members of his society. Yet, despite distributionist policies that made the poor unswervingly loyal to him, his economic initiatives spurred inflation and undercut the economic growth that might have been the surest aid to the lower classes in the long run. In his private life, in his sexuality, for example, not only was he at various times a chaste widower and a traditional Latin American ladies' man, but also he was open and cheerful throughout in his relations with women, with a degree of candor that became fashionable in the United States only in the decade of his death. In his political relationship to women, he was extraordinary: his second wife was the most politically influential woman in the history of the American republics, and his third wife was the first female chief executive in the Americas. Unique in some ways, prototypical in others, Perón established a highly controversial record over the five decades of his public career, a record that has often been interpreted in narrow or partisan ways. Perón should be far better understood, not only in his native Argentina but also in other nations of the world.

In political terms, the Peronist phenomenon again affirms the ambiguity of democracy. On the one hand, Perón having been elected in 1946, 1951, and 1973, in a multiparty system, with between half and two-thirds of the vote, Peronists can make a tangible, irrefutable argument for their leader's popular support. A careful analysis of the March 1973 elections by Manuel Mora y Araujo and Peter Smith in one of the following chapters shows just how widespread was the support for Perón's return. Mora y Araujo and Smith correlate voting patterns and socioeconomic indicators for the 479 *departamentos* of Argentina, finding an important negative correlation between the level of development and support for Peronism which was not evident in Perón's first election in 1946. By 1973, Perón was able to win especially strong backing not only in industrial, working-class districts, but also in the least developed and most impoverished rural areas. Far from being supported only by industrial workers or by people in certain parts

3

of the country, Peronism in its triumphant resurgence proved once again to be a multiclass movement that, in drawing major support from rural as well as urban areas, overcame the much-publicized split between Buenos Aires and the interior of the country.

On the other hand, if democracy is interpreted as "a government of laws and not of men," then the highly personalistic Peronist regimes do not fit that interpretation. From 1946 to 1955, and again in 1973 and 1974, legislators hastened to change the laws of Argentina to fit the predilections of Perón. Indeed, as Marysa Navarro demonstrates with underlying pathos in her chapter, perhaps the greatest failure of Peronism was its *verticalismo*, its extreme dependence upon one man who could not be replaced after his departure or death, a man to whom vast loyalty and allegiance were given by the common people, enhanced in considerable part through the personal devotion and activities of his second wife, Evita.

If one interprets democracy as involving a skepticism toward absolutes, the Peronist movement was again far from the fundamental tenets of democratic faith. The late Kalman Silvert, who knew Argentina well, has summed up one element of democracy by saying, "We do not know, nor have we ever known, whether we are right or wrong. . . . This rock-hard unsureness is the best reason for establishing a contained and relativistic system of governance that has as its first principle the separation of what is changeful and secular from what is permanent and sacred."[1] Peronists have believed absolutely in Perón, his movement, his policies, finding them at best to be part of what Silvert calls that which is "permanent and sacred," and therefore incapable of being lessened or bargained away through democratic compromises with those individuals and those sectors of Argentine society that have not shared the Peronist faith.

In the creation of this faith, Perón's charisma, his gift for eliciting emotional commitment from those who came in contact with him, was certainly one important element. Several of the authors represented in this volume have heard and watched Perón's speeches from tightly packed crowds or have marched past him beneath the reviewing stand, each time with the surprising, arresting feeling that his eyes were for a time riveted upon theirs during the encounter. But Perón cannot be dismissed as just one more charismatic, "mesmerizing" historical figure. Noting that Perón increased the share of national wealth going to the workers from 38 percent in the early 1940s to 46 percent in 1948, Juan Corradi quite rightly points out that the workers' support for Perón came from a rational perception of their interests rather than simply from their admiration of Perón's special gifts of leadership style.[2]

During Perón's eighteen years of exile after 1955, the durability of support for him came, therefore, not only from his charisma but also from his redistribution of income in the workers' favor during his first terms as

Perón (right) as a cadet at the Argentine Colegio Militar, where he was an excellent boxer, equestrian, and champion fencer. (Courtesy Wide World Photos)

FREDERICK C. TURNER

president. This created what Gary Wynia analyzes as the "incomes policy" problem, one that various governments during the intervening eighteen years then found it especially difficult to deal with because of the popular expectations that Perón awakened and increased. Although it created serious problems by focusing attention on distribution rather than on productivity, and encouraging inflation by printing more and more money to meet popular demands, the incomes policy of Perón's first presidency built a foundation for his political support that, according to surveys, lasted intact until 1973.[3]

In one sense, therefore, tragically but importantly, the experience of Peronism in Argentina shows that neither good intentions nor charisma can assure the success of a leader or a political movement. One of the continuing appeals of Peronism was that it had a heart, not just a head, that it was concerned with people and their needs in the present, rather than — like Stalinism or the economic strategies of the Brazilian military in the decade after 1964 — sacrificing present living standards for future economic achievements. Its advocates saw the citizens of their times as people with present needs to be met, not as producers in a quantitative game plan. When, for example, a Peronist slogan said *Los únicos privilegiados son los niños* (the only privileged ones are the children), it stressed the need for immediate aid to children, thus evoking the desire that so many of us have to see our children better off than ourselves, the hope that our children will enjoy a period of greater material and emotional security than did we. The failure of economic growth under the first phase of Peronism meant that the next generation had a lower standard of living than it might have had, but even that failure could not overcome the people's loyalty toward Peronism engendered by the psychologically satisfying ideals that the movement continued to uphold. By the early 1970s, when a series of other governments had proved unable to achieve stable and impressive growth, it was only natural that many Argentines should look again to Perón for leadership. At least the slogans and the ideals of his movement had remained intact, and the people's hopes had not diminished.

Besides generating a powerful symbolism associated with egalitarianism, Peronist policies had already had other effects. By 1949, Perón had brought a large segment of the working class into positions of economic and political strength from which subsequent governments could oust them only temporarily. However, as I have noted, by stressing redistribution rather than the creation of income, by neglecting the agricultural sector and fiscal reform, and by spurring inflation, the economic policies of the three Perón presidencies — in the 1940s, the 1950s, and the 1970s — undercut the long-term possibilities of raising incomes in Argentina. While Perón's rhetoric and personal aura created a fervent and dedicated following, his personal qualities also gained him inveterate opponents, establishing a pattern of continuing confrontation rather than compromise after his ouster in 1955 and his death in 1974. For other nations, the general lessons of Peronism stand out clearly: government officials should care for the welfare of the underprivileged by raising their economic productivity as well as by redistributing benefits in their favor; they should use the all-too-rare qualities of charismatic leadership to build broad coalitions, institutions, and a consensual acceptance of the rules of the political game so that balanced, progressive policies can be continued after the charismatic leader passes from the scene.

The critics of Perón stress the dangers of these periods of transition when a major leader leaves office. They claim that Perón's failures in 1973 and 1974 were like his failures before 1955, that he had learned nothing of value in the interim, and that death saved him in 1974, just as exile had done in 1955, from witnessing the collapse of the economy while he was still in office. Of the 1973–1974 period, and the subsequent government of Perón's third wife, Isabel, for example, a satirist has recently written:

> His rule was short and his death was well timed. . . . His followers could always believe that he might have saved his country had he lived longer. Just as the 1955 coup enabled him to escape the consequences of his misrule, so his death rescued him from those same consequences in 1974. The responsibility for saving Argentina was shifted to his widow, a woman whose previous professional experience had been working as a hostess in clip joints like the Panama City night club where she met her husband during the early days of his exile.[4]

Would Perón have been able to change Argentina more constructively had he lived another five years? The answer is not as clear as the above quotation suggests. Wayne Smith, a former officer in the United States foreign service and hardly a "follower" of Perón, suggests in his chapter that if *anyone* could have done it, Perón was the most likely candidate, that his untimely death prevented the continuation of the coalition that he was working to fashion. H. S. Ferns, a British analyst, was even more optimistic. Writing at the time of Perón's death, he found that, with inflation moving downward and export prices rising, and with a social accord backed by labor, business, and the armed forces, Perón had bequeathed the nation "a recipe for success which only a super-abundance of idiocy [could] destroy."[5]

More broadly, Perón was neither as uneducable nor as cowardly as his enemies have portrayed him. In 1955, it was said, he left before the house of cards tumbled down because he feared for himself and preferred to live in luxurious exile, leaving the myth of his generosity intact and the way open for a possible return. Actually, a more central motive, as Perón himself

FREDERICK C. TURNER

explained, was the desire to keep Argentina free from a destructive civil war; before coming to power, he had witnessed the carnage and desolation in Franco's Spain at the conclusion of the Spanish Civil War. During the years of exile, most of which were spent in Spain itself, Perón did come quietly to modify the distributionist wage policies which were the hallmark of his first presidency. When he returned in 1973, for example, he rejected the widespread, irresponsible calls upon him to double all wage levels for the workers. Instead, he gave everyone a wage increase of about forty dollars a month, which aided those most in need but did not wreck the economy, as it typically doubled the wages of the domestic servants in the homes of the Buenos Aires rich, but made little difference in the salaries of the Peronist leaders of the working class whom Marxists derided as the "trade union bureaucrats."

Perón's failures were more prosaic than stupidity or cowardice: unfortunately, like so many of us, he failed to understand economics and relied far too much upon his own judgment. To the faithful, it is sacrilege to talk of a charismatic figure in these terms, but charisma, with all its appeal to the populace, may by its very nature cause a leader to overlook the necessity for careful planning and limitations on his own leadership. Perón understood the warm, human issues of political symbolism and the generation of mass support, not the colder constraints of budgeting and sacrificial strategies for economic growth. He allowed and by example encouraged too much personal enrichment on the part of those in government service, and by printing money to meet public demands he heightened levels of inflation that cut into the buying power of everyone. Without sufficient institutional limitations on his rule, choosing his lieutenants, like his wives, on the basis of their loyalty and submissiveness rather than their brilliance or their academic credentials, Perón *did* make too many major decisions personally. Having surrounded himself with admirers, he did not benefit from the critical responses of insiders that might have improved the quality of those decisions and therefore also their public acceptability in the long run.

In this sense, but only in this sense, Perón was like Mussolini and Hitler, two other charismatic leaders to whom he is frequently likened. Perón was not in fact the "fascist" that his enemies have so long and so consistently claimed him to be. He did admire the social and economic benefits which, as a military observer in Italy during 1939 and 1940, he believed that fascism had brought to the Italian working class, and like Hitler and Mussolini he concentrated power so much in his own hands that, when he made a mistake in judgment, it was very costly indeed. But Perón never shared Hitler's vicious anti-Semitism nor Mussolini's romantic glorification of war. A number of Argentine Jews were active Peronists, and — speaking without fear of harming his own interests, given the undiminished electoral strength of Peronism and the weakness of its enemies — Perón repeated that govern-

Perón goes into exile ten days after the Revolución Libertadora, 16 Sept. 1955. (Courtesy Juan Carlos D'Abate)

ments should come to power by elections and not by civil wars. Perón never sent his armed forces to conquer other nations, as did the European fascists. It was easy for the Marxist guerrillas whom he allowed to fight for his return in the late 1960s and early 1970s, and then ruthlessly ousted from his movement once he regained control of the nation, to see Perón as a fascist traitor in the mold of Mussolini, one who would abandon the international socialism that he had professed, to lead a nationalistic, self-serving revolution. Yet, Marxist stereotypes aside, Perón was simply reverting to type, persecuting left-wing critics of his own national "revolution" in his third presidency as he had during his first two terms in office, having used some of his enemies to fight his battles and to gain himself office just as Marxist — Leninists had done earlier during the long course of the Bolshevik Revolution.

In contrast to emotional writings against Perón, the chapters that follow tend to portray him and his movement as far more reasonable and rational than has often been acknowledged. Wayne Smith contends, for example, that in 1971 Perón genuinely favored consensus rather than grabbing all power for himself, that it was Lanusse's apparent determination to remain president that made Perón replace Jorge Daniel Paladino with Héctor J. Cámpora and turn away from more coalitional politics. Later, Smith affirms, Perón actually favored a government of national unity and, in September 1973, even favored a vice-presidential candidacy for Ricardo Balbín; however, he was unable in his old age to withstand pressures against this coalition from old stalwarts in his movement, and from within his own household, pressures that led him to name Isabel vice-president. In a similar vein, Marysa Navarro convincingly demonstrates Evita's organizational efforts to aid the poor. Whereas detractors have described the Fundación Eva Perón as a corrupt device to exploit companies in the private sector, Navarro shows it as one of the few government agencies with funds enough to construct the buildings and programs that the poor needed. Rather than being deified as a secular saint or pilloried in a psychological interpretation as a woman who tried through her largesse to make up for her own early poverty, in Navarro's chapter Evita emerges as one who worked tremendously hard and with considerable immediate success to aid those Argentines who needed help most. By the same token, in a stinging, intriguing critique of early interpretations of Perón, José Miguens concludes that North American and European academics have generally failed to see Perón as the Catholic nationalist that he was because their nations' cultures, ideologies, and interests were frequently so far from those of Argentina.

Other chapters in this volume bring out contrasting dimensions of the political situation during the Perón era. From inside the Argentine labor movement, Juan Carlos D'Abate chronicles in detail not only how Peronist governments brought various benefits to workers but also how Perón encouraged far greater participation by workers both in the public sector and in the shaping of their own lives. Since D'Abate was also campaign director for major Peronist candidates for political office, his chapter can also be read — rather importantly — as a retrospective on the movement by one deeply committed to it. By contrast, my chapter deals with business executives and *estancieros* rather than workers. In my study, I use survey data to demonstrate that, despite many areas of continuity among the private-sector elite, the chief executives of Argentina's largest corporations have felt a striking alienation from the landowners of traditional rank and privilege. In a chapter using a similar data base regarding popular attitudes surveyed just before the 1973 elections, Roberto Guimarães provides one of the first detailed evaluations of popular support for terrorists anywhere in the world. He analyzes the characteristics and attitudes of those who sympathized most with Argentine guerrillas. Finally, in dealing with the most important religious sector of Argentina, Antonio Donini portrays the Catholic church during the Perón era as beset with the same social tensions as Argentine society as a whole. He demonstrates how many churchmen have come to the enforced conclusion that their safest strategy is to concentrate on their pastoral and religious roles rather than answering the siren calls of politics, unlike those who sided with the early Peronists, as did the church hierarchy in 1945, or with the Marxist guerrillas, as did the Movement of Third World Priests in the late 1960s, or with the government of President Jorge Videla, as seemed tempting to accommodationists in the late 1970s.

Readers unfamiliar with the sequence of events in the long career of Juan Perón may want to begin with the chronology of his public career that Marisabel Brás Castro has compiled in the appendix. Laura Dalton has compiled a comprehensive bibliography of books, dissertations, and articles on Peronism which was originally to appear as an appendix to this volume, but the bibliography has grown to such great size that it is being published as a separate monograph. Those seeking more bibliographical references than appear in the notes to the chapters in this book can order the Dalton bibliography directly from the Center for Latin American Studies, University of Connecticut, Storrs, Conn. 06268.

Of the vast literature on Peronism, what works require special emphasis and interpretation? The chapters that follow provide diverse answers to this question, but, quite understandably, the scholarly analyses omit references to one of the ways in which tens of thousands of people are currently obtaining a view of Perón: through *Evita*, the malicious, one-sided, anti-Peronist musical that has been playing to packed houses in London and New York. As theater, it is arresting; as history, it is false. The musical cheaply exploits the image of Evita as a harlot and perpetuates such myths as her great participation in bringing Perón to power in 1945. It alleges the dangerous charisma, the essential opportunism of Perón. Yet, in a perverse manner, even this historical travesty underlines the importance and the continuing attraction of Perón and Evita; its creators may occasionally touch upon the truth quite by accident rather than through design or understanding. In the haunting refrain of its most popular song, a message comes from Evita on her deathbed:

> Don't cry for me, Argentina;
> For the truth is I shall not leave you,
> Though it may get harder
> For you to see me.
> I'm Argentina
> And always will be.
> Have I said too much?[6]

Even in misrepresentations, Juan and Evita Perón always will represent Argentina, at least twentieth-century Argentina, in the eyes of many observers. Both the appeal of their visions and the more prosaic reasons for their failures to implement those visions, however, give them a pressing need to be more realistically understood, ample reason to be seen upon a much broader stage.

NOTES

1. Kalman H. Silvert, *The Reason for Democracy* (New York: Viking, 1977), p. 99.

2. Juan E. Corradi writes, "To interpret Perón's appeal as exclusively charismatic, that is, as the irrational attachment of undereducated, unorganized masses of migrants from the countryside to a Latin *caudillo*, is to forget the important role played by older, mature worker organizations." ("Between Corporatism and Insurgency: The Sources of Ambivalence in Peronist Ideology," in Morris J. Blachman and Ronald G. Hellman, eds., *Terms of Conflict: Ideology in Latin American Politics* [Philadelphia: Institute for the Study of Human Issues, 1977], p. 109.)

3. For both urban and rural workers, the political support for distributionist policies came out particularly strongly in a survey that I conducted during Perón's final electoral campaign in August and September 1973. Question 7 asked respondents what respect they felt for decisions taken by various governments, including (rated separately) the first and second presidential terms of Perón. See Frederick C. Turner, "The Study of Argentine Politics Through Survey Research," *Latin American Research Review* 10, no. 2 (Summer 1975). Survey data are available from the Roper Center, University of Connecticut, Storrs, Conn. 06268.

4. Peter Witonski, "The Legacy of Perón," *New Republic*, 17 June 1978, p. 16. Some denunciations of Perón at this juncture are even more bitter. For instance, Carlos Rangel [Guevara], a Venezuelan journalist, writes, "Perón evidently succeeded in bringing Argentina back to nativist obscurantism. Having ruined the country politically and economically in his ten years of government, he spent the following seventeen years of exile exerting himself to prevent Argentina's recovery from its first Peronist bout; he managed to make the country ungovernable, and it remained so even after his return, despite the fact that he was granted almost absolute powers. When he learned he was ill and dying, Perón crowned his 'achievement' by committing the final indignity: imposing as his successors his wife, a former showgirl,

and his 'private secretary' [José López Rega], a former police sergeant, self-appointed astrologer, and the author of a book recounting his personal conversations with the Archangel Gabriel." *(The Latin Americans: Their Love-Hate Relationship with the United States*, trans. Ivan Kats [New York: Harcourt, Brace, Jovanovich, 1977], p. 76.)

5. H. S. Ferns, "How Socialism Broke Argentina," *Review of the River Plate*, 23 July 1974, p. 93.

6. The text of the musical may be found, along with a frequently inaccurate history of Evita's life and an excellent set of pictures from throughout her career, in Andrew Lloyd Webber and Tim Rice, *Evita: The Legend of Eva Perón (1919–1952)* (New York: Drama Book Specialists, 1979).

2

MARYSA NAVARRO

Evita and Peronism

Few political figures in the history of Argentina have aroused as much violent hatred or passionate love as Eva Perón. To her followers, she was Evita, a selfless woman who worked tirelessly to improve the lives of workers, destitute women, and needy children, totally dedicated to the downtrodden because she was born poor like them, and so committed to them that she sacrificed her own life on their behalf. To her enemies, however, she was only an ambitious actress, a trollop who rose to the top by using countless men, a hypocrite interested in money, jewels, and luxurious clothes, and a vengeful woman intent on accumulating power to make Argentine society pay for the shame heaped upon her because of her background.

Shaped during her lifetime, these two irreconcilable images of Evita have remained unchallenged for the past thirty years. They permeate the numerous biographies and articles written about her, and even scholarly works on Peronism.[1] Fascinated with the mythology of Evita, Argentines and foreigners alike have transformed her into a paradigmatic figure, a saint or a parvenue, either endowed with superior qualities or worthy of the greatest contempt, according to their ideology. In the meantime, this fascination has obscured another Evita, the one who gave origin to the myths and who played a significant role in Argentine politics as General Juan Domingo Perón's co-leader of the Peronist movement, his liaison with organized labor, president of the wealthy social aid organization, the Fundación Eva Perón, and also president of the Partido Peronista Femenino, the women's branch of the Peronist party. Indeed, from 1948 to her death in 1952, although she was not a member of Perón's cabinet and was never elected to public office, Evita was nonetheless the second most powerful and influential person in the Peronist hierarchy. There is therefore a need to concentrate on Evita as a political figure and to examine her relationship to and her impact on Peronism during Perón's first presidency.

Evita's participation in Argentine politics came about not as a result of a conscious decision or a long preparation for public life but because of her personal relationship with Perón. For much of her life, she had one ambition, to become an actress, and it was only after she met Perón that she discovered the world of politics and began to show an interest in it. Born in 1919 in Los Toldos, a village of Buenos Aires Province, the fifth illegitimate child of Juan Duarte and Juana Ibarguren, Evita left her family at the age of fifteen. Once in Buenos Aires, she tried the stage but only managed to obtain walk-on parts or minuscule roles in second-rate plays, and her attempts to break into films gave her minor parts in three forgettable movies. On the other hand, after 1938 her radio career blossomed. By 1943, she had become a successful soap opera star, heading her own company.

In January 1944, Evita met Perón, then undersecretary of war and secretary of labor in General Pedro Pablo Ramírez's government. At that time, Perón's actions from the Secretariat of Labor were already drawing much attention and would eventually make him the most controversial member of the military government. Ending successive governments' anti-labor policies, he supported workers' demands for unionization, enacted new labor legislation, and forcefully implemented existing laws. While he met with resistance among Communists and Socialists, who controlled much of organized labor, his supporters grew consistently. His success was made possible by favorable economic conditions, a largely nonunionized, substantial working class, and a divided, highly bureaucratized labor movement. Furthermore, workers responded not only to the concrete benefits they obtained through his actions but also to his personal style. He met daily with labor leaders and rank-and-file workers, visited their factories, and spoke at their rallies emphasizing workers' rights and announcing the beginning of a new era in which exploitation would no longer exist.

When Evita met Perón, she was twenty-four and he was a forty-eight-year-old widower, tall, handsome, and dashing. She became his mistress, but contrary to what usually occurs in such situations, Perón did not isolate her from his public life; he introduced her to his fellow officers, went to visit her in Radio Belgrano when she was at work, and in fact treated her as if she were his wife. The rumors about Evita's questionable past date from this period, when she was "the colonel's mistress"; Perón's behavior toward her became the source of endless gossip in Buenos Aires salons and among many of his fellow officers. As for Evita, she soon found herself in a totally different world, where every political event was discussed heatedly and where the latest government crisis was the subject of interminable debates. Her interest in her career as an actress, however, continued to be paramount in her life, although she took part in a propaganda series praising Perón's actions as secretary of labor and also helped to organize a union of radio employees. Indeed, she even used her relationship with Perón to get a starring role in a new film. Ironically, *La Pródiga* was never shown publicly, because, by the time it was ready to be released, a major political crisis and her marriage to Perón had put an end to her acting career.

The October 17, 1945, crisis began on the ninth when Perón, then not only secretary of labor but also minister of war and vice-president, was

Before her marriage to Perón, Eva Duarte was a radio star and played in several Argentine films. (Courtesy Wide World Photos)

forced by his military opponents in the Campo de Mayo garrison to abandon his three cabinet posts.[2] Perón's dismissal caused other cabinet members to present their resignations, and President Edelmiro J. Farrell was left with only two ministers. On October 14, the day after President Farrell ordered the arrest and jailing of Perón on Martín García Island, under renewed military pressure, the crisis took a new turn. The news of Perón's confinement, accompanied by rumors that his life was in danger, prompted both blue- and white-collar workers who had benefited from his actions as secretary of labor to seek his release.[3] Helped by his collaborators in the secretariat, they began to mobilize. On October 15, sugar workers in Tucumán went on strike and that same day, the CGT (General Confederation of Labor) met to consider a general strike motion. After a long session, the CGT voted to strike, and set the date for the eighteenth.[4]

Disregarding the CGT orders, however, on the morning of the seventeenth thousands of workers abandoned their work places and marched towards the Casa Rosada, demanding Perón's release, gathering supporters along the way. Once in the Plaza de Mayo, they stayed until late at night, when Perón appeared on a balcony of the Casa Rosada and addressed the crowds.

October 17, 1945, marked the transformation of Perón's relationship with the Argentine working class into a bond that would unite them until his death in 1974. It had the significance of a founding act, and in the years to come, the ceremony would be reenacted every October 17. The descamisados (the shirtless ones) would gather in the Plaza de Mayo and Perón, the leader, would address them from a balcony of the Casa Rosada as he did that night.[5]

Most of the literature on Peronism attributes a crucial role to Evita during the October crisis.[6] Notwithstanding the numerous accounts of her attitude during the crisis, she did not play a major role in the workers' mobilization. She did not rally Perón's supporters or prompt them to act on his behalf because, among other reasons, her political involvement until then had been minimal; she did not meet most of the labor leaders who organized the workers until after the crisis exploded, and she therefore lacked the necessary contacts to influence the CGT vote or the massive walkout.[7] On the other hand, the workers' actions undoubtedly altered her life radically. Four days later, the actress of dubious origin, the infamous "colonel's mistress," married Perón in a quiet civil ceremony, and the following month, when he announced his candidacy in the forthcoming elections, she found herself transformed into the wife of a presidential candidate.

As soon as the campaign got under way, Evita began to act in a most unusual manner for an Argentine woman. She accompanied her husband on his trips into the interior, attended meetings, and even addressed a women's rally in the Luna Park stadium. After he was inaugurated in June

1946, she clearly refused to follow the pattern established by previous Argentine first ladies. Instead, she attended rallies with Perón, visited slums, factories, and union headquarters, and went on the air to urge support for her husband's new economic policies. More importantly, however, she also began to act as his substitute and met with labor leaders in an office made available to her in the central post office. By September 1946, her office was moved to the old Secretariat of Labor, now transformed into a ministry. By December, she had become Perón's liaison with labor, and a presidential press release made her new role official.

Neither Perón nor Evita has explained satisfactorily his decision to allow her to become his liaison with labor or her reasons for wanting to do so. Evita's favorite explanation is that on October 17, 1945, she contracted a "debt of gratitude" with the men and women who forced Perón's release and that her debt could only be repaid by loving the *descamisados* as they had loved Perón and by dedicating her life to them.[8] While perhaps essentially true, Evita's explanation is nevertheless insufficient in view of her extraordinary actions at a time when women were not expected to take part in politics, especially in a society where they voted for the first time in 1951 and where presidents' wives were relegated to an occasional ceremonial role. For his part, Perón is no more helpful than Evita on this subject. During his exile, Perón wrote that he decided that Evita should abandon her acting career and work in the ministry because he saw in her an "exceptional" woman, "truly passionate, motivated by a will and a faith comparable to those of the early Christians."[9] Perón's claim is rather exaggerated, because there was little indication in early 1946 that Evita could turn into the charismatic leader she eventually became. Moreover, his sequence of events is slightly off: her acting career ended when she married him in October 1945, and she moved to the Ministry of Labor in September 1946 when she had already demonstrated her usefulness to him.

Whatever personal reasons may have influenced the decision,[10] Perón allowed Evita to act as his substitute and become his liaison with labor because she helped him to solve one of the two major problems created by his election to the presidency. On the one hand, if Perón wanted to retain and strengthen the social base of his power, he could not let his charismatic relationship with the *descamisados* deteriorate. Yet his election endangered that relationship, because, while his triumph in February 1946 was a ratification of his leadership, it was also a mandate to be president of *all* Argentines, not only of the *descamisados*. The duties of his new office no longer permitted him to be the rabble-rousing secretary of labor who dispensed favors, supported workers' demands, met with them every day, and spoke their language. Furthermore, the new ministry of labor was no longer under his exclusive control and might prove to be a dangerous weapon in the hands of an ambitious politician.

MARYSA NAVARRO

On the other hand, Perón needed to create a firm political base for his government, which was very shaky. Although he had received 52 percent of the vote, had seen his candidates win almost all the governorships, and counted on a majority in Congress, he did not have a cohesive party behind him. He had entered the presidential race backed by two parties hurriedly created after October 17: the Unión Cívica Radical (Junta Renovadora) and the Partido Laborista, founded by labor leaders like Luis F. Gay and Cipriano Reyes who were involved in the workers' mobilization. United mainly by Perón, the two parties were divided over issues, candidates, and strategies. During the campaign, disagreements had been frequent and heated. Furthermore, the Partido Laborista itself posed a serious difficulty for Perón because its organizers were veteran labor leaders who, while supporting him, also wanted to maintain some independence from him.[11] Moreover, since the leadership of the Partido Laborista overlapped with that of the CGT, the stance adopted by these labor leaders also affected the position of organized labor with respect to Perón. From his point of view, the existence of an independent labor movement was a danger to be avoided, especially at a time when the number of unionized workers was increasing substantially, when new unions were constantly created, and when workers continued to display a high level of militancy.

Perón moved against the Partido Laborista even before his inauguration; he dissolved it in May 1946. His decision was openly resisted by certain labor leaders like Cipriano Reyes, then a deputy, but the majority accepted it. His next step was to create a political organization, the Partido Peronista, which he controlled totally; in fact, it remained under his absolute authority until his death.

The CGT proved to be a more delicate problem, but Perón also succeeded in bringing it under his control. In November 1946, Gay, the former president of the Partido Laborista, was elected secretary-general of the CGT over Perón's candidate, Ángel Gabriel Borlenghi. However, in January 1947, the visit of a U.S. delegation gave Perón the excuse he needed to accuse Gay of "collaboration" and to force his resignation. Gay's successor, Aurelio Hernández, was more pliable, but he was also a seasoned labor leader, and he did not owe his position only to Perón. Finally in December 1947, Hernández was succeeded by José Espejo, an unconditional Peronist who retained his post until October 1952. The Peronization of the top level of the CGT was paralleled by the Peronization of intermediate cadres in the labor movement and the organization of new unions totally committed to Perón.

The process was helped by the newly created Ministry of Labor, headed by a former labor leader, José María Freire, and by Evita, who, since shortly after Perón's inauguration, had begun to meet with blue- and white-collar workers as he had done when he was secretary of labor. She listened to requests, passed them along to Perón or to Freire, and made sure that they were answered promptly. Workers needing support in a union election, or facing a confrontation with a business executive who refused to comply with the new labor legislation, went to see her because she was Perón's wife and therefore his extension — the person closest to him. Furthermore, they soon recognized that she could speed paperwork and obtain quick results. On the other hand, while making herself useful to those who courted Perón, she also proved to be beneficial to him because she identified those who resisted the Peronization of the labor movement; she backed his supporters and, in so doing, helped to weed out his most dangerous opponents.

Her office in the former Secretariat of Labor reminded workers that Perón, the president, continued to be secretary of labor, Freire notwithstanding. In her speeches, she spoke of "the secretariat" not the ministry, and, while Perón was now a general, she still referred to him as "the colonel." However, she was not entirely accepted as the intermediary between Perón and labor, the link between the past and the present, until Espejo became secretary-general of the CGT, that is to say, until the labor movement was effectively Peronized.

Evita's incorporation into the political structure, albeit in an informal way, allowed Perón to maintain close contact with the rank and file, to strengthen his control of the labor movement, and to continue to be responsible for its gains. It also permitted him to retain his leadership with the *descamisados* by avoiding sharing it with another man. As a woman and his wife, Evita represented no danger to him. Moreover, she soon proved to be exceptionally good at her new job. At first shy and somewhat ill at ease, she gradually gained confidence and seemed to enjoy thoroughly the continuous meetings, the frequent trips, the visits to factories or union locals. Uninhibited by any fear of microphones because of her radio experience, she made short speeches in which she declared her love for Perón and the *descamisados* and her commitment to work for them, and her audiences received her enthusiastically.

By 1948, Perón had consolidated his position and Evita was clearly established as an influential member of his government. On that October 17, she not only stood on the balcony of the Casa Rosada with Perón, but also addressed the crowds for the first time. Congressional elections were held that year, and all lukewarm Peronists were replaced by enthusiastic supporters of the new regime, some of them selected by Evita. Her influence continued to grow consistently in the following two years, especially after the 1949 reform of the Constitution had assured Perón's candidacy for a second term and removed all potential challengers to Perón or to Evita from within the Peronist ranks.[12] In August 1951, she attempted to formalize her position and sought the nomination for the vice-presidency, with the backing of the Peronist party and the CGT, but she had to withdraw her

Up until her death in 1952, Evita labored hard on behalf of workers and the underprivileged, exercising considerable political influence. (Courtesy Juan Carlos D'Abate)

candidacy under pressure from the military. Less than a month later, as Perón easily crushed General Benjamín Menéndez's revolt, she began her long and painful battle against cancer. Already quite ill, she attended the October 17 rally, this year dedicated to her. Unable to campaign actively for Perón's reelection, she nevertheless managed to record speeches and on election day, November 11, she cast her vote from her hospital bed. Pale and thin, she found enough energy to address the *descamisados* one last time on May first and to attend Perón's second inauguration the following month. She died on July 26, 1952, and sixteen days later, after an extraordinary explosion of public mourning, her embalmed body was finally laid to rest in the CGT headquarters.[13]

Evita's central activity between 1948 and 1951 was the work she performed with organized labor from the Ministry of Labor. Every day, she met countless delegations of workers who came to visit her in order to thank her for whatever help she might have given them, to pay their respects to her before returning to the provinces after attending a congress, or to bring her a contribution from a union for the Fundación Eva Perón. Accompanied by members of the CGT secretariat, especially José Espejo and Ministry of Labor officials, she spent the morning with the various delegations, chatting with every group, gathering information, granting requests, or assuring petitioners that their concerns would be dealt with promptly by the proper authorities. The sessions usually ended with Evita making a short speech expressing her pleasure to meet with workers in the "old secretariat," reminding them to be alert against the enemies of Perón and asking the *descamisados* to remain loyal to him, as they had been in October 1945.

While Perón met with the CGT secretariat only once a week and addressed workers only on special occasions, whenever Evita attended a Labor or Peronist party rally, toured a new Fundación project with foreign dignitaries or traveled to the provinces, she was accompanied by union officials or labor leaders who were also members of Congress or the CGT secretariat. Her contact with the *descamisados* was therefore far more close and direct than Perón's.

Although she occasionally took part in contract negotiations, Evita cannot be credited with having shaped Perón's policy toward labor or to have had a profound impact on the gains obtained by the working class. Indeed, long before Evita was able to exert any substantial influence, Perón had already demonstrated his commitment to the same policy toward labor that he had implemented as secretary of labor and that Argentina's favorable economic conditions in the post–World War II period undoubtedly allowed him to carry out. Yet, because she was the direct personal link between Perón and the *descamisados*, "the bridge of love" between them (as she liked to call herself), as working conditions continued to improve, as unions kept signing favorable contracts, as labor organizers became members of Congress or labor attachés, and as workers acquired better fringe benefits, Evita was perceived to be as responsible as Perón was for these gains. That is why she could speak with Perón and Espejo from the Casa Rosada every May first or October seventeenth and be heralded as the *abanderada de los trabajadores* (the workers' standard-bearer).

On the other hand, while Evita's impact on Perón's labor policy was less significant than the CGT secretariat constantly claimed, she did carry out numerous projects which directly affected workers' lives and in so doing reinforced their allegiance to Perón — as well as to herself. She accomplished this through the Fundación Eva Perón, a social aid foundation over which she presided and whose funds she controlled exclusively.

Organized in 1948, the Fundación's main objective in its first years was to extend Perón's social policy to those sectors which could not profit from it because of their marginality — for example, to women, to children, and to old people who lived in such poor conditions that they could not get social security benefits. Besides granting old-age pensions, building *hogares para ancianos* (homes for the aged) and *hogares de tránsito* (halfway homes) for women and children, organizing soccer championships for children and teenagers, and every Christmas distributing *sidra* (cider) and *pan dulce* (raised bread), dolls, and soccer balls, she gradually expanded the Fundación's goals to include the construction of schools, union headquarters, a building for the CGT, luxurious hotels where workers could spend their vacations at low cost, four modern hospitals where they received free medical care, numerous clinics, and housing projects.

In the meantime, however, Evita did not abandon the initial objectives of the Fundación and continued to practice what she called "direct social action," which her critics insisted was pure and simple demagoguery. Every afternoon, Evita received long lines of people who came to see her with the most varied requests: young couples who wanted to get married and did not have money to buy furniture; mothers with sick children who needed expensive medication; old men without relatives who wanted to apply for old-age pensions; a young man who needed an orthopedic leg and could not afford it; unskilled women asking for sewing machines to earn some additional money while their children were still at home. Surrounded by Peronist party officials, members of Congress, ministers, and foreign visitors, Evita sat at her desk personally interviewing each petitioner and deciding each case on the spot. Sometimes she left to attend an official function but she returned and continued her "audiences" until late at night.

According to Evita, her daily contact with human misery during these audiences spurred her desire to assist all those who needed her help and intensified her commitment to them. As she wrote in her autobiography,

Because I know the personal tragedies of the poor, of the victims
of the rich and the powerful exploiters of the people . . . because
of that, my speeches often contain venom and bitterness. . . .
And when I say that justice will be done inexorably, whatever
it costs and whomever it may affect, I am sure that God will
forgive me for insulting my listeners, because I have insulted out
of love, because of my love for my people! But He will make
them pay for all that the poor have suffered, down to the last
drop of their blood![14]

From a formal point of view, the Fundación Eva Perón was a private
institution which Evita ran like an autocrat. Displaying incredible energy,
she made every decision, from the selection of its personnel and the approval
of construction plans to budget allocations; she supervised all its operations
and even managed to pay unexpected visits of inspection. On the other hand,
since its explicit objectives were to complement Perón's social goals, Evita
was quite open about the political nature of her social work. Her first speech
for the 1951 presidential election campaign, for example, was made to
coincide with the inauguration of the Ciudad Infantil, four homes for the
aged, a sanatorium, eight home-schools, and 150 regular schools, which,
according to her, were all proofs of Perón's concern for the welfare of his
people.[15] The Fundación was therefore part of the political structure but,
unlike any other government agency, it was unrestricted by institutional
constraints. Evita ran it following the pattern that she had adopted when
working with labor unions. She exerted pressure on private firms or
ministries to make her projects top priorities or to obtain whatever she
needed, except that now her power to influence decisions had risen
appreciably and she found little resistance to her wishes. She could even
summon ministers and government officials to her office and demand explanations when her orders were not carried out to her satisfaction.

Perón did not put a stop to Evita's interference in the affairs of these agencies and ministries. By 1950, when Argentina was beginning to undergo
financial strains, the Fundación was the only agency rich enough to give
away a building to a union, to subsidize workers' holidays, or to construct
luxurious hospitals, thus demonstrating Perón's continued dedication to improve the lives of the *descamisados* when in fact real wages were already
declining. Evita began her organization in 1948 with some 10,000 pesos,
and, by the time it was dismantled by the Revolución Libertadora in 1955,
it had an annual budget of one billion pesos and assets totaling 3,408,196,500
pesos.[16]

The question of how Evita obtained funds to run the Fundación Eva
Perón has been a major source of controversy in Argentina. Anti-Peronists

have insisted that she got most of her undisclosed funds by blackmailing businesses and individuals who were opposed to Perón. Although pressure was undoubtedly applied on both anti-Peronist and pro-Peronist businesses, as well as on ministries and other government agencies, the only report published by the Fundación states that its funds came from a variety of sources — among others, a gambling tax collected on casinos, the national lottery, and a percentage of all wage increases agreed upon in labor contracts. The largest item included in the report, "contributions," does not reveal who the contributors were.[17] While some individuals or corporations may have been forced to "give" large amounts, it is also true that since 1948 labor unions competed with each other with donations in cash or goods; besides giving a percentage of wage increases, from 1950 onward the CGT also committed all wages received on May 1 and October 17 to the Fundación.

Evita saw the Fundación as her own contribution to the New Argentina created by Perón. She took pride in every new building erected and frequently toured the projects with visiting dignitaries. While her critics accused her of irresponsibly squandering ill-gotten funds, Evita saw in her homes and her hospitals the symbols of the *descamisados'* new life under Perón, where the poor and the exploited had a right to live as only the rich had done before. "I wish them to accustom themselves to live like the rich . . . to feel worthy to live amid the greatest riches. For when all is said and done," she wrote in her autobiography, "everyone has a right to be rich on this Argentine soil . . . and in any part of the world."[18]

Beginning in 1949, besides her intense activity with the Fundación projects and her daily work with the labor unions, Evita also spent a great deal of her seemingly endless energy organizing the Partido Peronista Femenino. Her decision to organize a political party exclusively composed of women came two years after women were granted the right to vote.

Evita did not play a significant role in the campaign for women's suffrage. Indeed, before she made her first public statement in support of women's suffrage, the Senate had already approved a law project granting women the vote. The final approval of the bill was the culmination of a long, difficult struggle waged by Argentine feminists during the previous decades, when repeated attempts to extend political rights to women were blocked by a Conservative-dominated Senate. Perón had stated his support for women's suffrage as early as July 1945 and included it in his five-year plan. With the Conservatives no longer in Congress and a Peronist majority assured, the bill did not encounter difficulties. Evita was very active in the voter registration campaign for women launched by the Peronist government and was the major force behind the organization of Peronist women into a political party.

The Partido Peronista Femenino was not the first political party exclusively composed of women. The first was the Feminist party founded in 1918 by one of Argentina's earliest feminists, Julieta Lanteri de Renshaw. Despite the efforts by Lanteri and feminists like Alicia Moreau de Justo, Carolina Muzzili, and many others, women's political participation during the twenties and thirties remained very low and was mostly restricted to communist, socialist, and anarchist militants. In the early forties, especially after the June 1943 military coup, women became more politicized. They attended marches and rallies in increasing numbers, and during the 1946 presidential campaign they organized numerous groups to support the candidates.

The Partido Peronista Femenino was founded on July 26, 1949, at a meeting held in the Cervantes Theater, where Evita delivered a long speech in which she declared that the fundamental principle of the Women's party had to be "the strictest fidelity to the doctrine, the work and the personality of General Perón. . . . For a woman to be a Peronist means above all loyalty to Perón and blind trust in Perón."[19] A few days later, she began to select personally the first *cencistas* (census takers) who went to all the provinces to organize first a women's registration drive and then *unidades básicas* (party cells). As she did with the Fundación, she supervised their activities, demanded frequent reports, and insisted on knowing the most minute details of the steps they followed.

For two years, the *cencistas* crisscrossed Argentina and, working tirelessly, founded cells in the most remote corners of the country. The November 11, 1951, elections showed that their efforts had paid off. Perón received 62.5 percent of the vote, and, of the 3,816,460 women who voted, 2,441,558 (63.9 percent) did so for the Peronist ticket.[20]

Evita ran her party as an organization parallel to the men's branch although totally separated from it. While both were supposed to coordinate their activities through the *Consejo Superior*, the Superior Council, of which she was the only female member, they rarely did so, because she did not allow any interference in her organization. She only accepted orders from Perón and was the only one who could transmit them or give them to the *rama femenina*, as the women's branch was known. Imposing her authority in the name of Perón, she directed her party with an iron hand. Internally, her control was complete and never actually challenged. She demanded strict discipline and she obtained it, perhaps because she personally selected all the party members who eventually occupied relevant positions, including the six women who became senators and the twenty-three who became deputies.

Together with the CGT and the Peronist party, the *rama femenina* formed the third component of the Peronist movement. The three were united not only by Perón but also by Evita, because she was the nexus that connected them to him and because the three groups acknowledged the leadership of Perón and Evita. While he was the undisputed leader, she

Perón and Evita are cheered on the day of his second inauguration as president of Argentina in June 1952. Eva Perón died less than two months later. (Courtesy Wide World Photos)

was his partner and complement. Evita's own charismatic leadership of the *descamisados* not only originated in Perón and was legitimized by him, but also existed because of him and for him. As Evita once explained to a CGT congress in her inimitable style: "I am here among the working classes representing General Perón's wonderful heart; I am here to receive the concerns and the hopes of the working people and place them in the wonderful hands of General Perón; I am here to bring you the love that the general feels for you."[21]

Evita occupied a privileged position in the Peronist hierarchy. In all official ceremonies, except those directly related with the armed forces, she stood by Perón, while the vice-president remained in the background. Together with Perón she addressed the crowds in the Plaza de Mayo every May 1 and October 17. Whenever foreign dignitaries visited Argentina, they not only went to the Casa Rosada to be received by Perón, but also paid their respects to Evita in the Ministry of Labor. Her name appeared as frequently as Perón's on buildings, streets, schools, or ships; when two new territories were transformed into provinces, one was given his name and the other became Eva Perón. She was inferior to Perón only within the Peronist movement. But she had, above all, the power to influence decisions, especially in selecting congressional candidates, diplomats, party officials, and governors. She does not seem to have had an impact on major policy decisions, whether concerning labor, nationalizations, or foreign policy, but she was free to act and use her influence as long as Perón did not limit it. Her acceptance of Perón's decision not to further irritate the military by making her a vice-presidential candidate is perhaps the best example of his final and absolute authority over her actions.

Evita's leadership was defined on the basis of Perón's superiority not only as a man but also as a leader. She praised him shamelessly: "Sometimes I think Perón is no longer a man like the others; that he is an ideal incarnate," she declared in 1949. "Perón is the Argentine ideal in the form of a man."[22] While he was the ideologue who had elaborated a "superior doctrine," *justicialismo* (the Peronist doctrine of social justice), the strategist who defined the objectives and the means to attain them, she only concerned herself with repeating his ideas and introducing innovations only when they would serve his cause. When she said that she owed everything she was to Perón,[23] she was not merely using a convenient rhetorical formula to eulogize him. The words had a very real meaning to her. She had no politics before becoming his mistress, and she learned what to believe by listening to him and doing radio programs for him. Barely educated, she never liked to read, and did not improve her faulty education after marrying Perón. Had it not been for him, she might have been a radio and film star, no better and no worse than many others. Instead, her marriage to him metamorphosed her into Evita, the "Lady of Hope," the "bridge between Perón and the people," the "standard-bearer of the *descamisados*," or, as

Congress declared her to be in May 1952, the "Spiritual Leader of the Nation."

Evita transformed her personal relationship with Perón, her love for him and her gratitude, into political values that every Peronist had to uphold. Stating unequivocally her fanaticism toward Perón,[24] she demanded — and obtained — that same commitment from his followers. In so doing, she was responsible for the creation of a cult of the leader that required absolute loyalty to him, complete trust in him, unconditional allegiance to him, and blind obedience to his word.

Repeated endlessly, her pleas and demands for unity, discipline, faith in Perón, and obedience to Perón created an atmosphere in which criticism and challenge were successfully eliminated and which transformed Peronism into a movement run by lackeys totally subjected to the leader's will. Of course, Evita was by no means the only architect of Perón's absolute leadership. He too wanted it; he never took steps to prevent or to curb Evita's fanatical idealization of him during her lifetime and managed to retain it during his eighteen-year exile. The cult of Perón shaped by Evita also survived that exile. When he returned to Argentina, it was given a new name, *verticalismo*, and it continued to be a major tenet of the Peronist movement.

Evita's death was a great loss to Perón. Because she had accumulated so much power, albeit informal, no single person could inherit it and replace her in all her activities. Perón understood the situation, and, while continuing with his presidential duties, he attempted to become her substitute, including taking her place in long afternoon sessions in the Ministry of Labor. But he soon gave up. By September 1952, he had named a committee to direct the Fundación Eva Perón, and, that same year, he appointed Senator Delia Parodi to head the Partido Peronista Femenino. He did not name anyone his liaison with the CGT, keeping that job for himself. Although many tried, no one succeeded in praising Perón with the passion and sincerity that Evita had demonstrated.

The impact of Evita on Peronism, once Perón came to power, was substantial. She allowed him to retain his charismatic leadership intact.[25] She was instrumental in widening and strengthening the social basis of Peronism insofar as she reinforced the allegiance of the working class to Perón, organized the massive incorporation of women into the political process through the Partido Peronista Femenino, set up the Fundación, and thus extended Perón's social policies to other groups, and secured the support of marginal sectors for him.

With respect to women in particular, Evita's actions had far-reaching effects. By no means a feminist, Evita urged Peronist women to enter the political arena, to be involved in politics, and to become militant activists, but to do so without forgetting their "duties" as women. They responded to her appeals by flocking to the Partido Peronista Femenino, by voting for Perón, and, especially after 1955, by maintaining a high level of militancy. In fact, Evita made politics a legitimate activity for Argentine women, Peronist or not. Furthermore, while her vice-presidential aspirations were thwarted, she paved the way for the eventual candidacy of another woman, Isabel Martínez de Perón.

For Kalman H. Silvert.

NOTES

1. See Mary Main (María Flores), *The Woman with the Whip: Eva Perón* (Garden City, N.Y.: Doubleday, 1952); Román J. Lombille, *Eva la predestinada. Alucinante historia de éxitos y frustraciones* (Buenos Aires: Ediciones Gure, 1953); Robert J. Alexander, *The Perón Era* (New York: Columbia University Press, 1951); Richard Bourne, *Political Leaders of Latin America* (Middlesex: Pelican Books, 1969); J. M. Taylor, *Eva Perón: The Myths of a Woman* (Chicago: University of Chicago Press, 1979); and the Broadway musical *Evita*.

2. See Félix Luna, *El '45: Crónica de un año decisivo* (Buenos Aires: Editorial Sudamericana, 1969); Eduardo Colom, *El 17 de Octubre: La revolución de los descamisados* (Buenos Aires: Editorial La Época, 1946); Hugo Gambini, *El 17 de Octubre de 1945* (Buenos Aires: Editorial Brújula, 1969); Robert A. Potash, *The Army and Politics in Argentina, 1928–1945: Yrigoyen to Perón* (Stanford, Calif.: Stanford University Press, 1969): Alain Rouquié, *Pouvoir militaire et société politique en République Argentine* (Paris: Presses de la Fondation nationale des sciences politiques, 1978); and Ángel Perelman, *Cómo hicimos el 17 de Octubre* (Buenos Aires: Editorial Coyoacán, 1961).

3. For Perón's actions as secretary of labor, see Luna, *El '45;* Juan José Hernández Arregui, *La formación de la conciencia nacional (1930–1960)* (Buenos Aires: Ediciones Hachea, 1960); Luis Monzalvo, *Testigo de la primera hora del peronismo. Memoria de un ferroviario* (Buenos Aires: Editorial Pleamar, 1974); Samuel L. Baily, *Labor, Nationalism, and Politics in Argentina* (New Brunswick, N.J.: Rutgers University Press, 1967); Hobart A. Spalding, Jr., *Organized Labor in Latin America: Historical Case Studies of Workers in Dependent Societies* (New York: New York University Press, 1977); Miguel Murmis and Juan Carlos Portantiero, *Estudios sobre los orígenes del peronismo* (Buenos Aires: Siglo Veintiuno Argentina Editores, 1971); and David Tamarin, "Argentine Industrial Unionism During the 'Infamous Decade' and the Emergence of Perón," presented at the 1979 meeting of the Latin American Studies Association, Pittsburgh.

4. See the CGT debate in "La CGT y el 17 de Octubre," *Pasado y Presente* 4, nos. 2, 3 (July–Dec. 1973), 403–23.

5. The word *descamisado* is generally translated as "shirtless" but it really means "coatless." It was first used to describe the men who took over Buenos Aires streets on October 17, 1945, and who, unlike gentlemen, did not wear coats and ties. The derogatory connotation was clear, and, because of it, the Peronists adopted the word as their banner shortly afterward. Perón's campaign train in the 1946 elections was called El Descamisado. Throughout this chapter, *descamisados* is used as a generic term describing the men and women, the blue- and white-collar workers, the rural and urban citizens who voted for Perón in 1946 and again in 1951. The social composition of Peronism continues to be a source of great controversy. See Peter H. Smith, "The Social Base of Peronism," *Hispanic American Historical Review* 52 (1972), 55–72; Gino Germani, "El surgimiento del peronismo: El rol de los obreros y de los migrantes internos," *Desarrollo Económico* 14 (July –Sept. 1974), 385–98; Walter Little, "The Popular Origins of Peronism," in David Rock, ed., *Argentina in the Twentieth Century* (Pittsburgh, Pa.: University of Pittsburgh Press, 1975); Darío Cantón, *Elecciones y partidos*

políticos en la Argentina: Historia, interpretación y balance, 1910–1966 (Buenos Aires: Siglo Veintiuno Argentina Editores, 1973); and E. Spencer Wellhofer, "Peronism in Argentina: The Social Base of the First Regime, 1946–1955," *Journal of Developing Areas* 11 (1977), 335–56.

6. See George I. Blanksten, *Perón's Argentina* (Chicago: University of Chicago Press, 1973); Pierre Lux-Wurm, *Le Péronisme* (Paris: Pichon et Durand-Auzias, 1965); Baily, *Labor, Nationalism, and Politics;* Main, *The Woman with the Whip.*

7. See Luna's evaluation, *El '45,* p. 340; and Marysa Navarro, "Evita and the Crisis of 17 October 1945: A Case Study of Peronist and Anti-Peronist Mythology," *Journal of Latin American Studies* 12, pt. 1 (1980), 127–38.

8. While Evita may have expressed this idea publicly at an earlier date, it was first reproduced in *Democracia,* 12 Jan. 1947.

9. Juan Domingo Perón, *Del poder al exilio: Cómo y quiénes me derrocaron* (Buenos Aires: n.p., n.d.) p. 52. Unless otherwise indicated, all translations are mine.

10. See Marysa Navarro, "The Case of Eva Perón," *Women and National Development: The Complexities of Change,* special issue of *Signs* 3 (1977), 229–40.

11. The tensions and divisions within the CGT surfaced explicitly in the October 15 debate over the general strike. See Juan Carlos Torre, "La caída de Luis Gay," *Todo es Historia,* Oct. 1974, pp. 89 – 100; and Baily, *Labor, Nationalism, and Politics,* pp. 84–90.

12. The only serious challenge to Perón in these early years came from Lieutenant Colonel Domingo A. Mercante, a son of a railroad worker and Perón's collaborator in the Secretariat of Labor. The Partido Laborista's candidate for the vice-presidency, he became instead governor of Buenos Aires Province. Until 1948, Evita repeatedly hailed him as the paramount example of "loyalty" to Perón during the 1945 crisis. After the Constitution was reformed, Mercante was gradually isolated and eventually expelled from the Peronist party.

13. Evita's body remained in the CGT headquarters until 1955, when in a cloak-and-dagger operation it was secretly buried in a graveyard in Milan, Italy.

14. Eva Perón, *La razón de mi vida* (Buenos Aires: Ediciones Peuser, 1951), p. 122.

15. *Democracia,* 28 Oct. 1951.

16. Argentina, Comisión Nacional de Investigaciones, *Documentación, autores y cómplices de las irregularidades cometidas durante la segunda tiranía* (Buenos Aires: CNI, 1958), vol. 3, p. 87.

17. Fundación Eva Perón, *Memoria* (Buenos Aires: FEP, 1953).

18. Eva Perón, *La razón de mi vida,* p. 145.

19. *Discurso de Eva Perón en el acto inaugural de la primera asamblea nacional del Movimiento Peronista Femenino* (Buenos Aires: n.p., 1949), p. 2.

20. Darío Cantón, *Materiales para el estudio de la sociología política en la Argentina* (Buenos Aires: Instituto Torcuato Di Tella, 1968), pp. 140, 142.

21. *Perón y Evita hablan en el acto de clausura del congreso nacional extraordinario de la Confederación General del Trabajo* (Buenos Aires: Presidencia de la Nación, Subsecretaría de Informaciones, 1950), p. 15.

22. *Eva Perón habla a las trabajadoras del país* (Buenos Aires: n.p., 1949), p. 14.

23. See Evita's last October 17 speech in *Democracia,* 18 Oct. 1951.

24. "The opposition says that this is fanaticism, that I am a fanatic [supporter] of Perón and the people, that I am dangerous because I am too sectarian and too fanatic. . . . I answer yes, I am a fanatic of Perón and the *descamisados." Eva Perón habla a las trabajadoras del país,* p. 14.

25. For analysis of Evita's own charisma and more details of her life, see Marysa Navarro, "Evita's Charismatic Leadership," in Michael L. Conniff, ed., *Latin American Populism in Comparative Perspective* (Albuquerque: University of New Mexico Press, 1982), pp. 47–66; and Nicholas Fraser and Marysa Navarro, *Eva Perón* (New York: Norton, 1980).

3

GARY W. WYNIA

Workers and Wages: Argentine Labor and the Incomes Policy Problem

Juan Perón achieved many things during his lifetime. Among the most enduring was his elevation of the Argentine labor movement to center stage in national politics. With the rise of organized labor came a host of new items for the public agenda, and few items were more troublesome for his successors after 1955 (and for Perón himself during his brief presidency in 1973 – 1974) than the question of equitable wages and salaries. Previously left to the forces of the market and the entrepreneurs who manipulated them, wages became a matter for public debate and political conflict under Peronism. Whether Perón was motivated by political opportunism or by a sincere concern for the well-being of the Argentine masses (or both) is not as important as the fact that he taught workers that what they were denied by their employers they could regain through the efforts of their friends in the Casa Rosada. In short, from 1946 onward income distribution became a political issue, or as Argentines say, *un problema político.*

To be sure, the central issue of Argentine politics after the ouster of Perón in 1955 has been the role of Peronism in national politics. The Peronist party was prohibited from electoral competition in 1958 and 1963, but allowed to compete in 1962, 1965, and 1973. At one time or another, union political activities have been proscribed or restricted. Perón himself was exiled for eighteen years and then allowed to return to the presidency in 1973. Yet, while most attention was focused on the issue of what to do with Peronism, the day-to-day problems of governing the country persisted. And it is here that we can find some of the most interesting examples of Peronism and its legacies. One of the most fascinating is what was done about the income distribution problem that the Peronists had placed on the agenda in the mid-1940s. An examination of how civilian and military governments have dealt with this issue not only teaches us something about Argentine labor and its political clout during the past thirty years, but also offers insights into how Argentines manage their public affairs.

33

GARY W. WYNIA

The Incomes Policy Issue

Argentines are not unique in their confrontation of the wage and salary issue. Nearly all capitalist nations in the industrial West have dealt with it in one way or another. With the rise of organized labor, social democratic parties, and economic intervention by the state in Europe, the United States, and Canada following the Depression, has come the politicization of the income issue. Various policies have been tried, ranging from minimum wage legislation to state arbitration of wage disputes. The most politically ambitious, however, is the incomes policy strategy.[1]

Incomes policy involves a deliberate attempt by government to affect the existing distribution of income within a society. Almost any economic policy affects personal income, of course, but the "incomes policy" refers here to the setting of specific wage level objectives and the design of policies to achieve them. Though it can be employed to raise working-class income, incomes policy is also used to contain wages during efforts to combat inflation. Inflation has several causes and a variety of policy remedies; many contemporary solutions, however, require that something be done about the wage-price spiral. That is, policymakers are asked to control the wage-price spiral by, among other things, using the authority of the state to hold down the rise in wages. Such decisions are, needless to say, highly political, especially where organized labor plays an active role in national politics. Consequently, government success with its policy will be determined as much by its political dealings as its economic expertise.

This is precisely the issue that faced each Argentine administration after 1955. Inflation remained a persistent problem, proposed solutions varied widely, and the response of organized labor to each proved critical to its success or failure. Simply put, the question before Argentine officials and the one of interest here is: how does one design and execute economic policies in an inflation-plagued, industrializing nation, when most of those policies appear to demand wage sacrifices unacceptable to a powerful labor movement? In other words, how can authorities cope with an adversary relationship in which one party to the dispute, organized labor, perceives itself to be involved in a kind of zero-sum conflict in which management and government appear to gain at labor's expense? Can such conflicts be resolved satisfactorily through the normal process of collective bargaining, or will greater state intervention be required? If the latter, what forms might it take? And finally, what about performance? Do any solutions "work" better than others; if so, which and why?

The Argentine Setting

Before we examine the experience of incomes policy in Argentina, we should consider labor conditions in that country more generally. The labor movement after 1955 was strong, and it exercised considerable control over the rank and file. Perón had transformed the General Confederation of Labor (CGT) into a powerful organization which tightly controlled the workers whose interests it protected. Moreover, after his forced exile in 1955, the CGT remained the dominant force in the labor movement despite repeated attempts to destroy it by anti-Peronist governments. Nevertheless, it would be a gross oversimplification to describe the post-1955 CGT as a unified movement that could keep its rank and file in line when enforcing unpopular wage guidelines or controls.

Leadership rivalries, often encouraged by governments intent on weakening the labor movement, caused frequent divisions within the confederation that resulted in substantial balkanization by the late 1960s. Moreover, the number of dissident unions that defied CGT leaders increased during the same period, making it almost impossible to hold the entire movement in line. To make matters worse for government policymakers, one of the principal sources of conflict within the labor movement was the issue of the collaboration of organized labor with non-Peronist governments that sought to implement wage and price policies. Thus the very issue which required labor unity and support for its resolution became a persistent source of division within the CGT. Given these conditions, it is not hard to understand why policymakers who had to adopt some kind of anti-inflation incomes policy held out little hope of securing the cooperation of the labor movement.[2]

Next come the entrepreneurs. Since the late 1940s Argentine industrialists and business leaders had contested as much with each other as with other economic sectors for influence over government economic policy. Prior to 1945, the Argentine Industrial Union (UIA) and the Argentine Chamber of Commerce (CAC) had represented most of the country's entrepreneurs, but in 1946 Perón closed the former and insisted that entrepreneurs join the government-sponsored General Economic Confederation (CGE).[3] After the overthrow of Perón in 1955, the UIA was legalized again and thereafter competed with the CGE for entrepreneurial support and influence. During the 1960s, the UIA represented most of the country's larger firms as well as many of the Argentine subsidiaries of multinational firms; the sales volume and powerful economic clout of its members surpassed that of the CGE membership by a substantial margin. The latter's membership was larger, however, since it included many of the nation's small and medium-sized firms.[4]

Not unexpectedly, UIA and CGE leaders disagreed on several economic issues. The UIA, the more conservative of the two, favored restrained fiscal and monetary management, deregulation, and the use of governmental authority to make organized labor more subservient to the dictates of management. The CGE, in contrast, preferred state promotion of economic growth using liberal fiscal and monetary policies; it championed business and labor involvement in the policymaking process through some type of official council on social and economic affairs. Regarding incomes policies, UIA leaders advocated heavy-handed government action against uncooperative unions, while the CGE supported more direct efforts to secure the coordinated collaboration of labor and business leaders in the execution of policy.[5]

Finally, it must be noted that in 1955, after ten years of Peronism, few Argentines were satisfied with their share of the national income. Farmers and entrepreneurs who believed themselves unfairly deprived by Perón's economic and welfare policies were anxious to recoup their losses at the expense of the workers whom they believed had benefited excessively from Peronist policies. Consequently, the *estancieros* and industrialists viewed economic policy not as a means of maintaining the existing distribution of wealth but as a way to regain the income that they claimed had been taken from them by the state and the working class.[6] In 1955 labor leaders were also dissatisfied with the prevailing distribution of income. Although real wages had risen significantly during the first half of the Peronist administration (24 percent between 1946 and 1948), they had declined steadily in subsequent years. Consequently, trade unionists too sought restitution, though they recognized that there was little hope of receiving it immediately after Perón's overthrow.

Three Policy Strategies

By now it should be apparent that in 1955 Argentina offered a very inhospitable environment for the execution of inflation-combating incomes policies. In order for such policies to stand any chance of success, something more than a laissez-faire approach appeared necessary. The approaches taken by Argentine governments after 1955 can be grouped into three basic types: the "bargaining strategy," the "autocratic strategy," and the "co-optation strategy."

The bargaining strategy involved government-supervised collective bargaining as the principal means of incomes-policy administration. It was tried during the Radical party administrations of Presidents Arturo Frondizi (1958–1962) and Arturo Illia (1963–1966). The autocratic strategy, in contrast, was the preferred mode of incomes-policy enforcement under military authoritarian regimes led by officers who were determined to apply force where necessary to halt inflation and to restore investor confidence in the Argentine economy. For those disillusioned with the more passive and conflict-ridden ways of democratic governments, autocracy offered what appeared to be the surest immediate solution to the country's economic problems. Its performance can be best examined in the administration of

General Juan Carlos Onganía (1966–1970). The co-optation strategy sought to secure the compliance of labor and management by involving the representatives of both in the design and administration of wage and price policies. It was seldom employed after 1955 because so few of the post-Perón governments enjoyed the confidence of the labor movement. It was revived, however, by the Peronists when they returned to power in 1973.

Collective Bargaining

The bargaining strategy aims to secure acceptable wage and price levels through a process of government-regulated negotiations between management and labor. It is a familiar mode of setting wage rates in industrialized, capitalistic societies. However, it takes on a special importance when used for the explicit purpose of halting an inflationary spiral during times of economic stress in an industrializing economy. Here it must demonstrate not just an ability to maintain an ongoing equilibrium between prices and wages, but also a capacity to induce labor and management cooperation in the solution of unusual economic problems. Since wage-price spirals often originate in or are sustained by collective bargaining, the bargaining strategy is usually given little chance of ending the spiral. Nevertheless, for both ideological and political reasons, many governments still prefer it to the available alternatives.

Several assumptions underlie the collective bargaining approach to incomes policies. Officials usually begin by assuming that organized labor cannot be subdued or transformed into a more docile instrument of government policy through other means. Consequently, the choice of a bargaining strategy represents the acceptance — albeit a reluctant acceptance, in many instances — of the labor movement as a legitimate bargaining agent for the working class. A second assumption, which complements the first, holds that the cooperation of labor can be won only by creating the kind of bargaining situation in which it participates willingly. This stems from the belief that labor leaders will prefer bargaining to other methods which the government might use to secure their cooperation, because negotiations offer them the best chance of satisfying their economic interests. Ideologically, bargaining also appeals to political liberals who believe that disputes among social groups should be resolved by regulated negotiations among the groups themselves, and it appeals to economists who have little faith in the long-term effectiveness of government-imposed prices and wage rates.

Presidents Frondizi and Illia struggled with the problem of chronic inflation throughout their tenures. Their responses to inflation differed, however, because of the contrasting economic situations each inherited. Frondizi was faced with a severe payments and foreign exchange crisis in mid-1958 and, in order to secure financial assistance, adopted a drastic International Monetary Fund–designed stabilization program which devalued the peso and freed prices and wages. The program, as anticipated, touched off a recession and an immediate and dramatic 114 percent increase in prices. Thereafter, one of the government's objectives was the restoration of relative price stability by blocking huge compensatory wage increases.[7] Illia, in contrast, inherited an economy that in 1962 was recovering from a recession and two years of drought. He therefore sought to promote economic recovery through increased mass consumption without igniting a new wage-price inflationary cycle. To that end he imposed price and exchange controls in the hope of reducing the demand for wage increases.[8]

As one might expect, several conditions led to the choice of collective bargaining. To begin with, Frondizi and Illia were committed to the restoration of constitutional government in a country whose citizens had demonstrated little confidence in it in the past. They were also convinced that their own legitimacy and that of their regimes could not be achieved without the reintegration of the working-class rank and file into the nation's economic and political mainstream. They also hoped to win the rank and file away from its Peronist leadership by demonstrating the fruits of participation in a collective bargaining process carried out within a constitutional framework. Finally, they believed that they had the authority and skill to secure economic conditions which would be conducive to restrained collective bargaining. They were leaders of a party which favored some regulation and intervention in order to promote economic growth. Illia was confident that price and exchange controls would do the job, while Frondizi, constrained somewhat by his IMF stabilization program, hoped that an economic upturn after a brief shock treatment would restore the confidence of both labor and management.

Were these assumptions justified by the conditions that prevailed in Argentina between 1958 and 1963? Did organized labor, for example, accept the rules of collective bargaining? Unfortunately, much of the labor movement, especially the majority of unions who were associated before 1955 with the Peronist-controlled CGT, distrusted both Radical administrations. There was, of course, some justification for their discontent. Both governments were elected in contests from which Peronist parties had been excluded; moreover, in their efforts to separate the rank and file from its Peronist leaders, the Radical governments threatened many vested interests in the labor bureaucracy. Frondizi, for example, prohibited the reconstitution of a united CGT and authorized the selective repression of labor protests by the more militant Peronist unions.[9] Illia, on the other hand, could not prevent Peronist leaders from recapturing control over the CGT when it was reconstituted in January 1963, nor could he deter general strikes by the CGT during 1964 and 1965 aimed at undermining his government. Frustrated by his inability to win favor from all but a small minority of white-collar unions, Illia finally went on the attack, intervening several unions in mid-1965 in an effort to undermine labor unity. In so doing, he reinforced the rank and file's distrust of his administration.[10] In sum, even though the CGT unions engaged in collective bargaining, they criticized and defied authorities, provoking occasional police intervention which, in turn, only reinforced their claim of discrimination by opposition-controlled government.

Both presidents made some progress on the economic front, though it was not sufficient to gain the trust and cooperation of labor. Frondizi secured a recovery in 1960 and 1961, and Illia succeeded in temporarily holding down consumer prices by using price controls. Under normal conditions, these achievements might have been enough to induce labor compliance, but these were not ordinary times. Labor leaders would not let the rank and file forget the shock of the 1959 price increases which had resulted in a net loss of 20 percent in average real wages. Rather than accept the improved condition of 1960, they demanded greater compensatory wage increases. Illia tolerated real wage increases of 5 percent and 3 percent in 1964 and 1965. Nevertheless, rather than limit its wage demands to the 12 percent as prescribed by the government in the wage guidelines it set for 1966, CGT unions demanded and received contracts granting 20 and 25 percent increases, adding pressure on prices.[11]

Labor opposition was not the only obstacle faced by Frondizi and Illia; for the most part, entrepreneurial support was lacking as well. Many industrialists, especially the larger and more conservative ones represented by the UIA, distrusted Radical party governments because of their interventionism and toleration of an activist labor movement. With memories of government manipulation of collective bargaining in labor's favor during the Peronist era still fresh in mind, they were not anxious to return to a bargaining mode of setting wages even if the government promised to promote conditions that would keep wages in line. Owners and managers had little choice but to negotiate with their employees, but they claimed that they did so under duress and never ceased their harsh criticisms of the wage policies of both presidents.[12]

The bargaining strategy did not thrive under Argentine conditions. Yet, before judging it a failure, we must examine several performance indicators more closely. Regarding the government's ability to secure labor's formal cooperation and support, Frondizi and Illia did poorly. Frondizi's inability to subdue labor was illustrated dramatically in late 1961 when railway workers struck to protest his plan to reorganize the deficit-plagued state railways and dismiss redundant employees. The strike, which lasted for over a month, was not settled until the president backed down and abandoned his reorganization scheme.[13] Illia could not get labor to follow wage guidelines in 1966 and was forced to resort to strong-arm methods to promote his objectives.

GARY W. WYNIA

Quantitative indicators of labor relations and their effects are also available. The utility of the data is limited by their high level of aggregation and the fact that strike data are collected only for the federal capital of Buenos Aires, where no more than half of the country's industries are located.

Table 1 shows that labor did not stand by idly in 1959 but engaged in protests at record levels. Though strikes dropped off significantly in 1960, they continued at a relatively high level until 1962, when the intervention of the military brought labor unrest to a virtual halt. Illia no doubt bought some labor peace with his expansionary policies and price controls. In 1964 and 1965, the strike volume was less than half what it had been a few years before. Nevertheless, it is evident that labor unrest continued.

Turning to the effects of collective bargaining on wage rates, it is apparent that the unions did fairly well after 1959, though under Frondizi their real-wage gains in later years did not compensate for losses in 1959. They did

TABLE 1
Strikes and Wages in Argentina, 1958-1965

		Strikes			*Industrial Wages*	
					Change in Monetary Income (%)	Change in Real Income (%)
	Frequency[a]	Duration[b]	Size[c]	Volume[d]		
Under Frondizi (May 1958–March 1962)						
1958	.015	22.52	3,302	1,115.40	37.9	4.9
1959	.008	7.14	31,357	1,791.67	58.8	− 25.8
1960	.005	12.78	5,002	293.98	35.1	6.4
1961	.008	7.42	5,499	318.26	26.9	11.6
1962	.003	6.34	2,826	50.17	18.9	− 3.8
Under Illia (October 1963–June 1966)						
1963	.004	3.92	10,361	154.36	25.0	1.0
1964	.005	4.41	5,342	117.79	36.8	12.0
1965	.006	2.90	6,362	105.18	39.3	8.4
1966	.005	4.25	8.738	178.45	33.9	1.4

Sources: Strikes computed from República Argentina, Secretaría de Estado de Trabajo, *Conflictos del trabajo,* June 1970, p. 25 (data for federal capital only); wages from Lorenzo Juan Sigaut, *Acerca de la distribución y niveles de ingreso en la Argentina* (Buenos Aires: Ediciones Macchi, 1972), table 16, p. 57.
a. Per 1,000 civilian wage and salary workers.
b. Work days lost per striker.
c. Number of strikers per strike.
d. Frequency "times" duration "times" size.

well under Illia, however, and by 1965 they had surpassed the 1958 level of real income. It seems obvious, then, that at least on the dimension of income, organized labor was served rather well by bargaining.

But what about the government's objective of combating inflation; how well was it served during this period? If we look only at the Frondizi period, the performance is quite mixed. After the anticipated skyrocketing inflation caused by freeing prices at the end of 1958, the annual increase in prices was reduced to only 13.7 percent by 1961; moreover, this was achieved at a time of rising real income and declining labor protests. Despite price controls, Illia did not do quite as well in 1964 and 1965. Instead, he was forced to live with an average annual rate of inflation of 37 percent (the lowest was 33.9 percent in 1966), which, though modest by some South American standards, was high enough to cause grave concern among Argentine industrialists and international lending agencies and to help weaken military confidence in Illia's ability to rule.[14]

What then can we conclude about the performance of the bargaining model in Argentina? Given the conditions that prevailed at the time, few thought that it would succeed. Nevertheless, it did better than expected by its critics. Despite the high level of conflict, wage contracts were negotiated under government supervision, and they did contribute to the partial achievement of incomes-policy objectives. These gains were transitory, however. The central issue in labor-government relations was not wage rates, it turned out, but the political legitimacy of governments which were elected in contests that excluded the Peronists. What labor leaders wanted and what the Argentine military refused them in 1958 and 1963 was public office. When the Peronists were allowed to flex their political muscles in congressional elections, they secured a plurality in 1962 and 1965. Each victory was nullified, however, by the officers who removed Frondizi in 1962 and Illia in 1966.

The Autocratic Way

If labor conformity cannot be secured voluntarily, then it must be gained through repression. So goes the argument of the autocrats. In practice, they should begin with the suspension of collective bargaining and the declaration of a wage freeze. Unions that refuse to comply with government policy should be intervened, their leaders jailed, and their offices closed by police. Simultaneously, labor ministers either should close national labor confederations or try to divide them so deeply that they would not be able to offer unified resistance to government policy.

Argentine autocrats blamed organized labor as well as vote-seeking politicians for the country's failure to combat inflation. Consequently, it was argued, the Argentine worker had to assume a large share of the burden in the fight against rising prices. Moreover, once the power and determination of the government had been demonstrated, the rank and file would have little choice but to comply. Or so it was hoped. What made this approach so appealing to officers was not just its familiarity but also its simplicity. In contrast to regulated bargaining and the co-optation of labor and business — both of which required skilled leadership — physical force, carefully and consistently applied, seemed so much more manageable. The strategy did not originate in 1966, of course. During the 1930s upper-class-controlled conservative governments had used much force to contain a growing labor movement. General Pedro Aramburu had also tried it after Perón's overthrow in 1955. In self-defense, the autocrats claimed that the economic development of their vulnerable country simply required the compliance of labor with a program of wage restraint and induced capital accumulation.

For this strategy to succeed, several things are necessary. Foremost among them is the state's capacity and determination to subjugate the labor movement. Uncertainty over the choice of methods, or an incapacity to intervene physically in concrete situations, will limit the application of the doctrine. So will an inability to deter armed opposition by workers or guerrilla movements. Second, the stronger the labor movement is organizationally, and the more determined its members to resist government repression, then the more difficult will be the task of subduing it. Where national confederations are weak, dependent on the state, or already divided by internal disputes, the subjugation of the labor movement is more manageable. Yet even then government control is not assured, since the rank and file can struggle on alone, especially if government repression radicalizes frustrated workers.

The military officers who overthrew the Radical party government of Arturo Illia in late June of 1966 indicated at the outset that theirs was to be a different kind of military regime. No longer would the military stay in power only long enough to purge the government of undesirable civilian officials and then return it to more acceptable politicians. This time they would rule until the country's more fundamental economic and political problems were solved. Under the leadership of General Juan Carlos Onganía, they set out to cure Argentina's economic ills and recreate political order.

Onganía's labor policy was an outgrowth of his economic strategy. While the military did not blame organized labor for all of the country's economic ills, it assigned to labor a critical role in their alleviation. Onganía and his advisors were convinced that the national malaise stemmed from the gross inefficiency of the economy. This condition, which pervaded the private as well as the public sector, had allegedly been caused by government policies initiated by Perón in the 1940s and reinforced by his successors succumbing to popular pressures. Most prominent among the inefficiency-building policies were price and tax disincentives to rural producers, overambitious welfare programs, rampant patronage, subsidies for public enterprises, high fiscal deficits, and tariffs that protected weak domestic firms. What the country required, the Onganía team concluded, was a nationwide attack on waste and inefficiency under the supervision of a strong government that would enforce technically correct decisions regardless of their political consequences. Such an approach, it was believed, would attract foreign investment to Argentina to finance the creation of an efficient industrial economy capable of sustained growth.

Of the many measures announced by minister of economy Adalbert Krieger Vasena in March 1967, none was more critical to his program than the wage freeze he proposed to combat inflation.[15] Onganía's advisors were convinced that labor would not willingly give up its economic conquests nor cooperate voluntarily with the freeze. They had witnessed labor resistance to wage guidelines during the last year of the Illia administration and recognized its antipathy toward non-Peronist governments. The only alternative, they reasoned, was the use of military force to impose the freeze on a resistant labor movement.

Even before he announced a two-year wage freeze in March 1967, Onganía had begun his assault on the labor movement in order to weaken its ability to resist his program. In August 1966 he decreed a compulsory arbitration law which permitted government intervention in any labor dispute. Two months later, when dockworkers refused to end a strike called to protest government reorganization of the port authority, he used force to halt the protest. Similar measures were employed to break up a strike of railway workers six months later. Through these unqualifiedly successful tactics, officials demonstrated their determination to deal harshly with labor. When the CGT tried to confront the government in early 1967 by calling a general strike, officials again intervened, this time closing several militant unions and jailing their leaders. Consequently, when the wage freeze was finally imposed three months later, labor was in no condition to resist.[16]

The growing organizational weakness of the labor movement also made the autocrats' task easier. It is clear that, when judged by most conventional criteria, the CGT was among the best-organized and most powerful labor movements in Latin America. How then was Onganía able to subdue it so quickly? First of all, its apparent strength could not hide the fact that the movement since 1955 had suffered from several weaknesses that authorities could exploit. Most notable were internal divisions over several issues, the most critical being labor's stance toward non-Peronist governments. One faction urged cooperation with all governments in order to secure limited economic gains, another advocated a mixture of cooperation and confrontation, depending on the issue, while a third group sought continuous confrontation. By skillfully exploiting these divisions through the use of concessions to some unions and the repression of others, Onganía managed to exacerbate them, making a united labor opposition against him unattainable.[17]

Onganía's apparent domination of the Argentine working class was short-lived, however. In May and June 1969, worker and student riots in the interior industrial city of Córdoba struck a devastating blow against his autocratic regime and its program; one year later Onganía was overthrown by military colleagues. The *Cordobazo*, as the Córdoba riots were labeled, demonstrated that the labor movement — or at least some parts of it — had not lost the ability to resist authority after all.

The fact that the riots came as a total surprise seems to be due to the government's fundamental misperception of labor's will to resist; Onganía had mistaken the submission and division of CGT leaders for the collapse of the entire labor movement. What he and his advisors did not appreciate was that the labor movement is held together in two distinct ways. The first is through its formal organization, which allows leaders to mobilize workers to protest government programs. The other is more psychological; it appears in rank-and-file resistance to authority. Onganía had closed CGT organizations, but in so doing he also provoked even greater resistance by the rank and file. The events in Córdoba bear this out. The industrial unions of Córdoba had never been as responsive to the leadership of the CGT as were those found in and around Buenos Aires, and, when CGT leaders succumbed to the military regime, the Cordobans resisted. The workers' resentment of the military regime and its policies continued despite the apparent quiescence of labor leaders, which had lulled officials into the belief that they had indeed won their battle against labor.[18]

There remains some debate over whether the *Cordobazo* was provoked more by discontent with political repression or by the economic deprivation caused by the wage freeze. Whatever the principal motives for the protest, it forced Onganía to use regular army troops against Argentine workers in order to restore order. While such methods had not disturbed military leaders in 1966, when they were confined to strike-breaking, the street war that took place in Córdoba led many to question the viability of the autocratic model. If the model had lived up to its promise, such confrontations would not have occurred, it was argued. With the *Cordobazo* came new doubts about the autocrats' capacity to manage public affairs.

Quantitative indicators of labor, price, and wage behavior indicate the autocracy's impressive short-term achievements. What they do not reflect, however, is its sudden demise in the face of the Córdoba protests. The data presented in table 2 make it easy to understand why Onganía's supporters within Argentina and in international financial circles were quick to conclude that the regime's harsh methods were responsible for the quick recovery of the economy. When contrasted with the performance of the democratic regimes of Frondizi and Illia, Onganía's achievement is very impressive. Labor protests were reduced to the lowest levels of the postwar period, wage increases were minimal, and inflation, if not completely conquered, was reduced to its lowest in two decades (7.6 percent in 1969).

TABLE 2
Strikes and Wages in Argentina, 1966–1970

	Strikes				Industrial Wages	
	Frequency[a]	Duration[b]	Size[c]	Volume[d]	Change in Monetary Income (%)	Change in Real Income (%)
1967	.0010	4.49	91	0.44	20.6	0.0
1968	.0012	9.63	230	2.66	15.0	−0.5
1969	.0013	22.44	837	24.41	11.7	3.8
1970	.0008	11.28	582	5.25	NA	−4.3

Sources: Strikes computed from República Argentina, Secretaría de Estado de Trabajo, *Conflictos del Trabajo,* June 1970, table 25; wages from Lorenzo Juan Sigaut, *Acerca de la distribución y niveles de ingreso en la Argentina* (Buenos Aires: Ediciones Macchi, 1972) table 16, p. 57.
a. Per 1,000 civilian wage and salary workers.
b. Work days lost per striker.
c. Number of strikers per strike.
d. Frequency "times" duration "times" size.

The short-term strengths of the autocratic approach to incomes-policy management are quite obvious. Even in a country as torn by political and economic conflict as Argentina, and with a labor movement as well organized and militant as the CGT, state power can be used to impose wage controls and other harsh measures on a resistant citizenry. The success of the autocratic model, however, should not be measured by a government's decision to adopt unpopular policies but by its ability to implement them. The pitfalls, it turns out, are many. The ability of the rank and file to resist the state despite widespread repression has been repeatedly documented. There is also the problem of government unity and determination. Despite the appearance of strength, Argentina's military governments have seldom been unified in their convictions about the use of force for domestic political purposes. Some officers prefer to make concessions to the popular classes rather than confront them with arms. Others believe that bargaining offers the surest means of labor peace, while from time to time a few have held out for the restoration of a Peronist government which can legitimately claim labor support. As long as these divisions persist, the sustained success of the autocratic strategy is problematic.

The Co-optation Alternative

The co-optation strategy seeks to win the favor of labor by involving it in the design and administration of government economic policy. It proposes a special kind of political solution to what is essentially an economic problem. By giving organized labor, along with farmers and entrepreneurs, major responsibilities in policy design and enforcement, the government hopes to secure cooperation.

Co-optation is not really new. Postwar experience in Europe has led some to argue that a labor government, as in Great Britain, or Social Democratic administrations in Scandinavia or Germany, can more easily extract sacrifices from organized labor than can conservative governments, because labor parties enjoy a solid base of working-class support. The trust of labor leaders in such governments, as well as their faith in the beneficial results of such policies over the long haul, is said to encourage blue-collar support. Labor involvement in Latin American governments is also a familiar phenomenon. Many of the political parties in the region have actively pursued labor support; once it was secured, they used it to win elections and implement reform policies during the 1950s and 1960s. Labor-government relations in countries like Mexico and Venezuela, to name two, have involved the co-optation of labor leaders and the workers' docile adherence to government policies even when the policies temporarily deprived them of wage gains.[19]

Argentina too has employed the co-optive strategy. Perón included organized labor in his administration and rewarded loyal unions with high wages in the late 1940s. When it became necessary to impose a wage freeze in 1952 and 1953 to deal with payments and price difficulties, Perón drew on this reservoir of working-class support and exacted substantial sacrifices from his followers. Like a general rallying his troops to do battle with their enemies, he gained acceptance of policies which under other political circumstances would have provoked vigorous protests. The temptation to replicate this approach to incomes-policy management did not disappear with the fall of Perón in 1955; however, its application was handicapped by the belief that only Perón himself could carry it off, something which his enemies were reluctant to permit.

The co-optive strategy rests on three assumptions. It begins with the notion that labor will cooperate only if its leaders participate in the design and administration of policy. But something more than token involvement is required; labor's price is, if not the domination of the policymaking process, at least a central role in it. Second, the strategy assumes that the rank and file will accept the decisions of labor leaders who represent them in government councils, even if those decisions do them harm in the short run. Third, it assumes that critical groups like entrepreneurs and military officers will tolerate a government that brings labor leaders into its inner circle.

A reluctant Argentine military allowed the election and inauguration of a Peronist government in 1973 and the return of Juan Perón to the presidency of the country from which he had been expelled eighteen years before. Disillusioned with non-Peronist democratic governments and frustrated by Onganía's failings, General Alejandro Lanusse and his colleagues decided that the only way to create a legitimate government was through the restoration of free elections. They had, of course, hoped that a coalition of non-Peronist parties would win the 1973 elections; but when the coalition did not materialize, the officers accepted the overwhelming Peronist victory in the belief that, despite their many faults, the Peronists might be capable of restoring social discipline through voluntary means.[20]

The promises of Perón and his supporters during their campaign reinforced the hopes of the military. Abandoning the combative rhetoric of the

CONCORDIA

A central political objective of Peronism was to create an accord among labor, youth, and the military, who had fought viciously before Perón's return in 1973 and continued to battle after his death. (Courtesy Juan Carlos D'Abate)

past, Perón returned to Argentina in 1973 promising public order, political unity and a cooperative approach to the solution of the country's economic problems. The Peronists had not relinquished their goal of progressive income redistribution, but they recognized in 1973 that, before they could address that objective, they had to deal with the recurring problem of inflation. This required measures that could not help but prove unpopular with their supporters in the labor movement. What they needed, they recognized, was not only a program of finely tuned fiscal, monetary, wage, and price measures but also some way of persuading the working class to postpone its demands for higher income and for increased social services until prices had been stabilized and until steady economic growth had been reestablished. They found it in the instrument of the "social contract."

The Peronists' social contract, or *pacto social* as it was termed, was a bold initiative that departed markedly from the practices of the past eighteen years. Rejecting the complicated and unpredictable process of open bargaining as well as the politically unacceptable methods of physical repression practiced by military governments, Perón chose instead the creation of a formal agreement between labor, industry, and government that suspended collective bargaining and froze most prices for two years.[21]

The *pacto* would not have been attempted had not Peronist officials believed that they enjoyed unique political strengths conducive to its implementation. They were convinced that organized labor would cooperate with an incomes policy if CGT leaders were among those who authored and administered it. Trust was critical to the program's success, and Peronist leaders believed that they still enjoyed the trust of labor. They were not alone in this belief. Many Argentines had voted for the Peronists, and many entrepreneurs and military officers tolerated their return, because they hoped that Perón would secure labor peace. The authors of the *pacto* also believed that, with the help of Perón, who appeared to retain his popularity despite nearly two decades in exile, labor leaders could hold the rank and file in line.

Peronist policymakers also expected to secure the cooperation of Argentine entrepreneurs. The latter, the Peronists were convinced, had little choice but to accept government policy, much as they had done when Perón took similar measures in 1952. Moreover, in the short term entrepreneurs stood to gain from policies aimed at halting inflation by holding down wages, though few welcomed the price freeze that went with it. What made officials optimistic was the presence of the General Economic Confederation among the signers of the *pacto*. Since the early 1960s the CGE had championed the idea of quasi-governmental arrangements that would bring labor, industry, commerce, and agriculture together in a "conspiracy" to manage economic policy. Peronist leaders had welcomed these efforts and incorporated many of the CGE proposals into their platform. After the election they appointed CGE president José Gelbard as minister of economy and assigned him responsibility for the execution of the *pacto*.

The *pacto social* might have become one of Argentina's greatest economic success stories. But, alas, it did not. Instead, after a brief period of apparent achievement, the *pacto* collapsed, and the Argentine economy plunged into one of the severest crises in its modern history. By 1976 ten Peronist cabinets had come and gone, all unable to halt the plunge of the Argentine peso and the rise of prices at astronomical rates, reaching 320 percent in 1975. Finally, in late March 1976, the Argentine military ended the brief Peronist experiment.[22]

One place to begin a search for the causes of this debacle is with the implementation of the *pacto social*. Several conditions were needed for its success, as noted above. First there was the trust of labor leaders in the *pacto*. When it was created in June 1973, they accepted it with enthusiasm. Their confidence was reinforced by the fact that the modest wage increase authorized before the *pacto* went into effect and the moderately successful price freeze yielded a slight increase in real wages during the second half of 1973. Trust was also fostered by Perón's enthusiastic backing of the agreement. Though many labor leaders distrusted each other as well as most of the officials who surrounded Perón, they still accepted him as the ultimate authority within the movement and placed their faith in his ability to hold all parties to the agreement in line.

When Perón died in July 1974, that ultimate authority disappeared. None of his successors, including his wife and vice-president, Isabel, could command the allegiance of labor leaders. The efforts of his principal lieutenants to fill the leadership vacuum touched off a struggle among Peronist politicians and CGT leaders that eventually undermined not just the *pacto* but also the Peronist government responsible for it.

The confidence of the rank and file and local labor leaders in the *pacto* had never been as great as that of CGT leaders. Tensions between the leaders of the heavily bureaucratized and increasingly conservative CGT and the more radical union locals had been a problem since the late 1960s. These conflicts did not disappear with the return of Perón, despite his pleas for conformity, but instead became manifest in frequent wildcat strikes that violated the terms of the *pacto*. After Perón's death, the power struggles among his successors touched off even more intense battles within the labor movement. Most provocative were the machinations of José López Rega, minister of social welfare and principal advisor to President Isabel Perón, who tried to discipline uncooperative locals and impose his personal control over the CGT. The final confrontation came in mid-1975 at the time of the renewal of the *pacto* when, after several unions had secured informal management agreements for up to 100 percent wage increases, López Rega annulled all labor contracts and authorized only a 50 percent increase.

The decision touched off an unprecedented confrontation between the CGT and the Peronist government; the former triumphed, and López Rega was forced to flee into exile.[23]

Finally, there was the matter of entrepreneurial confidence in the *pacto*. Nearly all industrial associations signed the *pacto* in June 1973.[24] During the first year entrepreneurs watched and waited, guided by their habitual skepticism of official promises. Then in October 1974, President Isabel Perón suddenly dismissed Gelbard, a casualty of the power struggles that followed Perón's death. As a potential rival to the ambitious López Rega, Gelbard had to go. But in expelling Gelbard from the inner circle, López Rega also cut off the government's only link with Argentine entrepreneurs and its only hope of retaining some support. In the months that followed, business confidence in the *pacto* and the government quickly disintegrated, as entrepreneurs joined ranks with the government's critics in an effort to prevent a descent into economic chaos.

The *pacto* required constant care and reinforcement. Unfortunately, Perón's successors ignored this fact in their struggle for power after their leader's death. It had been a bold instrument that came closer to the creation of a cooperative foundation for incomes-policy administration than anything the Argentines had previously tried. It was, however, doomed from the outset. Most serious among its problems were the lack of rank-and-file discipline within the labor movement and the absence of entrepreneurial confidence in anyone but ministers taken from the ranks of business. Moreover, the Peronists never really created the kind of quasi-governmental, representative institutions needed to sustain the *pacto*. Rather than reinforcing their precarious consensus through the use of a private sector–controlled council or some other corporate body, they relied instead on the kind of semisecretive decision making that had traditionally undermined public confidence in Argentine policymaking. This was especially true in early 1975, when the *pacto* came up for renewal. By then its symbolic value had dissipated and public confidence in it was lost. Only some form of intense campaign to involve critical groups in administering it might have saved it. But Peronist leaders were too busy fighting each other to attend to their policy responsibilities.

Conclusions

Argentina is clearly an extreme case in matters of labor relations and economic instability. To generalize from its experience is quite hazardous. Nevertheless, the Argentine case is instructive, because it does illustrate how difficult it is to create institutions and rules which are conducive to the peaceful resolution of income-distribution issues in an industrializing society. Argentina offers insights into what happens to economic policy when political and economic polarization becomes severe; its case suggests why efforts to deal with such problems often fail.

Wage pressures alone did not cause Argentine inflation. Periodic shortages of consumer goods, the rising cost of imports, frequent currency devaluations, deficit spending to maintain a bloated public sector, and expansionary monetary policies all contributed at some point to price instability. Yet, when faced with the necessity of stabilizing prices, Argentine leaders, like their counterparts in other capitalistic nations, have repeatedly turned to the wage-price nexus to deal with the problem. The appeal of incomes policies is obvious. In the short run, wage restraint can slow the growth of prices, thereby yielding the appearance of quick results. Moreover, for those who are also interested in long-term solutions to the problem of the wage-price spiral, greater stability in the wage-setting process is essential. What they must do is establish new rules for wage setting and then transform the rules into accepted norms through continuous enforcement.

Unfortunately, in 1955 Argentines did not welcome new rules with equal enthusiasm. After thirteen years of rigged elections and the repression of organized labor by conservative governments during the 1930s, followed by ten years of divisive populist rule under Juan Perón after 1945, there was no consensus on matters of political economy. Nor was there the kind of institutional infrastructure believed to be essential to cooperative public problem solving. Liberal democracy had been discredited during the 1930s, and Perón's pseudo-corporatism had made statist doctrines anathema to much of the Argentine elite and bourgeoisie. Attempts to restore constitutional government after 1955 were therefore handicapped at the outset by widespread distrust of its institutions and by deep antipathies among the groups whose support it needed to survive.

In the absence of conditions favoring the administration of cooperative incomes policy, Argentine leaders had to improvise, selecting measures and using procedures that compensated for the deficiencies they faced. Yet, to succeed, each of their remedies also depended on the presence or creation of certain conditions, many of which, it turned out, were lacking when they were most needed. In reviewing the Argentine experience in incomes-policy administration, we find two patterns most striking: (1) each strategy achieved what appeared to be modest short-term success only to flounder and collapse under extreme pressure; and (2) political considerations played a critical role in bringing them down.

Argentine governments could set new rules for wage determination. Nevertheless, despite some success in achieving price-stabilization objectives, each set of rules provoked political responses that eventually undermined their utility. The forces at work differed with the particular strategy attempted, but the outcomes in each case were similar. For example, bargaining worked modestly well under Frondizi and Illia; the former brought the rate of inflation down to acceptable levels, while the latter did not let it get out of hand. Nevertheless, labor leaders worked unceasingly to bring both governments down. Thus, even though Frondizi and Illia secured limited rank-and-file cooperation at the bargaining table, they could not achieve it at the polls. Their electoral defeat by the Peronists in 1962 and 1965 prompted military intervention and the termination of their experiments in bargaining. In the end, modest success in wage policies was swamped by larger political concerns.

The autocratic strategy appeared to achieve even greater success in the short run. But although the application of force could secure labor acquiescence to unpopular policies, it could not immobilize the rank and file nor destroy labor's hostility toward political regimes opposed to its interests. The capacity of the workers to protest against autocratic methods survived, allowing them to seize the opportunity when it arose to strike out against the regime and discredit its autocratic methods, albeit temporarily.

No approach to incomes-policy administration seemed more needed in Argentina in the early 1970s than that of co-optation. The exclusion of labor from the policymaking process had fostered political conflicts that made it impossible to sustain the execution of incomes policies. With the repression and exclusion of organized labor discredited as an option, labor involvement in policy formation — whatever its apparent costs — appeared to be the only alternative left. But, after 1973, Argentina's labor leadership was wracked by division, and the government that had co-opted it fell victim to political opportunists more intent on the acquisition of personal power than on effective policy management. As a result, the co-optive model never received the care that it required.

When in March 1976, ten years after General Onganía had overthrown a constitutional government, the military under General Jorge Videla brought the Peronist government to a halt, the outlook for Argentina was bleak, though not unfamiliar. This time the new government faced a well-organized guerrilla movement able to strike down nearly any government or private-sector leader as well as an economy plagued by one of the worst crises in Argentine history. To deal with the guerrillas, the government unleashed a violent campaign of repression; to cope with the economy, it adopted a graduated process of liberalization aimed at making Argentines live by the rules of the national and international marketplaces.

Autocratic rule once again brought the repression of labor unions, controlled wages, and prohibition against political activity. When in March 1981 General Videla relinquished the presidency to General Roberto Viola, a junta-chosen successor, Videla could boast that there had been no *Cordobazo* during his tenure. Moreover, as promised, the Argentine economy had been opened up significantly. Nevertheless, one should not rush to judgment, for if we have learned anything from the study of

Argentine politics, it is the need for caution when assessing its political renovations. In March 1981 Videla left to General Viola an economy plagued by high inflation, a record foreign debt, huge public sector deficits, and a deep recession, conditions which quickly undermined confidence in the new president and forced him to relinquish the presidency to General Leopoldo Galtieri eight months later.

Equally telling in light of Videla's promise to heal the country's political wounds was his failure to leave his successors any concrete plan for the reopening of the political process to civilian participation. No doubt one reason for the omission was his recognition of the fact that Peronism, though weakened by the loss of Juan Perón and the persecution of its leaders, retained the loyalty of most of a labor force that still outnumbered its opponents at the polls.

NOTES

1. For a review of incomes policy in industrial nations, see Lloyd Ulman and Robert J. Flanagan, *Wage Restraint: A Study of Incomes Policies in Western Europe* (Berkeley and Los Angeles: University of California Press, 1971).

2. Divisions within the CGT and the issues that caused them are discussed in Rubén Rotondaro, *Realidad y cambio en el sindicalismo* (Buenos Aires: Pleamar, 1971); and Roberto Carri, *Sindicatos y poder en la Argentina* (Buenos Aires: Editorial Sudestada, 1967).

3. The CGE was actually created by small businessmen from Argentina's interior provinces in the late 1940s. Its leaders supported Perón's promotion of industrialization and allowed their organization to be taken over and expanded by the government. It was closed after the fall of Perón in 1955 and legalized again in 1958.

4. For a discussion of the relative size and importance of these two organizations, see Dardo Cúneo, *Comportamiento y crisis de la clase empresaria* (Buenos Aires: Pleamar, 1967); and Robert Ayres, "The 'Social Pact' as Anti-Inflationary Policy: The Argentine Experience since 1973," *World Politics* 28 (1976), 478–80.

5. On policy differences, see Cúneo, *Comportamiento y crisis*; and José Luis de Imaz, *Los que mandan* (Buenos Aires: EUDEBA, 1964), ch. 7.

6. Unión Industrial Argentina, *Memoria y balance* (Buenos Aires: UIA, 1957).

7. His program is outlined in Arturo Frondizi, *Política económica nacional* (Buenos Aires: Ediciones Arayú, 1963), pp. 127–48.

8. See Consejo Técnico de Investigaciones, S.A., *La economía argentina – 1964* (Buenos Aires: CTI, 1965).

9. Rotondaro, *Realidad y cambio*, p. 288; Carri, *Sindicatos y poder*, p. 93; Santiago Senén González, *El sindicalismo después de Perón* (Buenos Aires: Editorial Galerna, 1971), pp. 28–32.

10. González, *El sindicalismo*, pp. 52–57.

11. Consejo Técnico, *La economía argentina – 1964.*

12. Ibid.

13. Democratic governments proved highly vulnerable to labor resistance in dealing with unionized public employees; repeated attempts to impose fiscal austerity in the public sector have thus met with failure. See Rotondaro, *Realidad y cambio*, p. 290.

14. Cost-of-living data are calculated from Centro de Información Económica, *La economía argentina: Treinta años en cifras* (Buenos Aires: CIE, 1971), p. 12.

15. Adalbert Krieger Vasena, *Política económica argentina: Discursos del Ministro de Economía y Trabajo* (Buenos Aires: Ministerio de Economía y Trabajo, 1968), pp. 23–36; see also Juan Carlos de Pablo, *Política anti-inflacionaria en la Argentina, 1967–1970* (Buenos Aires: Amorrortu, 1971), pp. 23–97.

16. Rotondaro, *Realidad y cambio*, pp. 325–29; Carri, *Sindicatos y poder*, pp. 162–64.

17. Ibid.

18. Daniel Villar, *El cordobazo* (Buenos Aires: La Historia Popular, 1971).

19. See Henry Landsberger, "The Labor Elite: Is It Revolutionary?" in *Elites in Latin America*, ed. Seymour M. Lipset and Aldo Solari (New York: Oxford University Press, 1967), pp. 256–300.

20. See Alejandro A. Lanusse, *Mi testimonio* (Buenos Aires: Lasserre Editores, 1977); on the Peronist restoration of 1973 as a process, see ch. 6.

21. The *pacto social* can be found in the *Review of the River Plate*, 19 June 1973; see Ayres, "The 'Social Pact' as Anti-Inflationary Policy."

22. Peronist economic policy of this period is discussed in Juan Carlos de Pablo, *Economía política del peronismo* (Buenos Aires: El Cid Editor, 1980).

23. Summarized in the *Review of the River Plate*, 22 July 1975.

24. Rural groups signed a separate agreement with the government called the *Acto de Compromiso del Campo*, which promised an increase in official commodity prices in exchange for increased production. See *La Opinión*, 9 Sept. 1973, p. 16.

4

JUAN CARLOS D'ABATE

Trade Unions and Peronism

The political situation in Argentina today is that of a country on the periphery, strongly connected to the international market, financially and economically intertwined with other powerful nations. Argentina is truly the most "developed" country in Latin America, considering its public awareness, cultural expression, high economic level, important raw materials, industrial power, and high population density in urban and manufacturing areas. In addition, one must remember that the political processes of the country have originated from a unique, deeply rooted historical experience which has not always been well understood. Errors frequently result from analyses of this experience based on European or North American concepts and methods which are in no way related to Argentine phenomena. In Argentina, the groups in power usually represent, at various times, leaders of the armed forces, the higher state bureaucracy, top government officialdom, the literary professions, and union management. These groups alternately assume positions of authority through coalitions, which are frequently unstable.

Complementing the influence of these groups is the power of the state. In the case of Argentina the classic state has been transformed from a mere instrument of the traditional power classes into a power in itself. At present, the state is the nation's most powerful proprietor and entrepreneur, controlling some 60 percent of the national economy. Argentina at this stage is atypical in the proportion of power held by the state, and therefore the usual patterns of power relationships, as found in other Western nations, do not apply in the case of Argentina. At the same time, the informed masses have become an increasingly strong undercurrent in Argentine politics during the twentieth century. These masses of the population now have to be, in one way or another, represented by the state leadership.

The Peronist movement drew strength from processes going on in Argentine society, and in turn it affected those processes. In studying the movement, one must not be misled by the picturesque nature of the first figures accompanying Perón; they were no more than mere instruments of the forceful motivations and drives underlying the evolution of Argentine history. One of these forces has been the internal migration from rural areas of Argentina to industrial centers, which has created an industrial working class of some seven million people. In a national population of 27 million, this large class of urban workers makes Argentina unique within the Latin American framework. The working-class population has gradually become concentrated, and sooner or later it would have imposed its presence upon the political scene. In Perón, this mass found a leader and a program which facilitated its transformation into the greatest single power behind national politics. Since Perón's death, the working class has remained a definitive part of the Argentine political scene; today and in the future no government can ignore its numerical force or its heightened self-confidence.

For the most part, the Peronist movement gathered its representation from the real transformations taking place in twentieth-century Argentina. While some leaders wanted to exploit the movement in order to enhance the socioeconomic development of Argentina, the urban masses could not be maneuvered by traditional patterns. As a result, Peronism utilized new political appeals and methods which enjoyed the warm and unconditional loyalty of a people who, by participating in the power structure and collaborating toward the general greatness of the nation, saw themselves as being understood, as being appreciated in their longtime desire to improve their standard of living. Under Perón's leadership, measures affecting the workers, and, consequently, the development of the country, were not adopted principally by the companies, but by those located in the decision-making centers of government. In other words, the Peronist movement found a reason to exist by connecting itself to the rise of the working class, which would, from that point on, become its "backbone," as Perón customarily stated.

Peronist governments granted the workers not only recognition but also the right to direct political participation. As a result of the workers' active presence, new state policies were developed. This occurred through the relationship between the chief of state and the organized working class, especially with the formation of a single General Confederation of Labor. Also, during Perón's three presidencies (1946–1952, 1952–1955, 1973–1974), labor leaders took their places in legislative bodies as deputies, senators, and municipal councilors, as well as in the executive branch—for example, in the Interior Ministry, in the national Department of Labor—in vice-governorships, in state banks, and in other government ministries and offices. To appreciate the dynamics and the impact of Peronism, one needs to understand more deeply this process of worker incorporation.

The Formation of National Trade Unions, 1943–1974

The "nationalization" of the working class came into being with the creation of the Secretariat of Labor and Social Security (Decree-Law 15.074

of November 27, 1943) and under the subsequent leadership of Perón. Up to that point, there were only a few organized unions affiliated to three different national confederations, and these were of foreign, internationalist orientation — anarchist, socialist, or communist. In 1943, however, the majority of union leaders began to confide in and collaborate with the person who would immediately become the most genuine representative and executor of the aspirations and unsatisfied needs of the labor force, Colonel Perón, who headed the Secretariat of Labor and Social Security. Labor unions increased the scope of their activities in the trades and in the social sphere. There were strikes for better wages, against employers' entrenched resistance. Most labor conflicts ended with agreements arbitrated by the Labor Secretariat and, in the most important cases, by Perón himself. Internal struggles also developed between the old union leadership and new supporters of Peronism, which resulted, in most cases, in the election of Peronist leaders in local and national unions. Despite the unorthodox methods used by those seeking power, there existed a truly effective rule by the majority that broadened the democratic character of the unions. Union members participated in the affairs of their organizations as they had never done before, even to the extent of opposing the established leadership. The 1952 national election held by the textile workers union offers an example: the official leadership, headed by Antonio Hermida (a representative in Congress), José Grioli (second vice-president of the Senate of the Province of Buenos Aires), and other members of officialdom were deposed by a newcomer, Andrés Framini, who at the time held a minor trade-sector post. Some 76,000 out of a total membership of 120,000 voted, and Framini's slate (Lista Verde) won by 4,000 votes.[1]

In 1943 there were twenty-two national labor unions organizing city, state, and federal employees, railroad workers, city transit workers, salespersons, and workers in banking, commerce, insurance, and the beer industry, among others. Between 1943 and 1953, approximately sixty new national labor unions were organized in industries such as communications, construction, utilities, health care, shipping, metalworking, the manufacture of food, tobacco, clothing, shoes, textiles, leather goods, paper, glass, plastics, chemicals, rubber, and automotive and petroleum products.[2] National union membership grew dramatically during this period; for example, the Federación Gráfica Bonaerense (the printers union) grew from 6,000 members in 1942 to 13,000 in 1946, and had 31,000 members by 1947.[3]

Besides stimulating sharp increases in membership, the rise of Peronism also gave unions a political orientation. In 1929 there had been three national labor confederations in Argentina: the Federación Obrera Regional (FORA), led by anarchists; the Unión Sindical Argentina (USA), led by syndicalists; and the Confederación Obrera Argentina (COA), organized and led by reform socialists. In March 1929, these organizations agreed to

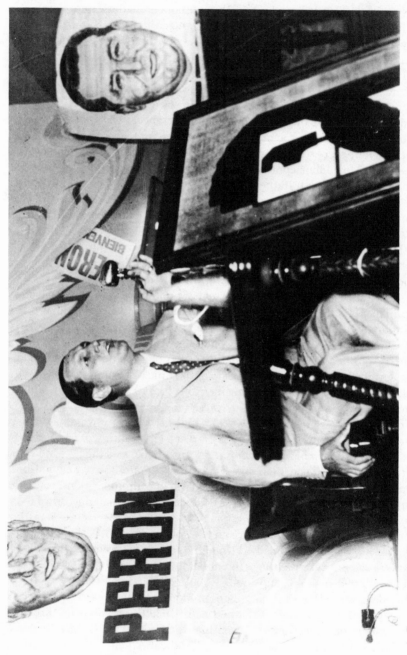

In December 1945 Perón begins his first campaign for the presidency with a two-hour speech. The Peronist party shield is before him. (Courtesy Wide World Photos)

organize a unique national organization, the Confederación General del Trabajo de la República Argentina (CGT), which was founded on September 27, 1930. The COA and the USA were dissolved, although the latter was reorganized in March 1937. During the second annual convention of the CGT, held in 1942, a split occurred and two national fronts briefly resulted, the first headed by José Domenech of the railroad workers union, and the second by Francisco Pérez Leirós, head of the city employees union. In 1945 the CGT was reunited and reorganized under a new set of rules. With this reform, the smaller unions were given greater representation and their influence and power therefore increased in relation to the larger organizations which had so long dominated the CGT. The confederation grew in membership from 330,000 in 1941 to 450,000 in 1946, and reached 2,500,000 members in 1951.[4]

An era of new Argentine social policies also began with Perón's activities in the Secretariat of Labor and Social Security. In this connection, the most fundamental achievements of the first Peronist decade were as follows:

1. Approval of the Agricultural Worker Statute by Decree-Law 28.169 of October 17, 1944, which sought to improve rural working conditions.

2. Creation and organization of the Labor Courts by Decree-Law 32.347 of November 30, 1944.

3. Creation of the National Commission of Apprenticeship and Professional Orientation by Decrees 14.538/44 and 6648/45, by which the state, together with labor representatives, assumed the responsibility for the supervision, control, and direction of the work and apprenticeship of minors between fourteen and eighteen years of age. Some 166 professional and technical schools and 208 factory schools, which also enrolled adults, were installed throughout the country.

4. Creation of the National Institute of Compensation by Decree-Law 33.302/45, for the purpose of instituting the minimum wage and assisting the executive branch with matters concerning salaries, prices, and the standard of living. The direction of this institute was distributed equally among company owners, blue-collar workers, and other employees.

5. An annual bonus (aguinaldo) to all workers, also established by the above decree. The bonus consisted of one-twelfth of the total salary received during the year.

6. Decree-Law 1740/45 establishing yearly paid vacations of from ten to fifteen days for all workers.

7. Decree-Law 23.852 of October 2, 1945 organizing professional and labor associations, granting exclusive defense and representation of the workers in a particular field to the union most representative in that field. This law also specified which practices by employers were considered disloyal and contrary to the ethics of professional labor relations. Unions were authorized to participate in political activities on either a temporary

or a permanent basis whenever a general assembly or convention of their members so decided.

8. The implantation within the companies of an inspection system carried out by union delegates and internal factory commissions to ensure that employers fulfill commitments made in collective agreements.

9. Creation of the National Workers University (known today as the National University of Technology) by Law 13.229/48, as an institution of highly technical instruction. Its first president was a labor representative.

10. Creation of the National Directory of Employment Services by Law 13.591/49, which organized free job placement services for workers throughout the country.

11. Law 14.250/53, providing a legal statute for the collective labor conventions which had been in use since 1944, a year in which 123 agreements were signed benefiting one and a half million employees. The agreements allowed free discussion of salaries and working conditions between labor representatives and employers for each line of national production.

12. The National Institute of Social Security, instituted by Decree-Law 29.176/44, extending retirement benefits to all labor activities. Retirement funds were started for commercial employees by Decree-Law 31.655/44; for industrial personnel by Decree-Law 13.937/46; for independent workers, company executives and professionals by Law 14.396/54, and for rural workers by Law 14.399/54.

13. Making the Secretariat of Labor and Social Security a national ministry, by amendments approved in the 1949 constitutional reform.

14. Granting constitutional status to unions, recognizing the "right to free unionization and participation in other lawful activities leading to the defense of professional interests while establishing essential labor rights that society must respect and protect, assuring free action and repressing any obstacle or preventive act." Article 37 of the Constitution granted a similar constitutional category to the following special rights: the right to work, just compensation, training, decent working conditions, health protection, social security, family protection, benefits for senior citizens, and cultural and educational opportunities. In short, a main philosophical principle of the Peronist doctrine was incorporated into the text of the Constitution: *respect for the personal dignity of the worker.* The concept of "institutional labor relations" replaced the free, capitalistic regime which was based on ownership of private property and the contracting of services individually arranged by the parties concerned. "Institutional labor relations"[5] were founded on labor laws not subject to personal will or desire, and by collective labor contracts consisting of standards established by professional groups, in which the workers became authentic legislators controlling their own working conditions.

The Constitution also declared that the right to personal freedom may not be interpreted as bringing advantages for some to the detriment of others. Furthermore, the constitutional reform of 1949 (repealed in 1956) specified that the abuse of personal rights, if deemed detrimental to communal welfare or if understood as the exploitation of one individual by another, would constitute a felony punishable by law. During the initial Peronist period (1943–1955), a total of 309 labor laws and 109 social security laws were passed, with 124 labor laws and 49 social security laws dictated during the initial twenty-six months (November 1943 to January 1946) of de facto government with Perón at the head of the Secretariat of Labor and Social Security. The rest were enacted during the constitutional period (March 1946 to September 1955) with Perón as president of the country. In addition to these laws, the Constitution of 1949 provided that the National Congress must initiate a code of social rights, although it is still non-existent after three decades.

The third, short-lived presidency of Perón brought further legal changes. Law 20.615 of December 11, 1973, affected professional labor associations. It exempted the unions from the payment of any charges, including taxes, improvement contributions, and assessments for administrative actions. In addition, unions could organize business associations which benefited from extensive exemptions as long as the union was the sole member of the corporation. Chapter 10 of the "Union Laws" establishes that (a) workers holding elected offices or representative positions in professional labor associations, workers who are subdelegates or internal commission members, and those active in similar representative posts are to be guaranteed job security during their terms of office plus one year more after the term of office; and (b) workers who participate in a union election (whether elected to office or not), and those who have helped to formulate the activities or the constitution of a union, cannot be dismissed or suspended from their jobs, nor can their working conditions be changed. No police authority may occupy, investigate, or inspect union premises without a proper court order based on reasonable cause to suspect a felony.

In the case of Law 20.744 of September 20, 1974, called the Labor Contract Law, a congress of labor attorneys from business employee affiliates studied and drafted a bill which was later passed on to the General Confederation of Labor. Together with the Department of Labor, the confederation put the bill into its final form before sending it to the National Congress, where it was adapted and improved until it became a national law. Compensating for the inequalities present in the traditional system of capital-labor relations, the law emphasizes the basic concept of social justice. It attempts to establish the principle of good faith as the standard and foresees a definite need to force corporations to assume a more socially constructive role. The law, which was structured into fifteen titles containing three hundred articles, drew together all accumulated legislative material, the teachings of national and foreign doctrines, the jurisprudence of the labor laws, the dispositions of diverse collective agreements, and the recommendations of national and international congresses and the International Labor Organization.

The Objectives of the Peronists, 1973–1974

Juan Perón appreciated the nature of Argentine industrialization. He knew that Argentina possesses a diversified production structure composed of advanced industrialization, high business productivity in comparison with other developing countries, large government firms that produce and distribute basic elements of the national economy, and sectors of the population with mature political consciousness. The economy gains strength from the fact that multinational firms are principally involved with marketing products manufactured within the country and with managing the national savings.[6] In short, the country is in a position to carry out an independent political policy geared toward the promotion of autonomous development.

Highly conscious of this reality in Argentina, Perón obtained the support of almost all the political and social forces in the country to achieve independent development and to bring about social justice. On December 7, 1972, with Perón as political leader and coordinator of an alliance of powerful groups, the so-called programmatic areas of agreement were approved and signed by the General Confederation of Labor and by the 62 Organizaciones. The agreement condemned any measures that would undermine the buying capacity of the internal market or weaken the operative power of the national production structure. A vital and flexible minimum wage was to keep real wages up; equal pay was required for equal work; the constitutional right to strike was guaranteed. Unions and companies were to participate in the management of companies, boards, banks, and other agricultural, industrial, and commercial organizations. Salaries, family allowances, and pensions were to be increased. Salary readjustments and annual transfers were to be based on the increase of the productivity of the economy. The construction of more than 500,000 dwellings was to begin within two years.

Perón worked to implement these goals after taking office. Having governed at the beginning of 1947 on the basis of two five-year plans, he produced a three-year plan of government in 1973. Regarding social security, the plan suggested that group interests must be subordinate to the general public interest, with the right to receive social security being equal to the right to receive salaries. The plan also sought to reduce unemployment through the training and rehabilitation of persons displaced because of technological or structural factors.

Perón understood that such policies, needed to transform the country, had to be supported by the agreed-upon participation of organized workers, business executives, and the state. As a result, the National Commitment Act was signed on May 30, 1973 by the Department of Finance, the secretary general of the General Confederation of Labor (CGT), and the president of the General Economic Confederation (CGE). This act tried to return to the workers the opportunity to share in the national income as they had

On Labor Day, 1974, workers gather in the Plaza de Mayo to hear Perón's address from the Casa Rosada. (Courtesy Juan Carlos D'Abate)

done in previous years. A national commission on prices, revenue, and the standard of living was created within the framework of the Socio-Economic Council; it was to analyze changes in the cost of living and to propose measures to defend the growth of the buying power of wages. In addition, a policy for salary improvements was determined, the minimum wage was established, and funds for retired persons were increased. All of these measures were subject to periodic readjustments in accordance with the growth of the economy's average productivity.

The act also supported an extensive housing program, with a housing plan in underprivileged areas being immediately initiated. It tried to provide drinking water, energy, and health services, among other necessities, to those in need. It also stipulated that 80 percent of the housing credit originating from private and official banks would be used to construct individual or multiple housing units with interiors measuring up to seventy square meters. Loan installments were not to exceed 20 percent of the borrower's salary.

Finally, the act made clear its underlying purpose of redistributing income and power in favor of workers. It stated:

> This act is based on the joint declaration of the CGT and CGE of September 7, 1972. This commitment was signed with the intent to do away with the injustices suffered by the workers for almost two decades as well as the economic unbalance and lack of control brought to us by the strategies of colonialism, for which this act requires and demands the unconditional observance of all. This Act of Commitment is not a circumstantial price and salary agreement. It is the definition of an irreversible political action to increase worker participation in the national income within the framework of a new concept of worker compensation and relations among the social sectors — a starting point for the process of national reconstruction and liberation.[7]

In December 1973, Perón himself announced the first concrete results of this policy. Referring initially to his earlier presidencies, he said:

> Our policy at that time was the same as the one we are following today — to establish a "life-line" whereby, after studying costs and salaries, it can be determined that no worker's family can be submerged below that line representing the necessities of life, despite the humble circumstances of his home. All salaries are scaled on that line, in accordance with the capacity, conditions, and effort put forth by each individual. The state only guarantees that no one will be submerged. The rest is up to the individual and the competition resulting from the capabilities, decisions, and

intelligence of each wage earner, who earns his salary within the limits of his capacities.

That was the doctrine that we implanted in 1946. We are at the same point today. . . . We feel that the distribution of benefits must be fair and divided into halves. In other words, we must not say that we have a per capita income of $1,350, as was customarily stated. That is a fantasy, because there are some with $5,000 and others with nothing. That is not the proportion that we are observing nor the one we want.

We recognize that the proprietor of the company has the right to his share, because he pays for labor and raw materials. He must cover management expenses and, in addition, must make a profit. That is covered perfectly well by 50 percent of what is produced. The other 50 percent belongs to the workers. This is not an easy index to reach, because it is the basis of a permanent struggle. . . .

I understand that this struggle must be regulated through a perfect equilibrium where possibilities and not aspirations are compared, since everyone wants to earn more. This is logical and necessary, but there is a limit to earnings set by any number of circumstances that must be recognized.

For that reason, I tell you that on May 25, 1973, we reached, through the distribution of profits, an index of 33 percent for the workers and 67 percent for the companies. This is not the balance we left in 1955, which was 47.7 percent for the workers and 52.3 percent for the proprietors. We continued to elevate that rising scale until reaching 50 percent. That percentage dropped to 33 percent during the eighteen years following 1955. That 33 percent worries me at this time. We must strengthen it more and more. By December 31, a few days hence, we will have established a proportion of 42.5 percent for labor and the rest for the companies. By 1977, we must reach that long-desired proportion of 50–50.[8]

The level of 42.5 percent of profits going to industrial workers, reached in 1974, was one of the highest achieved in national history, with the exception of the level reached in 1952 which gave the workers 61 percent participation in the national revenue.[9] At the same time, a drop in the unemployment rate from 6.6 percent in April 1974, to 4.5 percent in December of the same year was the lowest in the period from 1966 to 1976. As the chapter by Gary Wynia makes clear, this level of redistribution and employment could not be maintained, but its initiation clearly marks the priorities of Perón.

The Political Participation of the Working Class

During Perón's three presidencies, workers gradually rose to positions of political importance. The labor movement co-governed during these periods; in other words, the organized labor movement during the Perón governments ceased to be a power factor, a special interest, or pressure group, and became part of the government itself. Its functions were clearly established through custom (as in the case of the Ministry of Labor, which was always in the hands of the workers), through legal disposition (for example, the inclusion of representatives in the directories of official banks), and through party support (one third of the political candidates in the Peronist party coming from labor). This participation in power resulted directly from the unification of the General Confederation of Labor with the Peronist movement.

Perón's designation, in 1946, of Ángel Gabriel Borlenghi, secretary-general of the commerce workers union, to the key post of interior minister stands out as a sign of workers' political significance within the Peronist movement. Another example, in a different epoch and situation, was the Peronist candidacy in 1962 of Andrés Framini — a former textile worker who held the position of general secretary of the CGT — for the governorship of Buenos Aires Province. He was nominated and elected by a large majority. However, the election was later annulled by President Frondizi, who was himself soon deposed by a military coup.

Worker participation became very extensive from 1973 to 1976. In addition to occupying one-third of the seats in the national parliament, provincial legislatures, and municipal councils, workers were elected vice-governors of the most important provinces of the country, including Buenos Aires, Córdoba, Santa Fe, and Mendoza.[10] Following the traditions of the first two presidencies of Perón, the Ministry of Labor was placed under the direction of a union member who also gave the positions of undersecretary, various national directorships, and regional delegateships to workers.[11] Although never implemented, a decision was made to re-create the labor attaché offices in Argentine embassies abroad, with the offices being handled by workers as was the case from 1946 to 1955. Workers took part in the directories of the major banks, including the National Bank, the National Central Bank, the National Mortgage Bank, the National Development Bank, the Bank of the Province of Buenos Aires, the Bank of the City of Buenos Aires, and the National Savings and Insurance Bank.[12]

In less-structured areas, workers also gained new positions. Labor representatives formed part of the directories of the national subsidy institutions for the families of business employees, industrial workers, and longshoremen. Horacio Cuenca, administrative secretary of the construction workers union, occupied the presidency of the union's National Registry, an official organization which handled unemployment benefits. Abel O. Cuchetti, the communication workers union's adjunct secretary, headed the National Institute of Social Services, and its board of directors also included union representatives. Juan José Taccone, a member of the Argentine Federation of Utility Workers, gained the presidency of the state energy company, SEGBA. During that period, workers' self-government was established, the so-called *autogestión*. In 1976, after the military takeover, this worker's conquest was annulled. As a final highlight, the General Confederation of Labor (CGT) influenced the appointments of several high-level employees on a national scale, as in the case of the National Director of Chemistry, Dr. Evaristo Buezas, and the National Director of Adult Education, Miguel Cincunegui. This also happened in the appointments of the secretaries of commerce and housing, and the president of the University of Technology.

The Trade Unions' Economic Power

The possibility of strengthening the economic and financial situation of the unions originated with the first Perón government, which established obligatory union contributions and support of various social services by workers and company owners alike. That is, the workers of a given sector, whether union members or not, had to accept a salary deduction from their employers which (in addition to the company's own contribution) would be deposited in banks to the account of the corresponding union organization. The general obligation, included in all collective labor agreements, was based on the assumption that all workers, union members and non-union workers both, would benefit from the agreements negotiated by union leaders and management.

During Perón's first two presidencies, when the state was a proper and efficient provider of social services from medical aid to tourism, well-managed unions began to invest their capital by purchasing first the buildings occupied by their headquarters, then hospitals, sports fields, and hotels in tourist centers. After Perón's fall in 1955, the unions tried to maintain the social services begun in the Perón era. At the beginning of 1958, once the military government's intervention in the unions and the restrictions imposed on union leaders had come to an end, organized unions intensified their efforts. Their social services were developed to their maximum potential to cover the state's default regarding its social obligations and the evident decline in the workers' buying power. A powerful health organization was created through the direct purchase of existing hospitals and clinics, by constructing new health-care facilities, by purchasing new equipment, and by contracting for the services of private physicians.

Union buying and/or contracting of hotels in large tourist centers, vacation resorts, and sports centers also increased. For example, with 20,000 affiliates, the Insurance Union became the proprietor of nineteen hotels dispersed throughout the country. Construction also began for housing projects and high-rise apartment buildings. They were financed through agreements with state banks, through private cooperatives created for that purpose, and through international loans such as those arranged by the Light and Power Union from the Inter-American Development Bank.

Greater worker influence on government is also evident in the dramatic increase in social services during the Perón presidencies. In 1944, the creation of the Social Service Commission by Decree Number 30.655/44 made the Commission responsible for implementing social services in every establishment with salaried workers. Benefits included free medical attention, pharmaceutical necessities, and indispensable food, clothing, and household articles at cost price. Laws providing social services for specific unions also appeared — for railroad workers in 1944, for employees of the glass industry in 1946, for bank employees in 1950, and for insurance workers in 1951. In all cases, union representatives served on boards of directors.

At present, social service benefits are widely available through Argentine unions. Pharmaceutical services are offered through 165 pharmacies throughout the country directly managed by the social services system, not to mention union branches with their own pharmaceutical dispensaries. The service grants free medicine or a minimum 25 percent discount, according to the union's financial situation.[13] In about half the cases, unions offer other benefits through union-subsidized hotels, athletic fields, child care centers, homes for the elderly, consumer discount stores, housing projects, low-interest loans or loans at no interest, libraries, cultural and educational programs offering scholarships, training courses, education in union schools, and special cultural activities. The economic power of union-funded social service agencies is great indeed. To take one example, OSECAC (the social service organization for commerce employees) has one million direct members. When the families of members are also included, the number of beneficiaries rises to two and a half million persons. Services are completely free in Greater Buenos Aires, which encompasses about half the beneficiaries.[14] The monthly income of this organization in dollars is approximately $2,000,000.

Tables 1 and 2 indicate the vast extent of social benefits provided through unions in contemporary Argentina. Table 1 reflects the entire scope of union social services as compared to those coming from other agencies. With 17,500,000 persons covered out of a national population of 27,000,000, unions clearly provide the major support for social service activities. Table 2 suggests the large number of workers covered in various industries and the range of their activities. In addition to the clinics and subsidies mentioned in the table, each of these twelve unions, all Peronist in orientation, has its own publications, libraries, and training schools, while also running hotels, pharmacies, and sports facilities for its members.

TABLE 1
Sources of Social Service Funding in Argentina (1976)

	No. of Funds	Persons Affected (in millions)	Percentage of the Population Affected
Trade unions	362	17.5	70
Provincial and municipal governments	22	2.0	8
Armed forces and security forces	5	1.0	4
Totals	389	20.5	82

Source: Fundación de Estudios Geopolíticos, Económicos y Sociales, Obras Sociales (Buenos Aires, 1976), table 3.

Unions have also created their own, well-managed corporations, which have gone on to achieve very important economic surpluses. The General Confederation of Commerce Employees and its 347 affiliates, for example, own the Banco Sindical, S.A. (the Union Bank). The Instituto Asegurador Mercantil (the Institute of Mercantile Insurance) and the Companía Argentina de Seguros, S.A. (the Argentine Insurance Company) belong equally to the General Confederation of Commerce Employees and to the Proprietors' Coordinating Commission of Mercantile Activities. The Institute of Mercantile Insurance is connected with the International Association of Social Security and has 270,000 obligatory life insurance beneficiaries from 40,000 businesses throughout the country. Other similar corporations include the Insurance Cooperative formed by the insurance union, the Consumer Cooperative of the utilities union, and the Labor Cooperative of the naval workers union.

Final Considerations

With the death of Perón on July 1, 1974, the symbiotic relationship between the people and their leader was extinguished. Also his closest associates were removed as a consequence of the internal political turmoil that followed. Because of the rapidity with which events occurred, and the lack of contingency planning for them, neither trade unionists nor politicians could replace the leader with another chief executive or with a team that

TABLE 2
Characteristics of the Largest Nonstate National Trade Unions in Argentina (1976)

	Date Founded	No. of Affiliates	Members Represented (in thousands)	Workers Represented (in thousands)	Medical Clinic Ownership	Subsidies to Members
Textile Workers Association	27 Oct. 1945	45	110	155	yes	yes; 1,000-unit housing project built
Automotive Workers Union	1 June 1945	41	80	110	under contract	yes; has scholastic aid fund and strikes and emergencies fund
Banking Association	6 Nov. 1924	58	110	115	yes	yes; 500-unit housing project built
Argentine Federation of Health Employees	5 Feb. 1949	90	75	110	yes	yes; death benefits only
General Confederation of Commerce Employees	24 Mar. 1932	347	311	1,000	yes	yes; 25,000-unit housing project built; provides discount prices for medication and burial subsidies
Railroad Union	6 Oct. 1922	370	160	160	yes [a]	yes; 4,000-unit housing project built; gives academic scholarships and burial subsidies

Metal Workers Union	19 Apr. 1943	53	126	170	yes	no
Construction Workers Union	4 Sept. 1943	85	116	190	yes	yes; 300-unit housing project built
Federation of Meat Products Industry Workers	10 June 1947	75	65	90	yes	no
Federation of Food Industry Workers	1 Mar. 1947	40	40	55	yes	no
Federation of Workers and Employees of the Paper Industry	3 Apr. 1948	47	14.5	20	yes	yes; provides personal loans, academic scholarships, burial subsidies and assistance during illness
Fraternity [society of train engineers]	20 Aug. 1887	216	25.5	26	yes [a]	yes; provides personal loans, academic scholarships and death benefits

Source: Research done by the author in 1976.

a. Benefits from the Institute of Social Services for Railroad Workers, which has 88 medical clinics and a 2,000-bed hospital, and an old-age home.

had Perón's capacity to harmonize the diverse interests of all social sectors.

This led to a senseless division between the General Confederation of Labor, the official organization of the labor movement, and the 62 Organizaciones, which was a political expression of the workers during the non-Peronist period from 1955 to 1973. The 62 Organizaciones lasted in spite of the fact that the government was in Peronist hands, and despite the fact that the CGT publicly declared itself as Peronist in 1972 and demanded the return of its leader as a pledge of unity and peace. Both conflicting organizations tried to influence the president of the country, thus intensifying internal conflict. However, despite the evident lack of harmony, which tended to alienate union leaders from the true sentiments of their constituents, an effective labor mobilization took place which, although failing to prevent the military coup of March 24, 1976, nevertheless sought partial solutions to workers' problems. For example, when the government attempted to ignore the collective agreements signed earlier and still in effect, the CGT gave instructions for a general industrial shutdown on June 27, 1975. A crowd assembled in the Plaza de Mayo and demanded the removal of the minister of social welfare. Once again, the labor organizations assumed an aggressive role in the political process and, facing the persistent rejection of the collective agreements, a national 48-hour shutdown took place on July 7 and 8, resulting in the ratification of the collective labor agreements by the government. However, the division in union management intensified. One side insisted upon institutional continuity at any cost, while the other side accepted and incited the coup which reached a climax on March 24, 1976. The exile of some union leaders and the imprisonment of many others, the intervention of the CGT and all unions connected to the affairs of the state or to strategic sectors (the metal workers, construction union, and naval workers, for example) were the first measures adopted by the military government.

It is appropriate to end this brief analysis by pointing out the grave responsibility incurred by the present military government of Argentina by quoting the words of General Perón on December 21, 1973, that also defined his own responsibility. Perón said:

> Men of all nations must again practice the humility characteristic of the first Christians, and in that way find the path of understanding, because we are all human beings and therefore brothers. For that reason, we must respect one another. Those who are well off must give up something so that no one will be deprived of the essentials of a life of dignity and human pride. If we know how to proceed in this way, we will be rich in this world because, to the material goods that God has given us, we will add the social balance and economic equality which is ex-

pressed by justice for all who live by their work and the use of capital for an economy geared toward the well-being of all.[15]

Juan Perón, the movement that he led, and the growth of organized labor in Argentina have created a situation in which this message, this emphasis on social and economic equality and on assisting the deprived, cannot be ignored.

BIBLIOGRAPHICAL APPENDIX

1. Books

Abella Blasco, Mario. *Manual de sindicatos*. Buenos Aires: Editorial Peña Lillo, 1960.

Abós, Álvaro. *Delegados del personal: Comisiones internas*. Buenos Aires: Editorial IUS, 1977.

Actas de las jornadas nacionales de medicina del trabajo. *Medicina del trabajo al servicio de los trabajadores*. Buenos Aires: EUDEBA, 1974.

Angeleri, Luis A. *Los sindicatos argentinos son poder*. Buenos Aires: Editorial Pleamar, 1970.

Asociación Bancaria. *El contrato de trabajo bancario*. Buenos Aires: Edición propia, 1971.

Audi, Rodolfo, and Oscar Cardoso. *Sindicalismo: El poder y la crisis*. Buenos Aires: Editorial de Belgrano, 1982.

Belloni, Alberto. *Del anarquismo al Peronismo*. Buenos Aires: Editorial Peña Lillo, 1960.

Borlenghi, Ángel Gabriel, with a prologue by Juan Perón. *Evolución del movimiento obrero argentino*. Buenos Aires, edición oficial, 1950.

Cabanellas, Guillermo. *Derecho sindical y corporativo*. Buenos Aires: Editorial Omeba, 1959.

Capón Filas, Rodolfo E. *Derecho laboral*. La Plata: Librería Editorial Platense, 1980, vol. 2, ch. 15.

Centro Editor de América Latina. *Historia del movimiento obrero*, 5 vols. Buenos Aires, 1974.

Cerrutti Costa, Luis B. *El sindicalismo: Las masas y el poder*. Buenos Aires: Editorial Trafac, 1957.

Confederación General del Trabajo. *Hacia el cambio de estructuras*. Buenos Aires: CGT, 1965.

Correa, Jorge. *Los jerarcas sindicales*. Buenos Aires: Editorial Obrador, 1974.

D'Abate, Juan Carlos. *El antipoder sindical*. Buenos Aires: Editorial IUS, 1981.

Di Tella, Torcuato S. *El sistema político argentino y la clase obrera*. Buenos Aires: EUDEBA, 1974.

Garzón Ferreyra, Ignacio. *La convención colectiva de trabajo*. Buenos Aires: Editorial Arayú, 1954.

Iscaro, Rubens. *Historia del movimiento obrero argentino*. Buenos Aires: Editorial Anteo, 1972.

_____. *Origen y desarrollo del sindicalismo argentino*. Buenos Aires: Editorial Anteo, 1958.

López, Alfredo. *Historia del movimiento social y la clase obrera argentina*. Buenos Aires: Editorial Programa, 1971.

_____. *La clase obrera y el 4 de junio*. Buenos Aires: Editorial Juan Pueblo, 1945.

López, Guillermo A. F. *Derecho de las asociaciones gremiales*. Buenos Aires: Editorial La Ley, 1980.

Marc, Jorge Enrique. *Nueva ley de asociaciones profesionales*. Buenos Aires: Editorial Depalma, 1975.

Ministerio de Bienestar Social de la Nación. *Las obras sociales en la República Argentina*. Buenos Aires, 1972.

_____. *Síntesis informativa. Registro Nacional de Obras Sociales.* Buenos Aires, 1976.

Montuschi, Luisa. *El poder económico de los sindicatos.* Buenos Aires: EUDEBA, 1979.

Monzalvo, Luis. *Testigo de la primera hora del peronismo.* Buenos Aires: Editorial Pleamar, 1975.

Nápoli, Rodolfo. *Derecho del trabajo y de la seguridad social.* Buenos Aires: Editorial La Ley, 1969.

Oddone, Jacinto, and Alfredo López. *Los socialistas y el movimiento obrero.* Buenos Aires: Editorial Fundación Juan B. Justo, 1982.

Olmos, Amado. *Los mariscales de la derrota.* Buenos Aires: Editorial de la Fundación Raúl Scalabrini Ortiz, 1962.

Pontieri, Silverio. *La Confederación General del Trabajo, la revolución del 17 de octubre de 1945, el gobierno justicialista,* etc. Buenos Aires: Editorial Pirámide, 1972.

Prado, Pedro R. *El convenio colectivo de trabajo.* Buenos Aires: Editorial Abeledo Perrot, 1973.

_____. *Ordenamiento de las leyes laborales.* Buenos Aires: Editorial Abeledo Perrot, 1970.

Puigbó, Raúl. *La revancha oligárquica y el porvenir obrero.* Buenos Aires: Editorial Sigla, 1957.

Puiggrós, Rodolfo. *El proletariado en la revolución nacional.* Buenos Aires: Editorial Trafac, 1956.

Ramicone, Luis. *La organización obrera en la actualidad.* Buenos Aires: Editorial Bases, 1963.

Ramírez Bosco, Luis. *La función de los sindicatos.* Buenos Aires: Editorial Universitaria, 1976.

Reyes, Cipriano. *Yo hice el 17 de octubre.* Buenos Aires: GS Editorial, 1973.

Rotondaro, Rubén. *Realidad y cambio en el sindicalismo.* Buenos Aires: Editorial Pleamar, 1971.

Rudi, Daniel M. *Los derechos constitucionales del trabajador.* Buenos Aires: EUDEBA, 1974.

Senén González, Santiago. *El sindicalismo después de Perón.* Buenos Aires: Editorial Galerna, 1971.

Senén González, Santiago, and Juan Carlos Torre. *Ejército y política.* Buenos Aires: Editorial Galerna, 1969.

Sindicato de Luz y Fuerza. *Pautas para una política nacional.* Buenos Aires: SLF, 1972.

Taccone, Juan J. *Crisis . . . respuesta sindical.* Buenos Aires: Edición del autor, 1971.

Vázquez Vialard, Antonio. *El sindicato en el derecho argentino.* Buenos Aires: Editorial Astrea, 1981.

Via, Juan Vicente. *Coordinación regional de las prestaciones de bienestar de la seguridad social.* Buenos Aires: Ministerio de Bienestar Social, 1974.

Zorrilla, Rubén H. *Estructura y dinámica del sindicalismo argentino.* Buenos Aires: Editorial La Pléyade, 1974.

2. Articles, Addresses, Pamphlets

Benedetto, Orlando. "Sobre la Universidad Tecnológica Nacional." *Hechos e Ideas,* Jan.-Feb. 1974.

Confederación General de Empleados de Comercio. *En la era de Perón informamos de uno de los períodos mas intensos y proficuos de nuestra Confederación creada y conducida por Borlenghi.* Buenos Aires, 1954.

Corbiere, Emilio J. *La ley de asociaciones profesionales. Libertad y organización en el sindicalismo argentino.* Buenos Aires: Editorial As, 1966.

D'Abate, Juan Carlos. "Aspectos comparados de los sindicalismos argentino y norteamericano." *Derecho del Trabajo* 42 (1982).

_____. "Autonomía sindical en la Argentina." *Derecho del Trabajo* 40 (1980).

_____. "Consideraciones sobre el decreto reglamentario de la Ley de Asociaciones Gremiales de Trabajadores." *Derecho del Trabajo* 40 (1980).

_____. "Consideraciones sobre la nueva ley para el personal de la industria de la construcción." *Derecho del Trabajo* 40 (1980).

_____. "'El antipoder sindical' y la participación de los trabajadores en las decisiones de las empresas." *Derecho del Trabajo* 41 (1981).

_____. *La ley de asociaciones profesionales.* Buenos Aires: Editorial Cuadernos Peronistas, 1959.

Delich, Francisco. "Desmovilización social, reestructuración obrera y cambio sindical." *Crítica y Utopia* 6 (1982).

García Martínez, Julio A. "El movimiento obrero argentino y la libertad sindical." Editorial La Ley, *Revista Jurisprudencia Argentina* 90 (1958).

Informe de la representación obrera argentina en la 30° reunión de la Conferencia de la OIT. Buenos Aires: 1947.

Little, Walter. "La organización obrera y el Estado Peronista, 1943-1955," *Desarrollo Económico* 19 (1979).

Pérez Leirós, Francisco. *La revolución social que se pregona pero no se entiende.* Buenos Aires: Editorial Nueva Izquierda, 1963.

Perón, Juan Domingo. "Despedida a la delegación argentina a la OIT." *Síntesis Periodística, Congreso de la Nación,* Jan.-Mar. 1974.

_____. "Diálogo con el Ministro de Economía y dirigentes de la CGT." *Síntesis Periodística,* Jan.-June 1974.

_____. "Discurso a dirigentes gastronómicos latinoamericanos." *Síntesis Periodística,* Jan.-June 1974.

_____. "Discurso a los jubilados." *Síntesis Periodística,* Jan.-June 1974.

_____. "Discurso ante dirigentes de la CGT." *Síntesis Periodística,* Jan.-June 1974.

_____. "Discurso a una delegación de sindicalistas de la Provincia de Córdoba." *Síntesis Periodística,* Jan.-Mar. 1974.

_____. "El Plan Trienal y las organizaciones sindicalistas." Discurso pronunciado en la CGT el 27 de diciembre de 1973.

_____. "La capacitación del dirigente." Discurso pronunciado en la CGT el 8 de noviembre de 1973.

_____. "La doctrina: Fundamento de la organización." Discurso pronunciado en la CGT el 8 de noviembre de 1973.

_____. "La relación de costo de vida, precios y salarios." Discurso pronunciado en la CGT el 13 de diciembre de 1973.

_____. "Reunión con la CGT y las 62 Organizaciones." *Síntesis Periodística,* Jan.-June 1974.

_____. "Sindicalismo y política." Discurso pronunciado en la CGT el 30 de julio de 1973.

Pifarré, Roberto. *Sindicatos y ley de asociaciones.* Buenos Aires: Editorial Nueva Izquierda, 1965.

Rosembuj, Tulio Raúl. "Alcances de la extensión tributaria de las asociaciones profesionales." *Derecho del Trabajo* 35 (1975).

Rudi, Daniel Mario. "De la personalidad constitucional de las asociaciones profesionales de trabajadores." *Temática Dos Mil* 4 (1979).

Secretaría de Prensa y Difusión de la Presidencia de la Nación. *El sindicalismo en la Revolución Justicialista.* Buenos Aires, 1973.

Senén González, Santiago. *El poder sindical.* Buenos Aires: Editorial Plus Ultra, 1978.

Subgerencia de Relaciones Comunitarias, Servicios Eléctricos del Gran Buenos Aires. *Autogestión.* Buenos Aires: Edición de la empresa, 1974.

Torre, Juan Carlos. "El movimiento obrero y el último gobierno peronista." *Crítica y Utopia* 6 (1982).

NOTES

This chapter was translated by Francisco Di Blasi.

1. Andrés Framini and the author.
2. Confederación General del Trabajo, Departamento Técnico, documentación sindical (Buenos Aires, 1974).
3. CGT, *Anuario del Trabajo* (Buenos Aires, 1947).
4. Dirección de Estadística Social del Departamento Nacional del Trabajo, 1941 census. Also see Walter Little, "La organización obrera y el Estado Peronista, 1943–1955," *Desarrollo Económico* 19 (1979), 331–76.
5. Arturo Enrique Sampay, *La Constitución Argentina de 1949* (Buenos Aires: Editorial Relevo, 1963), p. 39.
6. Arturo Enrique Sampay, *Concepto y tipología del desarrollo político* (Buenos Aires: Facultad de Derecho y Ciencias Sociales de la Universidad Nacional de Buenos Aires, 1974), p. 7.
7. República Argentina, Poder Ejecutivo Nacional, *Plan Trienal para la reconstrucción nacional, 1974–1977* (Buenos Aires, 1973), p. 317.
8. Juan Perón, *El Plan Trienal y las organizaciones sindicales* (Buenos Aires: Secretaría de Prensa y Difusión, 1973).
9. Juan Carlos Esteban, *Imperialismo y Desarrollo Económico* (Buenos Aires: Editorial Palestra, 1961), p. 124.
10. For Buenos Aires Province, Vicente Calabró of the Metal Workers Union served as vice-governor, 1973–74 and as governor, 1974–76; for Mendoza Province, Carlos Mendoza of the Metal Workers Union served as vice-governor, 1973–74 and as governor, 1974–76; for Santa Fe Province, Eduardo F. Cuello of the Metal Workers Union served as vice-governor, 1973–76; for Córdoba Province, Atilio López of the Transport Workers Union served as vice-governor, 1973–74; for Entre Ríos Province, Dardo Blanc of the Meat Packers Union served as vice-governor, 1973–76; for Salta Province, Olivio Ríos of the Communication Workers Union served as vice-governor, 1973–74.
11. Serving as ministers of labor were José María Freire of the Glass Workers Union, 1946–53; Alejandro B. Giavarini of the Railroad Workers Union, 1953–55; Ricardo Otero of the Metal Workers Union, 1973–75; Cecilio Conditi of the Public Employees Union, 1975; Carlos Guillermo Ruckauf of the Insurance Employees Union, 1975–76; and Miguel Unamuno of the Banking Employees Union, 1976. Serving as undersecretaries to the minister of labor were José Mujica of the Textile Workers Union, 1973–75, and José Verón of the Textile Workers Union, 1975–76.
12. Serving on boards of directors of banks were Alberto Zibechas of the Banking Employees Union, Banco Central de la República Argentina, 1973–76; Florencio A. Carranza of the General Confederation of Commerce Employees, Banco Central de la República Argentina, 1975–76; Dámaso Sierra of the Banking Employees Union, Banco de la Ciudad de Buenos Aires, 1973–76; Juan Carlos Baslini of the Banking Employees Union and Alfonso Millán of the Glass Employees Union, Banco de la Nación Argentina, 1973–76; Otto Calace of the Health Workers Union and Pedro Eugenio Álvarez of the Entertainment Workers Union, Banco Hipotecario Nacional, 1973–76; Nicolás Amitrano of the Banking Employees Union and Maximiliano Castillo of the Glass Workers Union, Banco Nacional de Desarrollo, 1973–76. Cesareo Melgarejo of La Fraternidad [society of train engineers] was president of the board of directors of the Empresa de Ferrocarriles Argentinos, 1973–76; Félix Pérez of the Utility Workers Union was president of the board of directors of the Empresa Nacional de Agua y Energía, 1973–76. Constantino Zorila and Néstor Carrasco of the Meat Packers Union were members of the Junta Nacional de Carnes, 1973–76; Rodolfo M. Soberano of the Mill Workers Union

was a member of the Junta Nacional de Granos; Mariano Rubén Martín of the Metal Workers Union was elected president of the chamber of deputies of the city of Buenos Aires, 1973–74; Miguel Unamuno of the Banking Employees Union was elected president of the chamber of deputies of the city of Buenos Aires, 1974–75; and Lorenzo Pepe of the Railroad Union was consultant to the Comisión de Transportes y Comunicaciones of the national senate, 1973–76, and was author of the projected plan for the trans-Patagonian railroad.

13. Fundación de Estudios Geopolíticos, Económicos y Sociales, *Obras Sociales* (Buenos Aires, 1976), table 3.

14. In April 1976 OSECAC was intervened by the military government and workers were required to pay for medical care and other services.

15. Juan Perón, "El plan trienal de gobierno," un discurso de 21 de diciembre, 1973.

5

ANTONIO O. DONINI

Religion and Social Conflict in the Perón Era

Conflicts within the Catholic church in Argentina between 1945 and 1980 reflect the broader tensions of the society as a whole. Argentine Catholicism has been characterized as an intermediate type of religious organization.[1] The essential characteristic of this "intermediate" or "transitional" form is the coexistence of contradictory guidelines, due in part to the juxtaposition of two opposing sectors, one dynamic and modernizing, the other stagnant and traditional. This coexistence frequently provoked tensions and internal conflicts, and the predominance of a centralized, traditional leadership has made it very difficult for the church to adapt to the ever changing conditions of a vast, pluralistic society in transition.

The relationship between religion and society has been analyzed many times by classical and contemporary social scientists.[2] According to their studies, it seems impossible to understand a religious institution without analyzing its social context. Religion as a social institution lends itself to and acts in a concrete society.[3] The surrounding society exerts pressures and limitations on religion, like any other social institution, providing it with a specific frame of reference within which it must function and develop. It is safe to say that, to a certain degree, organized religion conforms to the cultural structure of the society in which it exists.

As various scholars have observed, Argentina is still a country in search of its identity.[4] It is a country approaching the end of a stage, and, like all endings, it is somewhat painful. In a transitional period, certain social values, forms, and life styles have lost or are losing validity. Therefore, it becomes essential to rediscover new values, new ways of living, a new form of expression.[5] Consequently, the internal conflict and uncertainties of Argentine Catholicism reflect the internal conflicts and uncertainties of the country itself — a social reality in search of identity.

An Imported Church

According to a leading theologian, Latin American Catholicism has always lacked human resources because it is a "transplanted" church.[6] In   79 fact, during the era of conquest and colonialism, the clergy was European by birth and education. At the beginning of the era of independence, its members remained European, if not by birth, by the adoption of European customs, because of the vast socialization process in Europe or in Latin American seminaries patterned after those of Europe. Moreover, Argentines believed their church, in its modus operandi, to be what de Hoyos calls the "depository of the faith." As in other absolutist structures of the past, church government was not carried out by community-elected representatives, but by those who represented the community without its consent or previous consultation.[7]

When Hispanic civilization imposed itself on Latin America, it provided not only a language but also a culture, which included Christianity. However, when independence came about two centuries later, the process of Christianizing the continent, beginning with the arrival of the first Spanish missionaries, had not yet ended. As Dussel puts it, "The church was the organization responsible for and aware of the Hispanic Weltanschauung, since the clergy created and controlled the universities, secondary schools, printing presses, etc. Most of the intellectual Hispanic elite was composed of clergymen. . . . In fact, the church committed itself to the task of bringing the Gospel and culture to the natives."[8]

For the most part, this strong cultural role explains the deeply rooted nature of Catholicism in Latin America. Ivan Vallier describes the notable sociological characteristics of the church as an organization: "First of all, the Church is the only formal organization that spans the four and a half centuries of Spanish-American history. . . . The Church is the only formal organization and value-transmitting agency that supersedes national boundaries."[9] The Latin American church is thus an entity in itself, maintaining a visible solidarity, having its own identity in relation to other sectors of the Catholic church, and providing the basis for a formal integration of society.

Clericalism in Latin America evolved along with the development of the church. On the one hand, the authority of the clergy was indisputable, not only because of the place of the clergy in the dominant culture of the conqueror, but also because it represented God. On the other hand, the religious-cultural distance between the clergy and the people accentuated the clergy's authority while simultaneously provoking submissiveness and passivity among lay persons. These relations between the church leaders and the people continue to prevail. As Gera and Rodríguez-Melgarejo point out, the Argentine church "lacks even today an organized group of laymen capable of expressing itself coherently before the other sectors of the religious community and before the country itself."[10]

However, in the 1930s, the most select members of the lay community were involved in a group called Catholic Action, which for twenty years represented a model of Catholic activism and social involvement. The deterioration and disintegration of this powerful movement resulted basically from the innate "clericalism" in the movement itself — its centralized organization in the diocese and in the parish, with strict and uniform rules and regulations. Ironically, these characteristics, which gave a great sense of unity and strength to Catholic Action, simultaneously provoked a marked passivity and lack of initiative and creativity among its members. Thus many of the most valuable members, who were displeased at times with the clerical sector, by the 1950s felt obliged to withdraw from the organization. In this way Argentine Catholicism lost an initial opportunity to reform itself from within and consequently found itself subjected to social innovations promoted by non-Catholic, liberal reformers outside its ranks. The fact is that, since around 1940, the institutional church had been largely taken over by conservative governing groups.[11]

Church and State

Relations between church and state in Argentina came into existence characterized by the Christian ideal behind the Hispanic conquest and colonization.[12] As Dussel sums it up:

The structure of the intended "world" of the Hispanic was the world of the medieval European man, plus certain elements of the Arab world. One of these elements is the tendency to indissolubly unite the objectives of the church and state, as did Constantine and the papal states. One must note that the Islamic doctrine of the caliphate demanded this unity, this politico-religious monism. However, that same monism was proposed by the various royalist schools. . . . Existing in Spain at the time was something like a "temporal messianism" which unified the destiny of the nation and the church — the Hispanic nation being the instrument chosen by God to save the world. This consciousness of being the chosen nation — a permanent temptation of Israel — is the basis of the religious politics of Isabel, Carlos and Felipe.[13]

Argentine Catholicism has fed upon this principle of church-state unity since colonial times. However, one purpose of the Second Vatican Council of 1962 was to lay the foundations for a new type of relationship between church and state worldwide, one without mutual interference. This objective has been pursued in other Latin American countries. But the degree of separation of church and state found elsewhere in Latin America has not yet been fully achieved in Argentina.

The position of the church hierarchy regarding the involvement of the church in politics is all the more anachronistic if one considers that, since the end of the nineteenth century, Argentina has been a pluralistic and even anticlerical country. To be sure, anticlericalism is only possible in religious countries. It is no more than an opposition to the dominance of the churchmen or, in other words, a form of thwarting the supremacy and power of the clergy. But Argentine anticlericalism differs considerably from European anticlericalism: for example, in Spain, France, and Italy, anticlericalism openly intends to annihilate religion. In Argentina, anticlericalism is not directly antireligious. Its objective is to relegate the clergy to the sacristy and to limit religion to the conscience.

Anticlericalism in Argentina has passed through periods of greater and lesser aggressiveness. For instance, during the later years of the past century and at the beginning of this century, Argentine anticlericalism took on violent characteristics due to the ideological influence of immigrants from Central Europe. As in other countries, anticlerical laws were passed but never enforced. These laws had contradictory results. On the one hand, they strengthened a secular tendency in the country, while on the other hand they also created a clearly antiliberal reaction among the devout. Catholics with political aspirations longed for a return to a time when nationalism was identified with Catholicism and was strengthened by it.[14] Thus anticlerical laws in Argentina have served, ironically, to bring the church closer to politics.

Peronism and the Official Church

The frequently implicit alliances of the church with political forces do not necessarily indicate an unconfessed desire for economic, political, or social power on the part of the church. These alliances generally carry the connotation of a "lesser" or an "inevitable" evil.[15] Reacting to the sting of anticlerical attacks, Monsignor Antonio Quarracino has answered frequent accusations of political interference by the church. In 1971 he affirmed, "I wish to point out that the conduct of the church throughout history has undergone evolutions—at times periods of darkness, at times periods of purification; and each time the church became involved in politics, the consequences were generally bitter."[16]

Although many were opposed to the church's political involvement, Argentine Catholicism, with few exceptions, lent its support to Peronism from the start. The populist tendencies of Peronism in 1945 evoked a traditional response from the Argentine church, especially from the clergy, which had always been devoted to popular movements—radicalism of the 1920s being an earlier example. This fact is partially explained by the social origins of the Argentine clergy and even of many bishops, who generally have come from the masses.

Perón attends mass at the Cathedral of Buenos Aires on the national day of independence, 1974. (Courtesy Juan Carlos D'Abate)

For his part, Perón wished to identify with the social doctrine of the church. Furthermore, on repeated occasions, he formally promised to follow the papal encyclicals.[17] For that reason many Argentine Catholics, from their own perspective, viewed Perón as a new Constantine, capable of restoring to the country the old national and religious traditions of God, country, and home. Thus it was natural that the opposing coalition, which called itself the "Democratic Union," blamed the church hierarchy for its electoral defeat. The bishops had in fact helped Perón with the famous pastoral letter of November 15, 1945. In that document, the hierarchy insisted upon the following points: (1) all citizens are obligated to vote; (2) when voting, one must choose the best candidate regardless of political party; and (3) no Catholic may vote for candidates or political parties whose programs include the secularization of schools, the separation of church and state, and the legalization of divorce. Strange as it may seem from an electoral standpoint, shortly after the publication of the pastoral letter, the political parties opposing Perón officially adopted in their platforms the three principles rejected by the bishops. Meanwhile, Perón publicly promised to maintain constitutional relations between the church and the state, to retain optional courses on religious education in public schools, and to make no changes in legislation regarding the indissolubility of marriage.

For Juan L. Segundo, this is a typical case of a "tacit alliance" between the church and political leaders in that "the church chooses as sufficient criteria (removed from all sense of lesser or greater evil) to maintain Christian privileges in a modern and really pluralist country. . . . Hence ten years later, when Perón failed to keep his promise, the church flatly confronted him without even recognizing the extent of his political and social achievements."[18]

Without concluding that the pastoral letter was in fact the deciding element in Perón's triumph — which also depended crucially on public opinion and on the nature of the defeated opposition — it is undeniable that, from 1946 until 1954, considerable cordiality and deep understanding existed between the church and Perón. Hence many observers were surprised at the abrupt change in relations that began with the president's famous speech of November 10, 1954, accusing the church of political interference.[19]

The first denunciation of "some bishops and priests" provoked a campaign against the Catholic church in general and a confrontation which culminated in the "burning of the churches." This conflict became more and more evident in social and judicial orders, dating from Perón's November 10 speech, such as the legalization of divorce, the suppression of religious education, the convocation of constitutional conventions to reform the Constitution and separate church and state, and the promulgation of legislation such as the law of equal rights for illegitimate children. All measures were systematically organized toward a secularization of society, despite the vehement and repeated opposition of the church.

This was a severe blow to Argentine Catholicism and above all to the church hierarchy which, intentionally or not, had supported the candidacy of Perón with the publication of the pastoral letter of 1945. Interpretations of the reasons for Perón's actions vary: some say that (1) Perón rejected the church when he found that he no longer needed its support, that (2) he did not want competition from Catholic reformers among the Christian Democrats and in the Federal Union, that (3) he came, over time, to feel greater compassion for couples who wanted divorces and for illegitimate children who needed wider rights, or that (4) his move against the church came not from his personal conviction but from the influence of some of his ministers and followers. Whatever the motives for Perón's initiative, the Argentine church hierarchy felt thwarted. With few exceptions, it came to attack Perón as a persecutor of the church and, at least in the early months, most bishops welcomed the Revolución Libertadora-Nacionalista y Católica, the coup which removed Perón from power.

The reaction against Perón's attack upon the church gave new strength not only to the Catholic laity but also to the political opposition. After 1954 many of the old elements of Catholic Action became involved in "civil commandos," the struggle of pamphleteers and various groups resisting Perón's regime. With General Eduardo Lonardi in command, given his orientation as a Catholic nationalist, the Revolución Libertadora seemed to open perspectives for many lay Catholics who aspired to collaborate in a "new socio-Christian order." The Federal Union, the Christian Democrats, and extreme right-wing groups began or renewed their political activities during this period. But many Catholics became frustrated after the forced retirement of Lonardi, who had led the rebellion against Perón mainly on account of his religious convictions. Ideological differences and a lack of political experience soon resulted in the breakup of the enthusiastic majority which had united against the "common enemy" in 1955.

The struggle for what a campaign slogan called "free education" and the possibility of offering a Christian education at the university level with officially recognized credentials again united Catholics momentarily in 1958. The Educational Freedom law of President Arturo Frondizi provided an alternative to the education given in the national universities, which had been predominantly antireligious — or at least non-religious — since 1918. The law officially recognized Catholic institutions of higher learning and has encouraged the education of new generations of lay Catholics since 1958.

On the other hand, Argentine lay Catholics, as an organized group, have not even been capable of exerting a noteworthy influence on the sociopolitical order. During the 1960s, dispersions, ideological conflict, disorientation, and discouragement characterized many lay groups, which, although well intentioned, lacked unity and common objectives. The Second Vatican

ANTONIO O. DONINI

Council was held during this time, marking a new era of Christian awareness and an "updating" of Argentine Catholicism.

The Second Vatican Council and the Medellín Conference

The highly institutionalized, hierarchical, and dogmatic Catholic church transcends national boundaries. It cannot, however, be considered a monolithic entity. Since certain aspects of religion are culturally conditioned, marked cultural and ethnic variations clearly distinguish a North American Catholic from an Italian, French, or Spanish Catholic. Such distinctions exist within universal Catholicism, and Argentine Catholicism is no exception. Among the most obvious social influences on the church in Argentina is the country's unstable political structure.

Vallier considers the central problem of development in Argentina to be a degree of political instability that prevents the coordination of its abundant natural and human resources. As one would imagine, the Argentine church shares in the general fragmentation and disorientation of the rest of society. The fragmented and insecure character of Catholicism in Argentina became particularly evident at the fall of Perón. Since 1955, the church hierarchy has assumed an attitude of great caution, a contrast to the optimism, security, and determination of the previous era. However, within the church lies the possibility of the restoration of order. Vallier quite rightly concludes that "the new Catholic elites of the pluralist variety thus appear to be one of the key agencies for building up the society's mobilization capacities. Their efforts are needed both within the Church and in the secular sphere. . . . In short, the Argentine society appears to require the institutionalization of a set of crossties that will form the normative basis for successful, long-range mobilization."[20]

In Argentina, as in the entire world, Catholicism has been characterized by: (1) a powerful hierarchy and a clergy independent of all lay control, (2) a conservative bureaucracy — the Curia Romana — prototype of a traditional organization, and (3) a detailed system of ceremonies, rites, and church laws with great emphasis on authority and obedience. Nevertheless, despite the church's reverence for tradition, in 1959 Pope John XXIII decided to call a general or ecumenical council with the intention of reviewing church policies and principles. After three long years of preparation, the Second Vatican Council was held in the fall of 1962. More than two thousand bishops and other church authorities from all parts of the world participated. It was the same John XXIII who prophetically gave the tone to the council when he described his objective as an "updating" of theology in church government, in its relations with non-Catholics, and in other areas. The Curia Romana, having assumed a determining role during the preparation of the council, drawing up documents for consideration by the bishops, lost control from the start.

As this historical moment has been described by some authors,[21] when the document folders prepared by the Curia and a list of names of the various commission presidents were handed out with the expectation of automatic approval, several cardinals (the French Cardinal Achille Liénart, in particular) expressed their displeasure and requested an adjournment to discuss and think over matters before voting too hastily. After an initial moment of general surprise due to the unexpected nature of the situation, 2,700 bishops who were members of the council burst into deafening applause. Without voting, they adjourned to prepare their own lists.

By the end of the Second Vatican Council in 1965, important changes had been made and a new spirit had rejuvenated the organization of the Catholic church. The authority of the bishops in relation to the pope was strengthened; a more open attitude regarding Protestants and Jews was imposed; and a reform of the ritual was ordered, permitting not only the use of modern languages in the liturgy, but also greater freedom and variety along with more community participation in religious ceremonies.

Unexpectedly, the range of the Second Vatican Council went beyond these adopted changes. A new spirit was taking shape in Catholicism. However, as one might imagine, a council of this nature was bound to cause varied repercussions. In Argentina there were two kinds of basic, dramatically opposed reactions.[22] First, the precouncil Catholics more or less openly rejected the conclusions of the council or at least attempted to prevent those conclusions from influencing national Catholicism; conservatives, for lack of more dynamic approaches to concrete reality, tried in vain to oppose any changes. Second, the postcouncil Catholics not only accepted the council's conclusions but also tried to put them into practice. This group included, among others, those who, for lack of theoretical knowledge and vision, hastened into anarchistic political activities as members of the so-called Third World Clergy.

In broad perspective, however, there is no doubt that the position of the precouncil Catholics was unable to sustain itself for very long. The Second Vatican Council dealt a harsh blow to this conservative and traditional sector. This was clearly observed in Argentina when the military coup of 1966 established "a Catholic government" under the presidency of General Juan Carlos Onganía and revived the old problem concerning relations between church and state. Since the fall of Perón, this problem had not been seriously raised again in Argentina. Facing this new government's attempt at Constantine-style clericalism, the bishops themselves, in various pastoral letters, have favored a mutual and independent autonomy between the powers, renouncing certain political privileges and demanding only the freedom to carry out specific church functions. At the same time, they have affirmed that Christians should intervene in politics and bear the consequences of their actions. This neutrality in the temporal and political order notably contrasts with what the hierarchy had traditionally considered to be its "pastoral duty" and its responsibility to guide and orient the consciences of Catholics.

Meanwhile, in August and September 1968, the Second Conference of the Latin American Episcopate was held in Medellín, Colombia.[23] During the conference, a clear effort was made to interpret the Vatican Council and define it within the reality of Latin America, beginning with an historical and sociological analysis of each country and of the continent in general.[24] Innovative sectors — including, but not limited to, priests in the Third World Movement — now felt supported by the conclusions of Medellín, by a growing number of bishops, and by the already famous "Manifiesto de los Obispos del Tercer Mundo" (The Third World Bishops' Manifesto).

The Declaration of San Miguel and the Third World Movement

In April 1969, the Argentine episcopate met at San Miguel, in the Province of Buenos Aires, to consider adapting the Medellín documents "to the current reality of the country." As might have been foreseen, the "Declaration of the Argentine Episcopate," published at the conclusion of the meeting, was a compromise between a conservative tendency, still dominant among the bishops, and a more prophetic tendency which had been acquiring strength and consistency in the heart of the episcopate. As Gera and Rodríguez-Melgarejo put it, this declaration, "after presenting a theology which could serve as a basis for a *Third World* position, arrives at a *conservative* clause; it neither renounces the institutional privilege, nor clarifies a confused type of relationship with the state." Yet these authors emphasize that, despite its ambiguity, this was the best document to emerge from the Argentine church for fifteen years, after the collective pastoral entitled "Promoción y Responsabilidad de los Trabajadores" (Promotion and Responsibility of the Workers), published on May 1, 1956.[25]

The Movement of the Third World Clergy dates from 1965, when groups of priests met in Quilmes, and the following year in Chapadmalal, to discuss the document of the Second Vatican Council entitled "The Church and the World." On August 15, 1967, the same priests met again to comment on "The Manifesto of the Third World Bishops," which was first endorsed by Dom Hélder Câmara of Brazil. Following these early beginnings, the first official meeting of the movement was held in Córdoba on May 1, 1968.

These priests were very active in work with lay Catholics, in the analysis of documents, in acts of protest, and in activities supporting labor demands. Their discussions and documents revolved around such topics as "The Church and Revolution," or "The Priesthood and Politics," with considerable emphasis on the theme of "liberation."[26] In concrete political situations, the Third World Clergy adopted an attitude of commitment and clearly established their protest position. Such an attitude was condemned by some as merely political and rebellious but praised by others as prophetic and committed.

As is usually the case in protest movements, not all Third World priests were innovators or prophets; some channeled their personal and emotional conflicts with the hierarchy into a movement that was able to give new meaning to their lives, drawing on their energies and even their failures. It is possible that this group did not consciously seek to oppose the hierarchy or create problems for it. In many of their declarations, they tried to fill a vacuum created by the silence of the bishops. But the fact that they considered themselves the leaders of the "liberated" church, whereas a great part of the hierarchy judged them to be rebellious extremists whose attitude overstepped and compromised their priestly mission, inevitably created problems within the official church.

There is no doubt that the Third World Movement has played an important role in the contemporary Argentine church, even though sympathizers like Enrique Dussel certainly exaggerate when they call it "the greatest event" in the history of the church in Argentina.[27] In spite of the simplifications and a certain ingenuousness in many of their documents, it is impossible to ignore their great human empathy. In accordance with the principles outlined at the Second Vatican Council and the conclusions of the meeting of the Latin American bishops in Medellín and of the Argentine bishops in San Miguel, the Third World Clergy declared that the Gospel must be applied to the real human condition and to the social and political dimensions of history. Furthermore, in the current historical circumstances of Latin America, they felt that "no commitment" meant the support of the unjust status quo, thus placing them in a paradoxical compromise with those who wield political power.

Herein lay the root of the dilemma of the Third World Movement: on the one hand, it committed itself to the struggle of marginal peoples for liberation and to the specific functions of the priest; on the other hand, it could not help but become involved in political action. There is no doubt that the Argentine church was connected, at least tacitly, to unjust structures and governments, maintaining a "Constantine clericalism." However, the Third World Clergy, perhaps without seeking to do so, was supporting a socialist or leftist type of clericalism. And yet, since the Second Vatican Council, the official position of the Catholic church had become clear and explicit: the church must stand free from any political, economic, or social structure.

A Church in Search of Identity?

A century and a half ago, when the cadres of Argentine Catholicism were destroyed after the end of the colonial rule, the church was directly reorganized by Rome. Under this system, the clergy and episcopate had juridical, normative, and institutionalizing tendencies which inevitably clashed with the activities of charismatic figures in the church and patterns of personal indentification by the clergy with historical, national processes. The same conflict emerged in this century. In the early 1950s, when the influence of the laity — especially in the ranks of Catholic Action — began to weaken, initiatives and ecclesiastical anxieties began to be expressed predominantly by the clergy.

After the Second Vatican council, a change took place in the language of many pastoral letters and in the style of communications with the people. A simple, austere way of life and paternal, straightforward qualities stood out as common characteristics among almost all the bishops and gained the esteem of the people. This spirit has not yet spread to the curias and other institutions, perhaps due to excessive concern for juridical formalities.

After Medellín, bishops came to speak out more often and to define their positions in concrete situations. For example, Monsignor Jaime F. Nevares, Bishop of Neuquén, after a meeting with his priests in August 1971, refused to participate in official acts so as not to project the image of what he called a "passive acceptance of the state of oppression from which our people are suffering." A few weeks before, Monsignor Antonio Devoto, bishop of Goya, had ordered the priests of his diocese not to officiate in outdoor masses for the armed forces, as a protest against student and labor conflicts. In 1974, the episcopal conference published a message condemning guerrilla activity, kidnaping, murder, and other types of violence.

Despite these episcopal activities, it was — beginning with the fall of Perón — generally not the church hierarchy but the clergy that originated the most profound questioning and posed the clearest options on political issues. In this sense, the episcopate often felt questioned or put upon by sectors of the clergy. The Third World priests frequently dispensed with the hierarchy and took the initiative in the preparation of declarations, denunciations, and prophetic statements.

Against this background, the prudent reserve and control which has characterized the ecclesiastical hierarchy since 1955 stands in notable contrast to the restlessness, dynamism, and protest of certain younger sectors of the clergy. The episcopate, which did not yield again to the temptation of Constantine clericalism during the presidency of Onganía (1966–1970) and even during the presidency of Alejandro Agustín Lanusse (1971–1973), succeeded in remaining neutral before and during the return of Peronism. This was true despite the fact that, as an astute Argentine political commentator wrote in 1973, the year of Perón's return, "A sort of left-wing neonationalism [in the church] followed the apparent internal logic of the 'Church of the poor' and the 'people of God,' in which the poor were identified with the working class, and the workers with Peronism. The necessary outcome of this process would be a coming together of the Church, now renewed, with Peronism."[28]

The reasoning of the Third World priests was exceedingly simple and popularly convincing, as they opted for and proposed Peronism as the only possible political solution for Argentina. They said of their decision: "(1) It is not a question of an option for a political party, but for a social force; (2) Peronism is a movement; and (3) Peronism is the highest level of consciousness and struggle reached by the Argentine working class."[29] This new encounter between a sector of the church and Peronism was relatively easy in the beginning. But by the middle of the 1970s, the Third World Movement had disappeared from the Argentine scene. Like guerrilla groups on the left, the Third World priests had — from a Peronist standpoint — ended their usefulness once Perón was back in power. Shortly after his election, Perón himself allegedly affirmed in a television interview that "if the priests wish to go into politics, let them take off their habits; if not, let them leave politics and dedicate themselves to preaching."

Considering in retrospect the two alliances of the church with Peronism (in 1945 and in 1972), we observe a great difference between them: in 1945, it was the hierarchy that supported the candidacy of Perón; in 1972, it was the Movement of Third World Priests — possibly 10 percent of the Argentine clergy — that actively intervened and proposed Peronism as the only solution. This opting for Peronism may have prevented the Argentine Third World Movement from reaching the Marxist extremes of similar movements in other Latin American countries.[30]

The position of this minority sector of the clergy contrasts with the behavior of the bishops. A declaration published by the Permanent Commission of the Argentine Episcopate shortly before the election of President Héctor J. Cámpora in March 1973 said, "Decisive hours are approaching for the entire nation. We must elect those who are to govern us. . . . Many ask us [the bishops], 'For whom shall we vote?' — a question that remains unanswered, but that points out the ambiguity of certain platforms and doubts about certain names."[31]

Looking back on the 1970s, one finds no glimpse of a dominant line in Argentine Catholicism. One cannot say that the Argentine church is conservative, liberal, or revolutionary. Before the Second Vatican Council, the Argentine church was predominantly conservative. From the 1962 council until the Medellín conference in 1968, a movement began toward renewal, and at the beginning of the conferences at Medellín and San Miguel, certain progressive and even revolutionary currents gained strength, as in the case of the Third World Movement. The only sector missing at each of these moments was the lay group.

Such a close look into the historical evolution of the Catholic church in Argentina suggests that Argentine Catholicism is gaining increased self-consciousness and maturity. In fact, the premeditated silence of the hierarchy in the face of concrete, legitimate political options has contributed to the maturity of both lower clergy and lay people; both groups see themselves as obligated to make decisions and to assume their responsibilities without waiting for direction or orders from the ecclesiastical hierarchy. This silence has caused confusion among many who were accustomed to obeying orders, without the risk of options, but this is a necessary price to pay for reaching adult age. The episcopate, on the other hand, maintaining a line of dialogue and persuasion, invites all to assume a personal and responsible commitment "as citizens and as Christians." At the same time, the church hierarchy seems less preoccupied with defending its rights and privileges than with safeguarding the exercise of its prophetic and strictly religious mission.[32]

The postcouncil Argentine church is clearly in search of its own identity; at the same time a new tendency is emerging in the relations between church and state, not only in Argentina but also in many Latin American countries. It is a new form of "clericalism" in which it is not the hierarchy that seeks unity with civil authority (Constantine clericalism), nor the Movement of Third World Priests (representing Marxist clericalism), but the Catholic governments — whether civilian or military — that demand unconditional support from the church in their struggle against communism, the guerrillas, and subversion (Arian clericalism).[33]

This new form of clericalism opposes the current noninvolvement of the church in the face of political options. However, on several occasions, many Argentine bishops have collectively or individually raised their voices in protest against injustices and violations of human rights and liberties.[34] Due to these repeated protests or, at least, the attitude of noninvolvement in political matters on the part of the hierarchy, relations between church and state are today at a critical level of coldness, and they could become aggravated to the point of dangerous confrontation. Needless to say, neither the military governments (generally Catholic, anti-Marxist, and firmly determined to prevent subversion) nor the church hierarchy want such a confrontation. Yet the lack of official church support of the government, plus frequent intervention in ethical matters by bishops opposing violence and violations of inalienable human rights and, above all, the undeniable fact that many guerrillas had been connected with priests or Catholic organizations at some point in their lives could exacerbate current resentments and provoke open conflict between church and state in Argentina.

In the early 1980s, relations between the church and the government in Argentina are characterized by understanding and mutual respect. To be sure, conditions are constantly changing; in the special situation of the war with Britain over the Islas Malvinas in 1982, Argentine churchmen patriotically backed the armed forces, urging the troops to "die like apostles" to repel the British advance, and Pope John Paul, after making a prearranged visit to Britain, also visited Argentina to demonstrate his concern for the country. However, in general, the church hierarchy and the clergy stay away from politics, concentrating their activity in their specifically religious and pastoral roles, while the government, for its part, has focused all its efforts — now that subversion has been controlled — on creating political and economic stability. Does this indicate that each type of clericalism is disappearing from Argentina? At least the Argentine church hierarchy is taking significant steps in this direction. One of its most recent documents strongly states the need for separation of powers in a pluralistic society, while rejecting clericalism and other church privileges even as a means for preaching the Gospel. The church is demanding from the state respect for its religious mission and freedom to exercise that mission.[35] After a close reading of such a document, one tends to believe that the Argentine church may be reaching a mature form of expression that will contribute to accelerating the process of growth and enhancing the maturity of a country that is searching for its own identity.

NOTES

This chapter was translated by Francisco Di Blasi.

1. Antonio Donini and Justino M. O'Farrell, "Tipología de la Religión Organizada en Países Subdesarrollados, en Transición y Desarrollados," *Actas del XX Congreso Internacional de Sociología* (Córdoba: Universidad Nacional de Córdoba, 1963), vol. 3, pp. 423–54.

2. See Emile Durkheim, *The Elementary Forms of the Religious Life*, trans. Joseph Ward Swain (Glencoe, Ill.: Free Press, 1947); Max Weber, *The Protestant Ethic and the Spirit of Capitalism*, trans. Talcott Parsons (New York: Scribner, 1930); Ernst Troeltsch, *The Social Teaching of the Christian Churches*, trans. Olive Wyon (New York: Macmillan, 1931); Ivan Vallier, *Catholicism, Social Control and Modernization in Latin America* (Englewood Cliffs, N.J.: Prentice-Hall, 1974); Frederick C. Turner, *Catholicism and Political Development in Latin America* (Chapel Hill: University of North Carolina Press, 1971); Thomas C. Bruneau, *The Political Transformation of the Brazilian Catholic Church* (London: Cambridge University Press, 1974); Daniel H. Levine, ed., *Churches and Politics in Latin America* (Beverly Hills, Calif.: Sage, 1980); and Brian H. Smith, *The Church and Politics in Chile: Challenges to Modern Catholicism* (Princeton, N.J.: Princeton University Press, 1982).

3. The study of religion as the investigation of "spiritual" or "divine" institutions pertains to theology and not to social analysis. As Max Weber emphasizes, the sociologist, when analyzing religion, must be aware of the limitations imposed by empirical knowledge.

4. See Félix Luna, *De Perón a Lanusse, 1943–1973* (Buenos Aires: Planeta Argentina, 1973); and Rubén J. de Hoyos, "The Role of the Catholic Church in the Revolution Against President Juan D. Perón (Argentina, 1954–1955)" (Ph.D. diss., New York University, 1970).

5. See Ezequiel Martínez Estrada, *Radiografía de la Pampa* (Buenos Aires: Losada, S.A., 1953), pp. 106–21, 385–90, and passim.

94

6. Juan L. Segundo, *Acción pastoral latinoamericana: Sus motivos ocultos* (Buenos Aires: Búsqueda, 1972), pp. 58–59. Unless otherwise noted, all translations are mine.

7. De Hoyos, "The Role of the Catholic Church in the Revolution," p. 52.

8. Enrique Dussel, *Hipótesis para una historia de la Iglesia en América Latina* (Barcelona: Editorial Estela, 1967), p. 47.

9. Ivan Vallier, "Religious Elites: Differentiations and Developments in Roman Catholicism," in Seymour Martin Lipset and Aldo Solari, eds., *Elites in Latin America* (New York: Oxford University Press, 1967), p. 222.

10. Lucio Gera and Guillermo Rodríguez-Melgarejo, *Apuntes para una interpretación de la Iglesia Argentina* (Montevideo: Centro de Documentación MIEC-JECI, 1970), p. 84.

11. See de Hoyos, "The Role of the Catholic Church in the Revolution," p. 76.

12. These relations are clearly stated in the Constitution of 1853. Article 2 affirms that "the federal government supports the Roman Catholic Apostolic faith," while article 76 states that "to be elected president or vice-president of the nation it is necessary . . . to belong to the Roman Catholic Apostolic church."

13. Dussel, *Hipótesis para una historia de la Iglesia en América Latina*, pp. 38–39. Dussel refers to the Emperor Constantine the Great, a convert to Christianity, who in 313 A.D. proclaimed religious liberty in the Roman Empire and worked throughout his long reign to strengthen the state by unifying the church. He called for the resolution of disputes and the eradication of heresies, even attempting to influence important decisions of episcopal councils. "Constantine clericalism," as opposed to "Arian" (see note 33), refers to a belief in a unity of powers linking church and state.

14. More generally, see Frederick C. Turner, "Catholicism and Nationalism in Latin America," *American Behavioral Scientist* 17 (July–Aug., 1974), pp. 845–64.

15. Noreen Frances Stack has concluded that the ties between Perón and the church after 1945 were considerably less close than has been generally assumed, as many Catholics supported Perón only as the "lesser evil." See "Avoiding the Greater Evil: The Response of the Argentine Catholic Church to Juan Perón, 1943–55" (Ph.D. diss., Rutgers University, 1976).

16. Antonio Quarracino, *Iglesia y política* (Avellaneda: mimeographed, 1971), p. 11. Before becoming the bishop of Avellaneda, a populous suburb on the outskirts of Buenos Aires, Monsignor Quarracino was a professor of theology at the Catholic University of Buenos Aires. Currently, he is secretary of the Latin American Council of Bishops (CELAM).

17. De Hoyos, "The Role of the Catholic Church in the Revolution," p. 88.

18. Juan L. Segundo y otros, *Teología abierta para el laico adulto* (Buenos Aires: Ediciones C. Lohlé, 1968–1973), vol. 1, pp. 41–42; and Segundo, *Acción pastoral latinoamericana*, pp. 143–44.

19. See de Hoyos, "The Role of the Catholic Church in the Revolution."

20. Vallier, "Religious Elites: Differentiations and Developments in Roman Catholicism," p. 219.

21. Michael Novak, *The Open Church* (London: Darton, Longman, and Todd, 1964), p. 9; and Enrique Dussel, *Caminos de liberación latinoamericana (Interpretación histórico-teológica de nuestro continente latinoamericano)* (Buenos Aires: Latinoamérica Libros, 1972), pp. 105–07.

22. See Gera and Rodríguez-Melgarejo, *Apuntes para una interpretación de la Iglesia Argentina*, pp. 63–64; and Enrique Dussel, "Fisonomía actual del catolicismo latinoamericano, considerando su génesis histórica," in Instituto Fe y Secularidad, *Fe cristiana y cambio social en América Latina* (Salamanca: Sígueme, 1972), p. 348.

23. This episcopal council, called CELAM, was founded in Rio de Janeiro in 1955, during the first General Conference of the Latin American Episcopate. Before Medellín, CELAM tried to hold a second meeting in Mar del Plata, Argentina, in October 1966, but failed partially because of a lack of support by the Argentine bishops.

24. For copies of the draft documents discussed at the conference, as well as its opening and closing addresses, see *Between Honesty and Hope: Documents from and about the Church in Latin America. Issued at Lima by the Peruvian Bishops' Commission for Social Action*, trans. John Drury (Maryknoll, N.Y.: Maryknoll Publications, 1970), pp. 171–227.

25. Gera and Rodríguez-Melgarejo, *Apuntes para una interpretación de la Iglesia Argentina*, p. 69.

26. See Movimiento de Sacerdotes para el Tercer Mundo, *Nuestra reflexión: Carta a los obispos argentinos*, versión definitiva (Buenos Aires: Mundo Nuevo, 1973); *Los sacerdotes para el Tercer Mundo: Crónica, documentos, reflexión* (Buenos Aires: Mundo Nuevo, 1972); and *Los sacerdotes para el Tercer Mundo y la actualidad nacional* (Buenos Aires: La Rosa Blindada, 1969); A. Mayol, N. Habegger, and H. Armada, *Los católicos posconciliares en la Argentina, 1963–1969* (Buenos Aires: Editorial Galerna, 1970). See also Juan José Rossi, ed., *Iglesia latinoamericana; ¿Protesta o profecía?* (Avellaneda, Argentina: Ediciones Búsqueda, 1969), pp. 97–144; Gustavo Gutiérrez M., "Apuntes para una teología de la liberación," in *Liberación: Opción de la Iglesia latinoamericana en la década del 70* (Bogotá: Editorial Presencia, 1970); Hugo Latorre Cabal, *The Revolution of the Latin American Church*, trans. Frances K. Hendricks and Beatrice Berler (Norman: University of Oklahoma Press, 1978), pp. 59–64; Enrique López Oliva, *Los católicos y la revolución latinoamericana* (Havana: Instituto del Libro, 1970); and José María Piñol, *Iglesia y liberación en América Latina: Diálogos con la vanguardia católica latinoamericana* (Madrid: Ediciones Marova, 1972).

27. Dussel, *Caminos de liberación latinoamericana*, p. 125.

28. Carlos Floria, "Church, Peronists Begin to Renew Alliances," *National Catholic Reporter*, 26 Jan. 1973, pp. 1, 16.

29. R. Concatti, *Nuestra opción por el peronismo*, 2nd ed. (Mendoza: Ediciones del Movimiento de Sacerdotes para el Tercer Mundo, 1972), p. 11.

30. See J. Rosales, *Los cristianos, los marxistas y la revolución* (Buenos Aires: Sílaba, 1970); and Moyano Coudert-Büntig, *¿La Iglesia va hacia el socialismo?* (Buenos Aires: Editorial Guadalupe, 1971).

31. *La Nación*, 6 Jan. 1973, p. 2.

32. Dussel correctly predicted this in "Fisonomía actual del catolicismo latinoamericano," p. 349.

33. "Arian" clericalism is named for the heresy condemned by the Council of Nicaea. Arian clericalism, like Constantine clericalism, allows civil authorities to intervene in purely ecclesiastical matters to preserve the unity of the faith and the security of the state. But in Constantine clericalism the civil authority intervenes with a common accord, tacit or explicit, with religious authorities, while in Arian clericalism the civil authority intervenes without the support and sometimes even against the religious authorities, so that civil and religious leaders may end by accusing each other of interference, ill will, and the violation of rights. See A. H. M. Jones, *The Later Roman Empire, 284–602: A Social, Economic, and Administrative Survey* (Norman: University of Oklahoma Press, 1964).

34. See Conferencia Episcopal Argentina, *Iglesia y Comunidad Nacional: XLII Asamblea Plenaria (4–9 de Mayo de 1981)* (Buenos Aires: Editorial Claretiana, 1981).

35. Ibid., p. 32.

6

WAYNE S. SMITH

The Return of Peronism

On May 25, 1973, General Alejandro Agustín Lanusse handed over the presidency of Argentina to Héctor J. Cámpora, the Peronist candidate who had won by a convincing plurality in elections held the previous March. The impossible had happened. The Peronists had not only returned to power — they had done so in elections organized by the very institution, the armed forces, which had ousted them in 1955. More was to follow. Less than two months after taking office, Cámpora resigned; new elections were then held in which Perón himself was swept into office by an overwhelming majority. To understand how the impossible had come to pass, we must analyze in detail the Argentine elections of 1973, focusing especially on two key questions: (1) what prompted the military to hold elections and to permit Peronist participation? and (2) how, after eighteen years in the wilderness and after appearing to have been so thoroughly discredited in 1955, did the Peronists win both the March and September 1973 elections so handily?

Failure of the Onganía Military Dictatorship

Probably the most compelling element which moved the military to convoke elections in Argentina was the failure of the Onganía dictatorship. On June 28, 1966, General Juan Carlos Onganía had overthrown Arturo Illia in a bloodless coup. It had been immediately clear, however, that his purpose was not simply to depose Illia and prepare the way for new elections, as had been the pattern when the military ousted Frondizi in 1962;[1]; rather, Onganía intended nothing less than the transformation of Argentine society, and thus his government took the grandiloquent title, "Argentine Revolution." As one general officer commented some years later: "In June of 1966, the armed forces did not act to correct a specific ill and then quickly return sovereignty to the people, its natural depository; rather, they acted to bring about change of a structural, revolutionary character."[2]

Onganía was to have remained in power for an indefinite period — for as long, indeed, as the transformation process might take. But such unlimited confidence in his leadership proved to have been ill founded. Onganía had little understanding of the political process.[3] Further, while the Argentine

Revolution had implied sweeping structural changes, there was no consensus within the ranks as to what form those changes should take. Nor could Onganía inspire a consensus, for he himself appeared confused about his objectives. Within three years of taking office, he faced growing public disillusionment and outright opposition. This came forcefully to the surface on May 29, 1969, in the form of labor and student violence in Córdoba. From that point forward, Onganía's days were numbered. As General Alejandro Lanusse himself was to comment years later: "The legitimacy of the Argentine Revolution lay in order — an order which, according to official theory, expressed a passive consensus. . . . The twenty-ninth of May made it clear that the oft-cited consensus, if indeed it ever existed, had disappeared."[4]

In May 1970, over the issue of increasing violence in the country, including the kidnaping (and eventual murder) of ex-President Pedro Aramburu, General Lanusse led the army in ousting Onganía, the man in whom only a few years earlier they had placed such trust.[5] The impact of Onganía's failure can hardly be exaggerated, for there had been a totality, an all-or-nothing character, to the Onganía experiment which now dictated an equally sweeping change of direction in the wake of his ouster. Onganía, in effect, had tried once and for all to demonstrate that the conviction which had motivated General José Félix Uriburu to lead the seizure of power back in 1930 had been valid — that is, that only the armed forces, with their code of honor, patriotism, and superior sense of organization and discipline, could provide the leadership necessary to bring about a national revitalization. Onganía's failure, in the minds of many Argentines, demonstrated just the opposite. Clearly, as Carlos Russo commented, "It was just as difficult for the armed forces as for the civilians to solve the country's major problems."[6] Hence the military's justification for retaining power was seriously undermined.[7] As one journal put it: "The armed forces, after five years lost in the experiment with the Argentine Revolution, which had achieved none of the objectives that had brought it into being, had no alternative but to return to the electoral system."[8]

Writing some years later, Lanusse phrased the thought differently, but agreed in substance. He said: "The military could not indefinitely go against the opinion of the vast majority of the nation. . . . The only intelligent alternative, given the situation, was to reestablish legitimate government, thus permitting the spiritual repair of the armed forces and the consolidation of order."[9]

The Armed Forces Move Toward Elections

The first steps toward returning the country to elected government appeared only a few days after Onganía's deposition when the new junta issued a document indicating that one of its goals was to assure political pluralism and a representative legislative power in which the people's will would be voiced through the various political parties. At the same time, it also became known that the junta had set up a board of three senior officers to begin planning for a return to political activity.[10]

However, if the junta's eventual objective — elections — was clear enough, the immediate steps toward that objective were confused. Rather than naming the army commander, General Lanusse, to the presidency, the junta named a virtually unknown general, Roberto Marcelo Levingston, who, at the time he was appointed, was serving as the Argentine military attaché in Washington. Why Levingston was chosen remains a mystery. It became apparent quite soon that his enthusiasm for elections was not as great as that of the junta. Many had assumed that his first moves would be to lift the ban on political parties and to set a date for elections. Instead, after months of convoluted "consultations," he announced just the opposite. He would not, he said, lift the ban on political parties, and it would be four or five more years before elections could be held.

Opposition to this general, who did not seem to understand what was expected of him, began to grow. On November 11, representatives of the Radicales (UCR), the Peronists, the Progressive Democrats (PDP), the Popular Conservatives (PCP), the Socialists, and Leopoldo Bravo's San Juan Bloquistas gathered to form a multiparty organization called La Hora del Pueblo, a name taken from its admonition to the military to recognize that this was "the hour of the people," and therefore that the generals should return to the barracks. The initial document issued by the new group called on the government, first, to permit the reestablishment of political parties and the resumption of political activity, and, second, to formulate a plan for political action which would include, among other things, a firm date for elections.

One month later, the new group issued another document entitled "The Hour of the People and the Armed Forces" in which it pointed out that the military had violated constitutionalism in 1962 and 1966, and since the latter year had made itself solely responsible for the nation's destinies. Military leaders could avoid responsibility neither for what had happened since nor for the continued suppresion of the public will.[11]

Levingston, however, paid little heed to the Hora del Pueblo or to other evidence of growing opposition to continued military rule. As discontent increased, bloody rioting broke out in March of 1971 — as usual, the worst occurred in Córdoba, but there were also a number of disturbing clashes elsewhere. Rather than bending to the pressure, Levingston on March 20 fired Brigadier Ezequiel Martínez, the top military planner for political reorganization; at the same time, the president reiterated that elections could not be held for another four years. Levingston had gone too far. On March

23, he was removed by the military commanders and on March 26, General Lanusse was installed as president.

Lanusse Takes Over

The stage was now set for two years of political maneuvering which often seemed to take on the aspects of a chess game between two of the wiliest political strategists the Argentine army has produced — Juan Domingo Perón and Alejandro Agustín Lanusse. As he took office, Lanusse faced difficulties, first, with a divided, confused military establishment for whom he had to indicate a new direction, a new institutional role, and, second, with a civilian population solidly opposed to military rule and suspicious of the new president's intentions. Indeed, public hostility had reached such a point that, as Lanusse himself was later to sum up the situation, the armed forces had only two options: to begin to work with the people and attempt to gain their confidence, or to continue to govern in isolation and become virtual occupation troops.[12]

As his principal instrument by which to gain the approval of the civilians and at the same time give the military a new sense of purpose, Lanusse launched the idea of a *juego limpio*, a clean political process leading to unconditioned elections guaranteed by the military. Accordingly, he immediately promised elections and called on Argentines of all persuasions "to actively join in the task of finding solutions to the country's problems through an extensive and generous accord that will overcome the animosities of the past."[13]

Lanusse's first two official acts were to appoint Arturo Mor Roig, a leader of the Unión Cívica Radical (UCR) as interior minister to oversee the political process, and to create a coordinating commission to formulate a plan under which those elections might be held.[14]

The appointment of Mor Roig was an especially astute move on Lanusse's part and helped greatly to gain public confidence. A long-time member of the UCR, Mor Roig had been president of the Chamber of Deputies when Onganía dissolved the Congress in 1966. A highly respected politician with a reputation for integrity and cool moderation, he had never hidden his belief that the country had to return to constitutionalism, and he was convinced that a solution could only come through a coincidence of views. He subsequently stated:

> I assumed the ministry with the hope that I could make some contribution to the achievement of consensus. . . . It had become clear over several decades that a spirit of national unity was needed if an electoral solution was to be lasting. I hoped, as I took the ministry, that through the electoral process that was to come, this unity could be generated.[15]

Political activity was now resumed, with the new government's abrogation of the law under which Onganía had prohibited it. Mor Roig invited those he described as "directors of public opinion," that is, the leaders of the soon-to-be-reconstructed political parties, including the Peronists, to begin a full and frank dialogue with the government.[16]

This was of key importance, for, clearly, if Lanusse was to bring off the electoral solution he was promising, he would need the support, or at least the participation, of the major political parties. Should any of their number abstain, as had the Peronists in 1963, the elections of 1973 would then come to represent little more than a repetition of past history. For their part, several of the key leaders of the new Hora del Pueblo saw that the kind of accord and political process that Lanusse was promising might coincide with their own aspirations for a move toward consensus through dialogue, and, eventually, to a national-unity government.[17] For once, there seemed hope that the three major poles of political power in Argentina — the military, the Peronists, and the UCR — might be moving in the same direction. The UCR at any rate was willing to give it a try. From the beginning, it accepted Mor Roig's invitation to sit down at the conference table and from the beginning took the attitude that as long as the elections were free and honest, as Lanusse promised, the UCR would participate.[18]

The situation with the Peronists was somewhat more complicated. Many of the Peronist politicians, including Jorge Daniel Paladino, wished to respond to Lanusse's call and to participate. Perón himself, however, clearly had doubts as to Lanusse's real intentions — and may have wondered whether Peronist participation in the proposed elections would enhance his own position, even if Lanusse proved sincere. Hence, before accepting Mor Roig's invitation, Perón called Paladino to Madrid for consultations.

To persuade Perón of his good faith, Lanusse sent him a conciliatory message through José Rucci, a Peronist labor leader who was traveling to Madrid. Rucci was to tell Perón that he would be issued a passport and allowed to return to Argentina, that there would be unconditional elections in which the Peronists could participate, and that the body of his late wife, Evita, would be returned to him.[19] Lanusse also dispatched one of his own men, Colonel Francisco Cornicelli, to confer secretly with Perón in Madrid. On April 22, 1971, Cornicelli was received by Perón, Paladino, and José López Rega, Perón's private secretary. In the lengthy conversation which followed, Cornicelli repeated Lanusse's assurances and tried to convince Perón of his chief's good faith.

Perón's reply, in essence, was that only facts, not words or promises, would win the public's confidence; in other words, he remained unconvinced. But at least for the moment, he said, he was willing to give Lanusse the benefit of the doubt. Paladino would return and begin to negotiate. "He will not, of course, decide; rather, he'll enter into negotiations. Then we'll see," Perón concluded to Cornicelli.[20]

Paladino returned to Buenos Aires on April 28, and on April 30 sat down for his first meeting with Mor Roig. The Peronists were now engaged in the process. The problem that Perón represented for Lanusse, however, went far beyond simple engagement. Lanusse needed the participation and cooperation of the Peronists in the coming elections, and for that he needed Perón's tacit consent. But, at the same time, he could not in fact allow Perón himself to be a candidate, for his brother officers were simply not ready to accept that prospect. Yet, had Lanusse openly proscribed Perón so early in the process, the latter doubtless would have called fraud and ordered his followers to boycott the elections. That Lanusse also could not afford. Hence, he had publicly to maintain the position that *no one*, including Perón, would be proscribed, while privately looking for some way to convince the latter to stand aside. Lanusse seemed confident he could successfully bring this off.[21] He was probably encouraged in this by Perón himself, for in a letter to UCR leader Ricardo Balbín, Perón had suggested that the Peronist and UCR candidates should be someone other than himself or Balbín.[22]

Meanwhile, Lanusse was moving ahead with efforts to advance the political process. On June 12, a new draft law for political parties was announced, and on July 6, 1971, it was promulgated as Decree Law No. 19,102. Political parties began formal steps toward reconstitution (or, in the case of new parties, toward organization) and registration. This went a long way toward convincing Argentines that Lanusse was sincere about holding elections, however skeptical they may have remained as to the outcome. Further, by early in the Argentine winter, it was clear that the majority of Lanusse's brother officers were willing to support — or at least accept — the political program he had put forward.[23]

Lanusse Shifts Emphasis to the Grand Accord

Feeling, then, that the first step — that of gaining public and military confidence — had been achieved and that his position was thus strengthened, Lanusse began subtly to shift emphasis from the straightforward concept of holding and guaranteeing clean elections *(juego limpio)* to a more complex and far-reaching definition of the Grand National Accord (Gran Acuerdo Nacional, GAN). Not that Lanusse had not previously spoken of such an accord; on the contrary, he had consistently referred to the need for an agreement among Argentines of all persuasions and had even used the term "grand national accord." But the emphasis had been on an electoral solution, and the role of the armed forces had been to guarantee the elections and their outcome, nothing more. Now, however, Lanusse began to add new dimensions both to his Grand Accord and to the role of the military within it. The military would still guarantee the elections, but it was now called upon to do a good deal more. The Grand Accord, Lanusse made clear, was not just political, nor would it end with elections;[24] rather, as he said in his "camaraderie" speech of July 7, 1971, social and economic transformations would be agreed upon by the participants and would then be guaranteed by the armed forces,[25] *guaranteed even after the elections.* "The Grand Accord has not been undertaken in order to remove the armed forces from the process for which they themselves are responsible," Lanusse assured his brother officers.[26]

As he developed his theme during the following months, it became clear that the new mission Lanusse was fashioning for the armed forces combined societal transformation with democratic restoration. The military would lead the country to elections and respect their outcome, yes; but first, it would also bring all parties together to reach agreement on the political, social and economic guidelines the new government should follow. The military would then act as a guarantor of the process. It would not govern, but neither would it retire to the barracks; rather, the military would continue to play a political role.[27]

Lanusse seemed also to hope that the forging of a Grand National Accord might bring about some agreement on a candidate—that is, a GAN candidate.[28] If Perón himself was not to run and if he intended to throw his support to someone else, Lanusse seemed to reason, then why could he not be persuaded to support a GAN candidate?

There were many who believed Perón might indeed order his movement to support an extraparty candidate rather than risk the creation of the second center of gravity within its midst to which the appointment of a Peronist candidate might lead.[29] This much was logical. To go beyond it, as Lanusse seemed to do in hoping that Perón might support a candidate identified with Lanusse (as a GAN candidate would have been), probably had been all along a miscalculation—even more so if Lanusse himself wanted to be that candidate, as most were beginning to believe he did.

Lanusse had not said that he sought the candidacy. On the contrary, he consistently indicated that he did not. But, just as consistently, he left the door open for a draft. In a television appearance on July 2, 1971, for example, he first said, "I will never present my candidacy"; but as to what might be his response if someone presented it for him, he was less categorical in his answer. The question of a draft was an extremely difficult one, he said, for his ambition was simply to be useful to his country during this most trying period, and no one could predict the future. In other words, he wanted to serve the nation and if it were decided that he could be most useful by accepting the candidacy, then he would have to do so.[30]

With Lanusse's shift from *juego limpio* to a Grand Accord with a continuing role for the military, and especially with indications that Lanusse himself might hope to be the candidate, Perón's suspicions deepened. As the gaucho saying goes, "Beneath his poncho, he gripped his knife still more tightly." In August, Perón sent a taped message to his followers in Argentina in which he warned of government chicanery. Lanusse's elections, he said, might simply be a plan to continue military rule under another name.[31]

The Turning Point: October 10, 1971

On October 10, the situation took a turn which to some observers marked the end of any hopes for a successful dialogue.[32] On October 8, there had been a revolt of the army garrisons in Azul and Olavarría, supported by elements in Buenos Aires. It was of little moment and was put down within twenty-four hours by forces loyal to Lanusse. Indeed, Lanusse emerged from the affair with his hand tremendously strengthened. With the exception of the small number of officers and men who had risen against him, the armed forces massively and enthusiastically gave him their support. Further, the revolt prompted an active expression of support from the civilian sectors. Lanusse felt himself to be riding the crest of a wave.[33]

Unfortunately, success seems to have gone to his head. The day of the revolt, Lanusse had called Mor Roig to say that he would follow the developing situation from army headquarters. The two remained closely in touch by telephone until the evening of October 9, when it became clear that the revolt had failed. Mor Roig, who had been ill to begin with, then went home in a state of exhaustion. Lanusse, on the other hand, spent the evening at army headquarters and had brunch there the next morning with several of his military comrades and civilian advisors, including Francisco Manrique, the minister of social welfare. Had Mor Roig been there, perhaps a more balanced view would have prevailed. As it was, however, swayed by the euphoria of the moment and the imprudent urgings of several of his advisors, Lanusse took a fatal step away from consensus.[34] First, he apparently decided that he was in a strong enough position to send up a trial balloon regarding his candidacy. This soon became apparent as several of those who had been at the October 10 brunch began to hint publicly that it was time to begin a "draft Lanusse" movement. Speaking on October 30, for example, Undersecretary of the Interior Belgrano Rawson stated that Lanusse's candidacy could be the culminating political product of the Grand Accord.[35] And Minister of Social Welfare Manrique observed on October 24 that "of course, Lanusse could be [the candidate] even if he did not want to be."[36] Only a few still doubted that Lanusse did want to be, and indeed his insistence in *Mi testimonio* that he did not seek the candidacy and his explanation as to why he did not rule himself out as a candidate at an early date are unconvincing. Whereas he says that declaring himself a candidate would have limited his room for maneuvering, it would likely have given him more. Certainly it would have given credence to his role as disinterested arbiter.[37]

Apparently as a corollary to his decision to edge toward the candidacy, Lanusse decided at the same brunch to begin forming his ministerial team. Heretofore, appointments had been made only after close consultations with the major political parties. In this case, there were no consultations at all; rather, on October 11, the appointments were announced. Cayetano Licciardo would become treasury minister; Bernardo Loitegui, the minister of industry and mining; and Bruno Quijano the minister of justice. None of the three was particularly well regarded by the forces represented in the Hora del Pueblo. But it was not so much the men themselves who caused concern as the manner in which they were appointed. Mor Roig was told of Lanusse's decision just before going into a meeting with Paladino. Stunned and still uncertain as to what Lanusse meant by it, Mor Roig said nothing to Paladino. The first the latter heard of the new cabinet appointments was the next morning. As he put it, "I had the new appointments for breakfast." Paladino minced no words as to the conclusion he drew: "The *juego limpio* is obviously finished," he announced.[38] Paladino may well have sensed at that moment that his days as Perón's representative were also numbered. If so, his premonition was well founded, for with Lanusse's ill-conceived cabinet appointments and the initiation of a transparent attempt to grab off the candidacy, Perón's suspicions of Lanusse hardened into convictions.

Paladino had come to represent dialogue, not only with the government, but, more importantly, with the other political parties. Among the Peronists, he was probably the strongest advocate of the new style of consensus politics embodied in the Hora del Pueblo. Paladino had believed—and had convinced Perón—that Lanusse was sincere in wishing to hold free elections in which he, Lanusse, would act simply as a disinterested arbiter. As it now appeared that Lanusse had other objectives, Paladino's position was fatally weakened.[39] He had urged dialogue with Lanusse. Perón now perceived that this dialogue, and any commitment to the Grand Accord, might well be used by Lanusse for his own purposes, that Lanusse might well be trying to maneuver not only Perón but also Balbín and the other parties aboard his own bandwagon in the name of consensus and unity.

Thus on November 10 word went out that Paladino had been replaced by Héctor J. Cámpora. This was a clear signal on Perón's part of a stand-down in his relations with the government. Paladino had encouraged dialogue. Cámpora would watch and wait. Further, there was a subtle shift in relations with the Hora del Pueblo as well as in those with the government, for although Cámpora came back from Madrid talking of increased emphasis on the Hora del Pueblo, and although the Peronists would remain within the organization for more than another year, something had been lost. It was not only that Cámpora was not Paladino; rather, it was that Perón's mind now seemed to be elsewhere. If Lanusse's focus was on engineering his own candidacy, Perón's was on the return to power of resurgent Peronism. In that Lanusse's Grand Accord posed a threat to that goal, Perón rejected it. Similarly, to the extent that the Hora del Pueblo did not serve the ends of resurgent Peronism, he would give it less attention.

Many have argued that no matter what Lanusse might have done, Perón would have pursued much the same course. According to this line of reasoning, Perón was not really interested in a dialogue with the government. If he had entered into one from April until August, it was only to draw the government on until it had committed itself irreversibly to elections. From that point on, his only purpose was to set rules of the game favorable to himself. Further, this argument holds, Perón was interested in cooperation with the other political parties only to the extent that they could help force the government to elections. Once having assured that objective, Perón lost interest in consensus politics.

The evidence, however, does not bear out the above line of reasoning. First of all, it was Perón in the first instance who had pressed for understanding among the parties, and, though he did it outside the framework of the Hora del Pueblo, he continued to emphasize a form of consensus politics even after achieving power. Moreover, there is no evidence of bad faith on Perón's part before August 1971. He reacted to the government's miscues, not the government to his.

Paladino, who probably had the most intimate knowledge of Perón's attitude during those early months of the political process, describes the latter's reaction to the October 10 decision in the following way:

> It took a good deal of persuasion on my part, but I had finally convinced Perón of Lanusse's good intentions—in other words, that Lanusse wished nothing more than to give the people a choice in elections in which he, Lanusse, would act as a disinterested umpire. If only Lanusse had been satisfied with that role, I am convinced the spirit of the Hora del Pueblo would have taken full root during the process leading up to the elections of 1973, and that out of those elections would have come the kind of government of national unity which could have been the real answer to the country's needs. But this required mutual confidence among the major political sectors—principally, among the armed forces, the Peronists and the UCR. From October 10 forward, that confidence no longer existed.[40]

Mor Roig's assessment closely coincides with Paladino's. Analyzing the situation some months later, he explained:

> There were doubtless many factors which caused Perón to shift toward a hard line vis-à-vis the government, and which in general terms soured the process initiated in March. If I had to

point to any one factor, however, it would be to "palace intrigues" and especially to those initiated on October 10. In retrospect, I believe I should have resigned at that point. Certainly from that day forward my dreams of a process which would produce a national-unity government met with little but frustration. That I did not resign was because it was not so clear to me then as now that an irreversible turning point had been reached. Hence, I wished to go on with the task I had undertaken and hoped the damage could be repaired.[41]

Feints and Parries

What had begun hopefully in March as a move toward national reconciliation now increasingly evolved into a contest of wills between Perón and Lanusse. For the rest of 1971 and the first six months of 1972, the contest produced little more than feints and parries on both sides. Each heaped invective and charges of bad faith on the other. Perón scorned Lanusse's Grand Accord and said the Peronists would negotiate nothing with the "dictatorship."[42] Lanusse just as tenaciously warned that he who did not participate in the GAN would not participate at all.[43] And he insisted repeatedly that there would be no "leaps into the void"; rather, the elections, and the program followed by the government they produced, were to be the results of prior agreements. It is not clear how Lanusse expected to persuade Perón to enter into these agreements. His optimism may have been fueled by the conviction that while on the one hand Perón did not really intend to return to Argentina to run, on the other, the great majority of Peronist politicians obviously did want to participate in the coming elections. Thus, Lanusse must have reasoned, Perón's own followers would exert increasing pressure on him to define himself. And as Lanusse was convinced Perón in fact did not want to return to be the candidate himself (no matter what he might say publicly), he was led to believe that Perón would have little choice but to give the nod to someone else. If Perón simply procrastinated, Lanusse reasoned, his followers might well break discipline and participate in the elections without him. In either event, it must have seemed to Lanusse that he had Perón over a barrel.

Lanusse's reasoning was rational enough. Its flaw was that it did not take sufficiently into consideration the wide margin of maneuver enjoyed by Perón as a result of Lanusse's own categoric promises that *no one* would be proscribed. Perón was now convinced that Lanusse would never allow him to be a candidate, and it seemed certain that Lanusse would wish to have the issue settled long before election day. Perón was well aware that Lanusse's brother officers were pressuring the latter to make it clear that Perón would not be a candidate in the elections. Perón, then, had only to sit back and wait, confident that Lanusse eventually would be forced to proscribe him. As one weekly political review described Lanusse's situation at the time: "In order for the government to comply with its word to provide elections without proscriptions, it must count on the autoproscription of the Peronist leader."[44] However, as the same article pointed out, Perón was not to be trapped into that. So far, he had turned aside all Lanusse's efforts to coax or force him to step aside, and he was quoted as saying: "I will not proclaim myself nor proscribe myself. That is something which must be in the hands of the Argentine people."[45]

A few weeks later, when asked about the government's position regarding his possible candidacy, Perón replied in high good spirits: "It's their problem, not mine; let them proscribe me if they wish."[46] Obviously, Perón was prepared to wait it out as long as necessary—right up to the time of the elections if need be. Lanusse had miscalculated. It was Perón who had *him* in a corner, not vice versa.

Although the Peronists were still in the Hora del Pueblo, in early July, Perón moved to create a second coalition group. Many believed his purpose was to fashion a multiparty organization he could more easily manipulate to his own ends. On July 6, representatives of various parties and groups met to form the Civic Front for National Liberation (Frente Cívico de Liberación Nacional, FRECELINA). At the first meeting, the new organization was described as a nonelectoral "alliance" which could develop into an electoral front. Its first undertaking, according to its organizers, would be to try to work out common guidelines. Once these were agreed upon, it was suggested that the parties in FRECELINA might form an electoral front with common candidates.

Present at the meeting, among others, were representatives of Frondizi's Movimiento de Integración y Desarrollo (MID), Vicente Solano Lima's Popular Conservatives, the José Antonio Allende sector of the Christian Democrats, later to become the Popular Christian Party (PPC), and a number of smaller groups. Notably absent was the UCR. Despite the creation of FRECELINA (the anagram prompted humorists to note that the elections might well come to be mistaken for a war of toothpaste commercials), the Peronists did not abandon the Hora del Pueblo; rather, Héctor J. Cámpora indicated their intention to remain in both.[47]

With Perón thus still on the loose, Lanusse's brother officers became increasingly unhappy with his management of the process. In fact, during the first week in July, for the first time in almost a year, there were persistent and widespread rumors of a coup.[48]

Lanusse Attempts to Seize the High Ground

Lanusse had to act quickly to regain the initiative. Most importantly, if he was to convince his fellow officers that he knew what he was doing and could be trusted to bring the electoral process to a satisfactory conclusion, he had to devise some dramatic formula to break the impasse with Perón over the candidacy. On July 7, 1972, at the annual "camaraderie" dinner, he announced just such a formula.

After reiterating that no candidate or party would be proscribed, Lanusse then presented a blueprint by which both he and Perón might proscribe themselves. Going back to his theme that in order to play the game, one had to be in the country, he set a deadline of August 25 for any who wished to be candidates to return to Argentina; likewise, by August 25, all major executive officeholders who wished to be candidates would have to resign.[49]

It was a clever move on Lanusse's part. He had kept his word; he had not proscribed Perón. He had simply brought into being a new regulation under which all candidates had to be physically present in Argentina. Perón and some of his followers might complain, but, Lanusse hoped, most Argentines would see it as a sensible requirement. Further, by providing for his own autoproscription unless he resigned both as president and as commander of the army by August 25, Lanusse balanced his move against Perón with what appeared to be one against himself. Did this mean that he had given up any hopes of being the candidate? Perhaps not altogether. He may have hoped that under changed circumstances a strong draft movement would begin and that the rules might then again be changed. Meanwhile, however, he was giving up very little, for his own trial balloon had fallen flat. Despite the strong hints dropped by his followers back in October 1971, no draft movement had yet taken fire; on the contrary, the public temper remained clearly against a military candidate. A sampling taken by a polling service in mid-1972, for example, showed that 87 percent of those polled in Buenos Aires felt that the military should leave power; in Córdoba, 90 percent, and in Rosario, 92 percent so believed.[50]

Still convinced that Perón would not come back, Lanusse thus hoped he had painted Perón into a corner and that his own GAN could go forward. With this in mind, in the same July 7 speech he again urged the political parties to come to the conference table.[51]

If one judges the July 7 speech by its results, one would have to give it low marks. Perón, as it turned out, had not been painted into a corner. He continued to avoid any clear definition and continued to have it in his power to disrupt the whole electoral scheme simply by announcing that he would be the candidate despite Lanusse's arbitrary ruling. He did quickly respond to Lanusse's deadline by saying he would not return by that date. The matter of the candidacy he left open, however, saying only that he still considered himself a possible candidate. "I cannot issue any such disclaimer. Whether or not I am to be a candidate is up to the people to decide," Perón concluded.[52]

The deadlock remained unbroken, but that was not immediately apparent. Lanusse's strategy, as noted above, had been based on the assumption that Perón would not return. Hence, believing that his assumption was proving correct, Lanusse pressed ahead with the project to get all the parties to sit down at the negotiating table with the government. By and large, this effort was designed to give substance to the floundering GAN and prevent what Lanusse called "a leap into the void." However, it was also at least partly aimed at providing a mechanism which might help lever the Peronists away from Perón. Whatever their leader might decide to do, if the Peronist politicians wished to participate in the elections, they would, Lanusse suggested, have to sit down at the government's table. And once that happened, he doubtless reasoned, it might be possible to engage them in the electoral process so firmly that even if Perón ordered them to boycott the elections, they would disobey and participate anyway.

But Lanusse was again overestimating his own position and giving Perón too little credit. All the Peronists had to do was wait. They knew that there could be no meaningful process without them, so they and their FRECELINA allies flatly refused to negotiate.[53] If Lanusse was trying to draw the Peronists away from their leader, two could play at that game. In a statement on July 25 clearly designed to drive a wedge between Lanusse and the rest of the military establishment, Héctor J. Cámpora said he was certain that the armed forces themselves wanted to see an honest process of institutionalization but that unfortunately the Lanusse government did not represent the armed forces.[54]

Angered by this blatant attempt to separate him from his military supporters and by Perón's continuing refusal to define himself, Lanusse, in a speech delivered July 27, attempted to break Perón's hold over the *descamisado* faithful by challenging his manhood. It was a long speech, but there were really only two major points: (1) that Perón could not participate unless he returned, which, Lanusse declared, "Perón simply did not have the guts to do" *(no le da el cuero);* and (2) that the right of the other Peronists to participate in the electoral process was guaranteed.[55]

It did not work. Perón called Cámpora to Madrid for consultations and then sent him back on August 16 with a flat No. The Peronists would not answer the government's call for dialogue, nor would their FRECELINA allies. Further, Perón continued to insist that he would return to Argentina in his own good time and that if the people wished it, he would be a candidate, no matter what the government said.[56]

With the Peronist refusal to sit down at the conference table came the collapse of Lanusse's efforts to involve the political parties in his Grand Accord. Obviously, if parties representing at least half the electorate refused to participate, there was no hope of achieving the kind of broad-based agreement that the GAN implied. Half-hearted efforts would be made in the months ahead to call for new consultations on specific topics, but nothing would come of them. For all practical purposes, Lanusse's GAN was now dead.

Lanusse and Perón Negotiate

Lanusse and Perón seemed to have worked themselves into a tight deadlock. But both were foxy political strategists who recognized that rarely does either side profit from a real deadlock; rather, the profit goes to the side which breaks it to its own advantage. With this in mind, the two began to communicate with one another through a secret emissary, José B. Gelbard, who was soon to become Cámpora's minister of economy, and who traveled back and forth from Buenos Aires to Madrid several times between August and November.[57] On Lanusse's side, he had little choice but to continue his efforts to persuade Perón to renounce the candidacy. Perón's principal aim was probably to bring about a more propitious atmosphere for his return. For return he would. He was already preparing to take Lanusse up on his challenge of July 27 and, as indicated in a *Las Bases* editorial of September 7, Perón wished his return to reaffirm the general desire for peace and reconstruction.[58]

The secret negotiations were not fruitless. By late September, well-informed Peronists were aware that Cámpora had received from Perón a new "plan for reconciliation" which Cámpora was to present to the government. On October 4, he handed to Brigadier Ezequiel Martínez a ten-point program for national unity.[59] Because this was a negotiated document (indeed, the principal drafters were said to be Mor Roig, José B. Gelbard, and Antonio Cafiero, a Peronist economist),[60] it is not surprising that the government reacted rapidly and favorably. Almost immediately after the Cámpora-Martínez meeting, presidential press secretary Edgardo Sajón held a press conference in which he emphasized the general coincidence of views between the Peronists and the government regarding the institutionalization process. He compared the ten-point program to the government's earlier call for dialogue and reconciliation.[61] Lanusse himself responded equally favorably. One might disagree with certain features of the program, he said, but the attitudes behind it were clearly new, positive, and encouraging.[62]

The two sides might have been expected to discuss the document and agree upon a program which Perón and Lanusse could endorse, upon the former's return, as the basis for a broad national reconciliation. However, they fell to arguing over who would discuss it with whom, with the result that it was never discussed at all. Despite Lanusse's earlier endorsement, and despite the assertion of *Las Bases* that the ten-point program represented an act of greatness which would set the stage for Perón's homecoming,[63] nothing concrete ever came of it. It did help to set the stage for Perón's return, however, for the very existence of a plan for reconciliation suggested to many that an accord was imminent. These hopes were further encouraged by Perón's statement just before his return that he was coming back to help in the task of national reconstruction. The government said that it favored dialogue and that he could return with guarantees. Very well, he would take them up on it. He would return in peace and perform his last service to Argentina.[64] Moreover, as many Argentines reasoned, simple logic suggested that Perón would not return and place himself in the hands of the military unless he already had an agreement with military leaders.

From all this emerged what came to be called the "golden vision" of Perón's return. He would come back, immediately meet with Lanusse, Balbín, and other politicians, and agree upon a single national-unity candidate. They would all then embrace and endorse an Act of National Reconciliation; Perón would return to Madrid as Argentina's statesman of the century.[65]

Perón Returns

It was a beautiful dream. Unfortunately, as with so many other attempts to forge a consensus in Argentina, it remained just that — a dream. As Perón's plane landed that drizzly morning of November 17, 1972, there was no high-ranking military delegation waiting to whisk him away to a meeting with Lanusse. Indeed, the military seemed curiously uncertain what to do with Perón once he was on the ground. There was a long delay before he could deplane, and when he finally did come down the ramp, it was only to be driven over to the airport's International Hotel. There he was greeted by the omnipresent Brigadier Martínez on behalf of the junta, but there were no embraces, no warm words of welcome, and certainly no invitation to meet with Lanusse. Instead, Perón and his party were kept at the hotel as virtual prisoners for some nineteen hours, at one point with machine guns trained on the entrance. Not until 6 o'clock on the morning of November 18 was Perón permitted to depart for the house in Vicente López, a suburb of Buenos Aires, which had been purchased and prepared for him by his followers, who soon converged upon him by the drum-beating tens of thousands, causing one of the worst traffic jams in Buenos Aires history.

After seventeen years, Perón was home again, and the world had not, as hard-line anti-Peronists had expected, turned upside down. That in itself was something. A cloud which had hung over the country for seventeen years was dispelled. But those who had expected a more positive result — agreements and solutions worked out among the major political actors — continued to be disappointed.

During the month that Perón remained in Argentina, there was no meeting with Lanusse nor any serious discussions with other military leaders. While in a news conference on November 22, Lanusse referred to Perón's return as a positive development,[66] he also stated publicly that he would receive Perón as he would receive any other citizen, by appointment. Perón would have to come to him.[67]

For his part, Perón might have been willing to request an appointment, but first he wanted a concession from Lanusse. As one well-informed Peronist described the situation:

> General Perón wants to meet with Lanusse, but he cannot do so until Lanusse rescinds the residency requirement; otherwise, he will appear to be going as the supplicant. Once Lanusse has made that gesture, however, Perón could go to him and make his own — that is, to renounce the candidacy and agree on someone else.[68]

The military strategists, however, were not sure that Perón would resign if the legal barrier to his candidacy were lifted. Further, they did not want to throw away their bargaining position even before Lanusse sat down at the table with Perón; hence, they pinned their hopes on the chance that Perón would agree to meet with Lanusse anyway, or, even better, that he would renounce the candidacy and then meet with him.[69] So they stood behind General López Aufranc's categoric statement on November 29 that the residency requirement would not be lifted.[70] As the weekly magazine *Panorama* put it: "The Casa Rosada intends to force the renunciation rather than negotiate it."[71]

Perón did not meet with the leader of the military party, that is, with Lanusse. He did, however, confer with the representatives of most political parties during his stay in Buenos Aires, including one large get-together with them at the Nino restaurant on November 20. This rekindled hopes for some degree of coalescence among the political parties and even of a Peronist — UCR ticket. Speculation concerning the latter possibility was further stimulated on November 21 when Perón and Balbín met privately. Newspapers the next day carried pictures of a smiling Balbín emerging from the meeting and quoted him as saying that he and Perón had agreed upon the need for national reconciliation. Further, Balbín commented about his old adversary: "Insofar as I can discern, Perón is dedicated to the achievement of a union of all Argentines within a democratic framework."[72]

The Possibility of a Peronist-UCR Alliance

The idea of a Peronist-UCR alliance was by no means new. In the 1940s Perón had embraced many of the reform principles of the Radicales and, indeed, had referred to his Peronists as "soldiers of Yrigoyen." In 1944, moreover, he had tried unsuccessfully to work out an electoral alliance with the Radicales through the leader of the UCR in Córdoba, Dr. Amadeo Sabattini.[73] Now he again seemed to be moving in that direction. In June 1972 he had made a concrete offer. Cámpora had lunched with Enrique Vanoli, Balbín's closest advisor, and transmitted a message to be passed on to Balbín. Perón suggested that the two parties agree to run a joint ticket, with the question of whether a Peronist or a Radical would be the presidential candidate to be negotiated in subsequent talks. Vanoli expressed interest, promised to inform Balbín of the offer, and said that the UCR would talk it over.[74] During the next few months the matter was chewed over by the UCR's top leaders. Balbín, Vanoli, Antonio Troccoli, and Carlos Pugliese, among others, were generally in favor. Raúl Alfonsín, Balbín's challenger for leadership of the UCR, was against any form of alliance with the Peronists, whom he continued to regard as fascists. Thus, while there was a growing interest on the part of the majority wing of the UCR, no definite decision was made. Even this inchoate interest was frozen in its tracks, moreover, when in October 1972 Vanoli asked Cámpora at an Hora del Pueblo meeting whether the offer of a joint ticket still held and received an evasive reply. "Many things have changed since June," Cámpora said.[75]

While Vanoli did not take Cámpora's reply as a flat rejection, it was not encouraging. The UCR left the proposal on the shelf — neither rejected nor acted upon. Meanwhile, the UCR was drawing closer and closer to its internal party elections slated for November 26.

Perón said nothing to Balbín about the idea of a joint ticket when he met the UCR leader on November 21. Some suspected that Cámpora had advised him not to. On November 23, however, Perón did send a message directly to Balbín asking if the UCR were interested in a joint ticket. After consultation with his lieutenants, Balbín told Perón that with the UCR's internal elections for candidates coming up in only three days, it was too late.[76]

Even then, Perón did not give up. On the eve of his departure, he offered the vice-presidential candidacy to Héctor Hidalgo Solá, a member in good standing of the UCR. Perón's exact motives in this will probably never be known. Some felt that he might have been mainly interested at that point in splitting the Radicales, who represented the only serious competition to his Peronists in the coming elections.[77] Others, however, including Hidalgo Solá, were convinced of the sincerity of Perón's offer and believed that it represented a last forlorn effort to join forces with the UCR. Whatever Perón's reasons for making it, nothing came of the offer, for after careful consideration, Hidalgo Solá turned it down.[78]

By the first week in December, it was not only clear that there would be no national-unity, or Peronist-UCR candidate, but by then also the individual slates were beginning to take shape. On November 26, Balbín and Eduardo Gammond had won the presidential and vice-presidential candidacies, respectively, of the UCR.

Further, on December 5, the Buenos Aires press reported a third force in the making in the form of a new coalition of provincial parties that Lanusse was said to be gathering to back the candidacy of Brigadier Martínez and Leopoldo Bravo of the San Juan Bloquistas.[79] This ticket did in fact run in the elections, and, while the government never acknowledged it, there was no doubt that Martínez was Lanusse's candidate and enjoyed official support, including the use of public funds.[80]

As for the Peronists, the coalition they were to lead began to take form on December 4, when, to the surprise of all, Cámpora proposed to a meeting of parties which had been represented at the Nino that they immediately join with the Peronists in forming an electoral alliance. This was entirely unexpected and caused an immediate uproar.[81] When Cámpora insisted, the UCR, accompanied by the Progressive Democrats, withdrew from the meeting.

The parties which remained — the Peronists, the Popular Conservatives, Frondizi's MID, the Revolutionary Christians (PRC), the Popular Christians (PPC), Héctor Sandler's UDELPA, Marcelo Sánchez Sorondo's Movement of the National Revolution, and various provincial parties such as the May 12 Front of San Juan — would meet the following day and formally organize an alliance, the Frente Justicialista de Liberación (FREJULI, the Justicialist Liberation Front). The PRC, UDELPA, and several other parties dropped out within a few days, however, leaving the Peronists, the MID, the Popular Conservatives and the Popular Christians as the only nationally recognized parties in the front.[82] The MID, the Popular Conservatives, and the Popular Christians were very minor parties with a total vote among them, based on past voting records, of no more than 8 percent of the electorate.[83] The FREJULI was an alliance, but it was hardly a substitute for the hoped-for national unity slate.

Who the FREJULI candidate would be, moreover, remained an open question. Cámpora had said at its founding meeting on December 5 that Perón was its candidate, and, as the various alliances registered on December 11, the FREJULI leaders again offered Perón the candidacy.[84] But clearly this was simply a matter of form. By then, no one expected that Perón would or could accept. During the nine days between the formation of the FREJULI on December 5 and Perón's departure on December 14, there was wild speculation as to whom he would name in his place. There was no longer any doubt that the candidate would be a Peronist, for Cámpora had indicated at the December 5 meeting that the various candidacies (for Congress, provincial governorships, legislatures, and other offices) would be shared by the Peronists with their allies on a three-to-one ratio and that the minority parties should prepare to choose the vice-presidential candidate from their own ranks, assuming that Hidalgo Solá turned down Perón's offer to him. It was therefore assumed that the presidential candidate would be a Peronist.[85]

Moderate Peronists hoped Perón would give the nod to a respected Peronist politician, to someone such as Italo Luder, Antonio Benítez, or Alfredo Gómez Morales. Unfortunately, this was not to be. Upon leaving

Argentina, Perón renounced the candidacy, as expected, but he did not publicly name a replacement; rather, he suggested in his departure statement that the matter of deciding upon an appropriate candidate was entirely up to the Peronist party congress, which was to meet the next evening as soon as Cámpora returned from Asunción, to which he had accompanied Perón .[86] Despite what he said publicly, however, Perón had indeed named a candidate. The morning of his departure, he called in Cámpora and told him he was the man. This could not have been altogether unexpected by Cámpora, for he had been angling for the candidacy for some time. Nonetheless, he feigned complete surprise and even shed a few tears.[87] Responsible Peronists, when they heard the news, would shed even more.

Perón left behind a confidential letter for key Peronist leaders indicating his wish that the party congress might nominate Cámpora. As the letter was read and word began to circulate the evening of December 14 and the next morning, reaction was sharp. The evening of the fifteenth, Cámpora returned from Asunción and the congress, meeting in the Hotel Crillón, got down to business. The FREJULI congress was in session at the same time on another floor of the hotel. Once the Peronists selected a presidential candidate, his identity was to be transmitted to the FREJULI and they, in turn, were to nominate him as the FREJULI candidate as well.

By the time the two congresses went into session, it was well known that Perón had given the nod to Cámpora. The only question was whether that fact would be swallowed by opponents within the Peronist movement — especially by the labor wing. Some clearly would not. Rogelio Coria of the labor movement walked out, accompanied by many other delegates, complaining of a pressure campaign to ram Cámpora's candidacy through. "We leave," he said, "hurt and embittered."[88]

Other representatives expressed strong disapproval of Cámpora, but no more walked out, and, after the arrival of a telex message from Perón backing the candidacy, active opposition to it ceased. Cámpora was elected by the Peronist congress in an after-midnight vote. Even so, his victory was greeted by jeers and catcalls from many in the hall. Shortly thereafter, the FREJULI congress also nominated him.

As for Cámpora's running mate, Perón had privately indicated his own preference for Vicente Solano Lima, leader of the Popular Conservatives, whom he had supported for the presidency in 1963. Almost as soon as he had been nominated by the Peronist congress, therefore, Cámpora went down to the FREJULI gathering and informed them of "his" choice. Frondizi's MID was strongly opposed to Solano Lima, but to no avail. Perón had spoken, through Cámpora, and his will was done. By dawn on December 16, the Cámpora–Solano Lima slate was an accomplished fact.[89]

Its troubles were by no means over. Provincial slates dictated by the national directorate of the Peronist party immediately began to run into the same sort of opposition that Cámpora had encountered from the labor wing. There were splits in the ranks and even outbreaks of violence as faction fought faction within the Peronist movement.

Why Cámpora?

In the end, the movement would hang together, but for the moment the Cámpora candidacy had wreaked havoc. Why, then, had Perón appointed such a man? Having known Cámpora some twenty years, Perón must have recognized him for the mediocrity that he was. Indeed, one possible explanation for Cámpora's appointment is that Perón felt such a man could never gather a following of his own or become a rival within the Peronist movement. Cámpora would be the candidate, but he would mindlessly do Perón's bidding. Or so Perón may have hoped.

There were other possible explanations. One line of reasoning, for example, was that Perón named Cámpora in an effort to abort the elections. Some evidence supports this. According to the late José B. Gelbard, Perón discussed the situation with him in early December, saying that he had lost his gamble that the military would deal with him reasonably and that his bargaining position was therefore so weak that he intended to abort the whole process. He would return to Madrid to await a more favorable moment. Shortly thereafter, he named Cámpora as the Peronist candidate. "There is no question in my mind," Gelbard commented subsequently, "that Perón expected the military to cancel the elections then and there."[90]

At least in retrospect, Lanusse himself agreed with that view. In *Mi testimonio*, published in 1977, he explains:

> The feeling we had was that Perón put forward that name so we would veto it. And with our veto, he would have put forward a replacement even less acceptable — such as Julian Licastro or Rodolfo Galimberti. That would have led the armed forces to choose one of two options: the suspension of the elections, or the proscription pure and simple of Peronismo.[91]

Finally, Cámpora's own running mate, Solano Lima, felt that Perón had given the nod to Cámpora in order to provoke the military to end the process. According to Solano Lima:

> General Alcides López Aufranc had told me in November the military would not accept Cámpora as a candidate. I reported that conversation to Perón; shortly thereafter, he decided Cámpora should be the candidate. I have no doubt that the one was related to the other. He had no thought that Cámpora would ever become president.[92]

The first explanation for Perón's decision, of course, does not necessarily exclude the second; that is, he may have hoped that Cámpora's candidacy would abort the elections, but in case it did not, and in case Cámpora actually won, Perón was still left with the most malleable candidate he could find who was at the same time ambulatory.

Why did the military *not* proscribe Cámpora at that point? One can argue that too much momentum toward elections had already built up and that the armed forces felt that the honor of their institution was already committed to Lanusse's promise that no one would be proscribed. Possibly. Certainly in the months ahead that was to be the case. But even had Lanusse believed in December that he could have proscribed Cámpora without provoking a civil conflict — or splits within the military — why should he have wanted to do so? On the contrary, given the dissension that Cámpora's candidacy had caused in the Peronist ranks, Lanusse must have seen it as a godsend, an instrument by which the Peronists might self-destruct and take themselves right out of the race. It seemed to make good sense, then, for Lanusse to bide his time.

Other Tickets

The Cámpora–Solano Lima ticket was allowed to stand. As the campaign got under way, it represented the largest party, plus allies. Balbín and Gammond represented the UCR. There were several other hats in the ring as well. As noted above, Brigadier Martínez and Leopoldo Bravo headed a coalition called the Republican Alliance, which was backed by Lanusse. Francisco Manrique, the same social welfare minister who in 1971 had advocated a draft-Lanusse movement, had subsequently left the Lanusse camp and was now the presidential candidate of a coalition called the Federalist Alliance.

Other candidates included Christian Democrats, old-line conservatives, and traditional socialists. Horacio Sueldo of the majority wing of the Christian Democrats, and Oscar Alende of the Intransigent party, joined forces with the Communists and Héctor Sandler's diminutive Union of the Argentine People (UDELPA) to form the Popular Alliance, which put forward an Alende-Sueldo ticket and was expected to do well, possibly to come in third. The New Force (Nueva Fuerza) was a new party, but hardly a new movement. Backed mostly by businessmen, it was laissez-faire in attitude and spent more than any other group on campaign propaganda. Julio Chamizo was its presidential candidate, Raúl Ondarts his running mate. The venerable Américo Ghioldi again ran for the presidency as the candidate of his Social Democrats. René Balestra was his vice-presidential candidate. Another offshoot of the old Socialist party, the Socialist Workers' party (PST), also put forward a slate. Juan Coral was its presidential candidate and Nora Sciappone his running mate. Finally, Jorge Abelardo Ramos and Jorge Silvetti formed the ticket of another new party, the Leftist Front.

The Campaign Begins

Altogether, then, there were nine candidates for the presidency in the March elections. As the campaign moved along, however, it became increasingly clear that only Cámpora and Balbín had a real chance of winning. Even so, the campaign never evolved into a slug fest between the two. This doubtless reflected some lingering spirit of the Hora del Pueblo, and the fact that there were few differences in the programs of the two parties also contributed to it. The principal explanation for the absence of campaign pyrotechnics between Peronists and Radicales, however, probably lay in the observation that if there was a single overriding issue in the elections it was one of sending the military back to the barracks, and on that, Peronists, Radicales, and most of the other parties were in full agreement. Further, as the Peronists calculated their electoral strategy, the party which most effectively capitalized on antimilitary sentiment would have the advantage; hence, they aimed their campaign squarely against the Lanusse regime, not against the Radicales, and they moved quickly to secure the foremost position. Once back in Madrid, for example, Perón lambasted the Lanusse government and declared that if he were fifty years younger he too would be out planting bombs.[93] Shortly thereafter, the Peronists began to put forward a slogan which was to characterize their whole campaign strategy: "A vote for Perón is a vote against Lanusse." This was refined as the campaign moved along and finally became: "Yesterday, Perón or Braden; Today, Perón or Lanusse."[94]

On January 21, the FREJULI kicked off its campaign with a violently antimilitary rally at San Andrés de Giles during which one of the milder chants heard was *Cinco por uno, no quedará ninguno* (five for one, then there'll be none — literally, we'll kill five of them for every one of us and soon there'll be none of them left).[95] From that point until the closing rally on March 8 attended by some eight thousand drum-beating stalwarts hurling defiance at the armed forces,[96] the Peronist campaign slogan never varied: "The military must be turned out, and Perón is the only one who can do it."

For their part, the military did not turn the other cheek. Even before the campaign was under way, they began placing impediments in the FREJULI path, such as denying Cámpora permission to charter a train for a barnstorming tour,[97] and bringing charges against Perón for his violent language of December 30 and against the Peronist publications *Mayoría* and *Nueva Plana* for reproducing them.[98]

The military also forbade Perón to return until after the elections,[99] raided the FREJULI headquarters in Córdoba, and ransacked the home of Peronist leader Juan Manuel Abal Medina in Buenos Aires.[100]

Probably none of this helped the military cause in the slightest. Denied a train, Cámpora flew from city to city. The charges brought against Perón and the Peronist publications simply gave both added prominence, while prohibition of Perón's return played right into his hands. He had given little evidence of wanting or intending to return for the elections anyway; now he had a perfect excuse not to do so and could assume the role of the in-jured party to boot — an innocent citizen denied his rights. Rather than hindering the FREJULI campaign, therefore, Lanusse's efforts to put obstacles in its path probably helped it, for this simply underscored the fact that he and the Peronists were adversaries, just as the Peronists wanted it. As one of Argentina's most astute political observers commented at the time, "The more measures Lanusse takes to block the Peronists, the more he translates the elections into a contest between himself and Perón. And that is the kind of contest Perón is certain to win."[101]

Lanusse Tries to Block the Peronists

But Lanusse was not inclined to back away. Having decided in December to let the Cámpora candidacy stand, now, over a month later and with the campaign getting under way, he probably regretted it, especially after the fierce Peronist rally at San Andrés de Giles. It came as no surprise when the day after the rally word went out that Lanusse had called an urgent gathering of senior generals, to be followed on January 24 by a meeting of the junta. Rumors had it that he intended to resign in disgust, or possibly that he would try to cancel the elections. A number of Peronists especially were convinced that Lanusse wanted to cancel the elections.[102] But Lanusse's meeting with his brother officers on January 24 produced neither. Some versions had it that he was prevented from calling off the elections only by the determined opposition of Army Chief of Staff López Aufranc, backed by the majority of the generals. The Peronist daily *Mayoría* ran headlines the next day proclaiming, "Lanusse Loses; Elections Go Forward!"[103] And one Peronist commented several days later that he and his friends were con-vinced that General López Aufranc had blocked Lanusse on January 24. They expected Lanusse to continue to try to halt the electoral process and López Aufranc to continue to prevent him from doing so. "We don't like López Aufranc and he doesn't like us," remarked the Peronist, "but we believe he, unlike Lanusse, is a man of his word. Thus, the process will probably go forward."[104]

Whatever López Aufranc's role, after the meeting with the generals, he stated flatly that the elections would take place and that if the FREJULI won, the armed forces would guarantee their right to take office.[105] At the same time, however, one strong threat did emerge. At the meeting's conclusion, the junta issued a lengthy statement which included a warning that the military expected political leaders to conduct the electoral campaign with serenity and in strict conformity with the norms established by the Law for Political Parties.

All doubts as to the meaning behind the warning were erased when in a meeting shortly afterward with provincial governors, Lanusse referred specifically to Articles 25 and 50 of the Political Parties Law. The first specified that the objectives of any party had to accord with the Constitution and the democratic system; the second warned against violation of public order and democratic norms. "Enough of this farce of supporting terrorism and then appealing to constitutionalism," Lanusse concluded angrily.[106]

Here, Lanusse clearly warned the Peronists to back away from their emphasis on "machetes and civil war" or face the possible dissolution of their party and coalition, the penalty prescribed by the law for violation of Article 50. Rumors immediately began to circulate that legal action would soon be initiated on the basis of these two articles, with the accusations referring specifically to the appeal to violence heard at San Andrés de Giles.[107] Abal Medina, the secretary-general of the Peronist party, noted in reply that Lanusse was a fine one to talk about violence. After all, he reminded his listeners, "Lanusse came to power by force of arms."[108]

But Lanusse was intent on pressing ahead, and on January 31 he reportedly convinced the senior generals that legal action should be initiated against the FREJULI. This, in turn, was approved by the cabinet on February 1,[109] and on February 5 the junta sent through the Ministry of Justice instructions to the federal attorney to begin legal action against FREJULI. The grounds were that its campaign rhetoric had violated Article 25 of the Law for Political Parties, and that its slogan "Cámpora to the Government, Perón to Power" violated Article 22 of the Constitution, which specified that the people were sovereign and could govern only through their *elected* representatives.[110] The FREJULI slogan, contravening Article 22, implied that someone other than an elected representative would rule.

Then, strangely enough, having launched what seemed to be an effort to proscribe the Peronists, on February 7 Lanusse reversed his field. The junta, he said, had no thought of proscription. "If we had intended to do that," he said, "we would have done it straight away."[111]

Yet, the federal attorney, in presenting the charges to the federal judge on February 6, had demanded the extinction of the FREJULI and its component parties.[112] Clearly, he could not have taken this step without orders from the highest levels. How then could Lanusse say the very next day that it was not his intention to proscribe anyone? What had happened from one day to the next to change his mind? The answer, in a few words, is that his initiative had encountered overwhelming opposition almost as soon as it was launched.

On the night of February 6 — immediately after the charges were presented — Interior Minister Mor Roig, who had all along advised against cancellation of the elections or proscription of any of the parties, informed Lanusse that he was very concerned as to the possible scope of the action taken. If its purpose was only to curb the FREJULI's excesses, then Mor Roig could go along with it. If its purpose, however, was the dissolution of the FREJULI, then he would immediately present his resignation.[113]

General López Aufranc, finding out that Lanusse was acting against Mor Roig's advice, also called on Lanusse that evening and warned that if he insisted on pressing for the dissolution of the FREJULI, he would do so without the support of López Aufranc and many of the other generals. The army, in following Lanusse's own lead, had promised clean elections open to all. The army would not dishonor its word, López Aufranc declared.[114] UCR leader Ricardo Balbín also reacted strongly, saying on February 5 that the FREJULI should not be proscribed, and on February 6 that he would convoke a multiparty meeting if it were.[115]

With his interior minister threatening to resign, the other parties reacting vigorously, and his support among his own generals uncertain, Lanusse not surprisingly felt the need to retreat. Thus, in the meeting of senior generals on February 7, he insisted that there was no intention of proscribing the FREJULI and put out the word that the only purpose was to warn the Peronists.[116] Simple logic, however, suggests that this had not been Lanusse's original purpose. One does not take an action one day designed to intimidate, only to tell the subject the next that he should not be intimidated, only warned.

In all this, in the legal action against the FREJULI, in banning Perón's return, and in the other jabs at the Peronists, Lanusse was really just thrashing around. He could not cancel the elections; his own officers would not have supported him in that. As General López Aufranc said at the time: "The point of no return has already been passed. Let's hear no more about a disruption of the electoral process."[117]

In other words, while Lanusse's fellow generals may initially have accepted his plan for elections somewhat reluctantly and had strong reservations about Peronist participation, and while they might at an earlier point have been delighted at the prospect of aborting the whole process, they now felt that they had come too far to turn back. Too many promises had been made, too much momentum had been generated. If Lanusse now changed his mind, they would not follow him in canceling, nor, indeed, would they permit him to cancel the process that he himself had begun.

To *La Nación*'s political observer Claudio Escribano, Lanusse was "his own prisoner." As Escribano phrased it:

> From the moment in which Lanusse first expounded his policy [of convoking elections open to the Peronists] in the opening months

of 1971, until the present, little by little the country has turned massively to the support of that decision, and now one hardly hears any voices opposed to the holding of elections or to the transmission of power to whoever wins. Today, then, the president is his own prisoner, or a prisoner of his own policies. . . . It must be he who presides over this process until the end.[118]

Unable to stop the process and unable to persuade or force the Peronists to play the game by his rules, Lanusse found himself equally powerless to proscribe them. Even his minister of the interior would not have supported him in that, and had he attempted to force proscription anyway (assuming his generals would have backed him, a most unlikely assumption), he would have taken the step into the past which he had sworn not to take. As *La Opinión* summed up his dilemma, he had the choice of proscribing the Peronists and thus bringing about elections à la 1963 (in which the major party did not participate), or of allowing their participation and thus confirming Peronist voting strength.[119]

In fact, by mid-February Lanusse had no choice. He had to swallow Peronist participation.

The UCR Platform

Meanwhile, the FREJULI was not the only group in the race. The UCR campaign was grinding along in its responsible and dignified, if somewhat uninspired, fashion. The UCR's campaign slogan was "Balbín, Solution," and in most of his speeches and interviews Balbín focused in measured tones on institutional solutions to Argentina's economic, social, and political problems. He criticized the government and the military, but he usually did so in a responsible, constructive manner. The public temper, on the other hand, was running strongly against the generals and seemed to want more dramatic attacks against them. As one Radical said after accompanying Balbín on some of his swings through the provinces, "The only times I saw crowds respond really enthusiastically were when Dr. Balbín used strong language in taking the military to task. But Dr. Balbín is a statesman, not a demagogue; hence,those occasions were rare."[120]

Why then did Balbín not compete with the FREJULI for the frontal position against the armed forces? His own answer is that, first of all, had both the major parties conducted such a hostile campaign, the elections might well have been canceled, and Balbín believed it imperative that elections be held. Second, Balbín saw clearly that the country needed a viable consensus. He did not want to burn during the campaign the bridges he would need to the armed forces during the period of national reconciliation that he hoped would follow.[121]

Lanusse's Last-Hour Appeal

On March 8, all the parties and candidates closed out their campaigns with rallies from one end of the country to the other, with the Peronists, as usual, heaping abuse on the military. Lanusse, however, was determined to have the last word. The evening of March 9, he went on nationwide television to deliver a special message to the Argentine people. He began by assuring them that the elections would be honest and that the armed forces would abide by the results. It quickly became apparent, however, that this would not be a may-the-best-man-win speech. The nation, he said, was faced with a choice. Its vote could bring into existence an authentic democracy, but it could also submerge the nation in "anarchy, messianism, the vilification of institutions, the curtailment of liberties, the implantation of terrorism, and the tyranny or subordination to the will of one man."[122]

Lanusse's references to "messianism" and to the "tyranny . . . of one man" made it clear that he was talking about Juan Domingo Perón and was, in effect, saying that a vote for Perón was a vote for chaos. He went on to call upon Argentine citizens to "reject false apostles."[123] There was no doubt as to Lanusse's message; he was almost openly urging the voters to cast their ballots against Perón and the FREJULI. It was an egregious error. It demolished any remaining claim on Lanusse's part to being an impartial arbiter; further, the public mood was running so strongly against the military that the average Argentine was simply not prepared to accept any advice from Lanusse — in fact, many may deliberately have rejected it and acted in a contrary manner. Whatever one might say about the validity of Lanusse's remarks, in delivering them Lanusse hurt his own cause far more than Perón's.[124]

The Peronist Victory

The campaign was over, and on March 11 the voters went to the polls. There was an air of tense excitement, but voting was orderly and well supervised. By late afternoon of March 12, 1973, it was clear that Cámpora and the FREJULI were building up a commanding lead which no other candidate was likely to overtake. Balbín called Cámpora to concede and congratulate him.[125] That evening, with the FREJULI having drawn even further ahead, Lanusse went on the air to recognize Cámpora as the inevitable winner.[126]

Of the 14.1 million Argentines registered to vote, 11,920,925 cast valid ballots. A few thousand voted in blank, but these ballots were not counted. The official results were as follows:

> Cámpora (FREJULI): 5,908,414 votes, or 49.56 percent
> Balbín (UCR): 2,537,605 votes, or 21.29 percent

Manrique (Federalist Alliance): 1,775,867 votes, or 14.9 percent
Alende (Popular Alliance): 885,201 votes, or 7.43 percent
Martínez (Republican Alliance): 347,215 votes, or 2.9 percent
Chamizo (New Force): 235,188 votes, or 1.97 percent
Ghioldi (PSD): 109,068 votes, or .91 percent
Coral (PST): 73,796 votes, or .62 percent
Ramos (Leftist Front): 48,571 votes, or .41 percent

The FREJULI had won a sweeping victory in the presidential elections. Its sweep was no less impressive in the congressional and gubernatorial races. The Peronists won every governorship.[127] FREJULI had 45 of the 69 senatorial seats, with only 12 going to the UCR. Had the FREJULI won just one more seat in the Senate, it would have enjoyed a two-thirds majority.[128] In the lower house, FREJULI had 142 of the 243 seat.[129]

There is no way of determining precisely how many of the votes cast for the FREJULI were cast *against* the military rather than *for* Cámpora, but most observers agreed that a good number had been. As *La Opinión* put it two days after the elections: "The vote was against the Argentine Revolution. It can be interpreted as a repudiation of the distortions of political reality, of the regimes lacking representation and based on force."[130]

If the Peronists had captured the antimilitary vote, Perón had also courted youth assiduously, even adding a youth wing to his movement. It paid off. Labor had always represented the backbone of the Peronist movement and assured it massive blocks of votes. In 1973, however, the Peronists and their allies had two strong blocks of votes, youth as well as labor, plus the many independents who were simply disgusted with military rule.

As an electoral tactic, the appeal to labor and youth had worked, but it carried with it the seeds of future conflict, for labor and youth were mutually antagonistic. Moderate Peronists, moreover, were deeply concerned over the increasing power and influence that radical youth organizations such as the Montoneros seemed to be gaining within their movement. The moderates were encouraged when in April Perón sacked Peronist youth leader Rodolfo Galimberti, who had imprudently suggested the formation of "special youth militia." This was like waving a red flag at the military, with whom, now that the elections were over, Perón wished to repair his bridges. Galimberti was called to Madrid, given a tongue-lashing, and fired.[131]

The Cámpora Government: A Political Disaster

Left-wing youth continued to have a major influence within the government-elect, however, and on inauguration day, May 25, seemed to be in control of the government and the city of Buenos Aires itself. Columns representing the various radical youth organizations marched into the city and soon filled the Plaza de Mayo and the streets leading from the capitol

Alejandro Augustín Lanusse hands to Héctor Cámpora the presidential baton, 25 May 1973. In September Perón was elected presi-dent for the third time. (Courtesy Juan Carlos D'Abate)

building to the Casa Rosada. There were inevitable clashes with military units guarding public buildings. These were especially serious in the area between the army building and the Casa Rosada, and by late morning the crowds around the latter were on the rampage, burning cars and stoning the vehicles of several foreign delegations attempting to reach the inauguration ceremonies. With the crowd out of control, Lanusse was warned to leave by helicopter from the roof, once he handed the baton of office over to Cámpora. He refused, saying, "I came in through the front door; I'll leave by it as well."[132]

The military parade and procession to the National Cathedral for the Te Deum had to be canceled. No one could get through the mob. Worse was to come. As night fell, crowds of young leftists began gathering at Villa Devoto and other prisons and jails in and around Buenos Aires. By 10 P.M., there were some twenty thousand people gathered in front of Villa Devoto alone. Terrorist prisoners shouted encouragement and draped Montonero and ERP banners from the windows, calling on those below not to disperse. The mood of the crowd became ugly, and it appeared they might storm the entrance at any minute. Frantic phone calls were made to Cámpora, who panicked and ordered all "political" prisoners released, including many convicted terrorists. Just before midnight, prisoners started filing out of Villa Devoto and other prisons around the country. In the confusion, many common criminals, including François Chiappe, a major international drug trafficker, were also released.[133]

Even Cámpora's directive to release prisoners did not prevent further disorders, however. Well after inmates had started to leave the prison, demonstrators clashed with guards at Villa Devoto, leaving two dead and many wounded. It was an inauspicious beginning for Cámpora's government. Its implications for the future disturbed thoughtful Argentines and convinced many that the Cámpora government was controlled outright by leftist extremists. Many even look back on it as a "Marxist revolutionary regime." This is something of an exaggeration, though understandable. Cámpora did move the government leftward, but his short-lived administration was very much a mixed bag, both in personnel and policies. Of his cabinet appointees, for example, Antonio Benítez (minister of justice), Jorge Taiana (education), and Ángel Robledo (defense) were old-line, orthodox Peronists, not leftists by any stretch of the imagination. Ricardo Otero (labor) may have been many things (including, some said, dishonest and incompetent) but he was no leftist. José López Rega (social welfare) had been Perón's private secretary. Without question he proved to be a bizarre character, but he leaned more toward fascism than leftism. José B. Gelbard (economy) was more difficult to define. A Polish Jewish immigrant, Gelbard had risen from poverty to riches. He was one of the sharpest (and, some said, shadiest) businessmen in Argentina. Despite this—or, perhaps, precisely because of it—he was often accused of being a communist, although no evidence was ever produced to back up such charges.

Esteban Righi (minister of the interior) and Juan Carlos Puig (foreign relations) were initially even more controversial than Gelbard. Neither was a Marxist, or, probably, even of radically leftist persuasion. But both were inexperienced and easily influenced by others. Righi was egged on by Cámpora's sons and nephews, members of the radical leftist youth movement. Puig was overshadowed by Jorge A. Vázquez, a young firebrand who was suddenly promoted from a minor position in the Argentine embassy in Santiago to be undersecretary of foreign relations. Righi and Puig made very poor showings, but less for ideological reasons than simple incompetence.

Internally, the Cámpora government did not move to alter the basic socioeconomic structure of the country. Rather, in line with Peronist doctrine, it initiated an economic program which aimed at income redistribution favoring the working class. But this was to be a gradual process, and most enterprises were to remain in private hands. Internationally, Argentina publicly identified itself with the Third World and stressed increasing trade with the communist countries. Cámpora reestablished relations with Cuba and gave special attention to Presidents Dorticós of Cuba and Allende of Chile who had come to Argentina for the inauguration. On the other hand, if relations with Chile and Cuba were good, they were even better with the right-wing dictatorship in Paraguay.

But if the Cámpora government's ideological directions were varied and often confusing, its inability to keep order presented a clear-cut problem. Disorders, which began the moment Cámpora took office, became worse. This largely resulted from Cámpora's own weakness and indecisiveness, as well as his appointment of inept and inexperienced people to key jobs. For example, in early June, the number of sitdown strikes and occupations of public buildings reached alarming proportions. Students who did not like their faculty deans seized university buildings. Hospital employees took over hospitals. State employees locked themselves in public buildings.

Esteban Righi, the thirty-one-year-old interior minister, was obviously out of his depth. For almost two weeks the government took no action at all to restore order. On June 14, Cámpora departed for Madrid (from whence he was to escort Perón on his final trip home), leaving matters in Righi's hands. The most Righi could do, however, was to argue that now that this was a people's government, there was no need for violent action.[134] This had not the slightest effect. Behind the scenes, however, Vicente Solano Lima, acting as president in Cámpora's absence, quietly ordered the police to begin arresting those who refused to surrender occupied buildings. A number of arrests were made and police took several buildings by force. Following this show of determination, the occupations quickly came to an end.

Perón's Return Marred by Bloodshed

Public order was temporarily restored, but there was to be a new breakdown of major proportions to mar Perón's homecoming. Some four hundred thousand of his followers had gathered near Ezeiza airport on June 20 to greet the returning leader. Left- and right-wing Peronists were determined to control the event and to plant their respective banners in the area around the speaker's platform. Who fired first has never been satisfactorily determined; both sides obviously came armed to the teeth and spoiling for a fight, and only a spark was needed to set it off. A full-scale battle broke out and raged until well after dark. With automatic weapons being fired at close range in the midst of the packed crowd, the carnage was tremendous.[135] No one knows exactly how many casualties there were, for the Cámpora government forbade the publication of a list. However, foreign correspondents and other neutral observers estimated that as many as two hundred lost their lives and over a thousand were wounded that bloody June 20.[136]

Perón could not have been pleased with this new demonstration of the Cámpora government's incompetence. Cámpora himself was not directly responsible; he was not even in the country when the fighting started. But his interior minister's federal police had failed completely to keep order. Indeed, after the shooting broke out, they had disappeared from the scene. The pro-Peronist daily *Mayoría* remarked, "It would be interesting to know who gave the order to the police not to act, even worse, to begin to withdraw as soon as the shooting started."[137] And yet, if there had been an absence of authority, if the police had received orders not to act, and if irresponsible elements had been given free rein, this was all very much in keeping with the past performance of the Cámpora government, which had allowed the occupation of public buildings and which had given in to the mobs in front of the prisons on the night of May 25.

Cámpora Forced to Resign

Perón was not blind to events. Just when he made the decision to ask for Cámpora's resignation was a secret he took to the grave with him. Solano Lima says that Perón told him as early as July 4, two weeks after the Ezeiza battle that Cámpora would have to go.[138] The first indication to the public, however, came on July 11 when Victorio Calabró, the vice-governor of Buenos Aires Province and a key leader of the Peronist labor sector, stated flatly that now that Perón was back in Argentina only he could be president and that Cámpora should step down.[139]

Calabró's statement took the country by surprise and caused instant consternation in Peronist circles. However, as Peronist leaders found that Cámpora's resignation was indeed "expected," they quickly endorsed Calabró's attitude. Labor began to mobilize to demand that Cámpora step down. For a short while on July 12 it appeared that there might be a general strike. This proved unnecessary.[140] At a cabinet meeting the morning of July 12, it was made clear to Cámpora that he was expected to resign.[141] Late that afternoon, word went out over Radio Rivadavia that he and Solano Lima would step down the following day.[142] On July 13, they did just that. Cámpora explained that he was stepping aside to make way for Perón, as he had always intended to do. He had run for the presidency, he said, because the Lanusse government had arbitrarily prevented Perón from being the candidate. But now that the Peronists were in power, the way was clear for the election of Perón, who was, after all, the only president the people really wanted.[143]

According to the constitutional order of succession, the provisional president of the Senate, Senator Alejandro Díaz Bialet, should have replaced Cámpora, inasmuch as the vice-president, Solano Lima, had also resigned. But Díaz Bialet was a close friend of Cámpora's and was thus ruled out. Arrangements were made to get him out of the way so that the presidency would pass to the president of the Chamber of Deputies, Raúl A. Lastiri, López Rega's son-in-law. Hence, Díaz Bialet was packed out of the country the night of July 13 on what was described as a special mission. Lastiri was sworn in that same night.

In his acceptance speech, Lastiri supported Cámpora's explanation and described the latter's resignation as a noble and historic gesture which did Cámpora proud.[144]

Perón also publicly backed Cámpora's story in full. In his own message to the nation, delivered about 10 P.M. July 13, Perón referred to the "unnatural proscriptions" and said that Cámpora had told him even before the elections that, if elected, the first thing he would do was declare the proscription unconstitutional and submit his resignation. In an extraordinary act of selflessness, he had now done so.[145] All this, of course, was the sheerest hokum and was obviously said with the aim of putting the best possible face on things publicly, even if no one was expected to believe it. As the retiring vice-president, Solano Lima, was to put it later:

> The idea that Cámpora had all along intended to resign was
> simply not true. Cámpora never mentioned any such intention to
> me while we were campaigning—or, indeed, on any occasion
> before Perón's return. Perón, on the other hand, had told me he

definitely did *not* plan to be president, that his health was not up
to it; rather, he planned to let Cámpora administer the country
while his [Perón's] role would be that of an elder statesman. . . .
Perón wanted to devote himself especially to hemispheric affairs
and to do what he could to promote Latin American
integration.[146]

Perón's comments to Solano Lima coincided exactly with what he had
been saying to other politicians. In March, for example, he had told a
Peronist politician, Rodolfo Tecera del Franco, that those who expected
Cámpora to be simply a shadow president while he himself ran the country were going to be surprised. He fully intended to let Cámpora be the
president, while he, Perón, as the head of the Peronist movement, would
only indicate general directions and provide philosophical orientation.[147]

No matter what those around Perón said on July 13 to save face, all other
evidence suggests that Perón had indeed intended that Cámpora should serve
his full term. But Cámpora failed him and had to be forced out. It is no
wonder that Perón tried to suggest that his resignation was a noble gesture
and all part of a previously conceived plan. To have admitted that the man
to whom he had given the candidacy was such a miserable failure as president that he had to be replaced after less than two months in office would
have been embarrassing in the extreme to Perón himself. What it might
have implied about his own judgment was a question that Perón obviously
did not wish to see raised. And few Argentines intended to raise it, at least
publicly, for most were too relieved to see Cámpora go to be inclined to
ask questions about his departure. Even to the anti-Peronists, after Cámpora,
Perón looked good. Though stunned and disoriented by Cámpora's ouster,[148]
even the left-wing Peronist Youth had to go along with it, at least initially.
In a statement issued July 16, for example, they declared that since
Cámpora's resignation would lead to placing Perón in the presidential chair,
they could only approve.[149]

New Elections Announced

Lastiri's presidency was an unimportant detail. The way had been cleared
for Perón, and it was obvious that he would soon be back in the Casa Rosada.
On July 13, Lastiri announced his intention to convoke elections almost
immediately.[150] Perón, in his own message an hour later, made it clear that
he would accept the candidacy:

I can have no aspiration other than to serve my country. . . .
The country has called, and when it calls one to its service, for-
tune stretches out its hand. God grant that we know how to take
that hand and fulfill the destiny now placed on us by history.[151]

In July 1973 it was rumored that Ricardo Balbín, leader of the Radical party, would become the vice-presidential candidate; however, Perón selected his wife Isabel instead. (Courtesy Wide World Photos)

Elections were soon announced for September 23, with the new president to be inaugurated on October 12. There was no doubt as to who would win. The only questions were: by how much would he win, and who would run with him?

A Perón-Balbín Ticket?

The ink was hardly dry on Cámpora's resignation before observers began to speculate that Balbín would be the running mate. Perón seemed to confirm this idea when in an interview on July 13 he described the possibility of a Perón-Balbín ticket as "beautiful" and said he "would go anywhere with Dr. Balbín."[152] The UCR, moreover, now seemed willing to go anywhere with Perón. UCR Senator Luis León, for example, stated on July 15 that he was convinced that a Perón-Balbín ticket was what the great majority of Argentines wanted to see.[153] Popular reaction in the days that followed suggested that he was right.[154] And no wonder. Such a slate might well have forged the kind of national unity Argentina needed but had never had. As Heriberto Kahn, one of Argentina's leading newsmen, summed it up: "With a Perón-Balbín ticket apparently a foregone conclusion, the kind of national unity which Mor Roig had hoped to see come out of the March elections and which the Hora del Pueblo seemed to have presaged, now might become a reality."[155]

But day after day passed and the hoped-for slate did not materialize. On July 28–29, the Radicales held a national convention at which, in effect, they voted to give Balbín a free hand in working out an alliance with the other party. Perón and Balbín met on July 31 and the country waited expectantly for an announcement of their joint candidacy. None came. Balbín emerged from the meeting insisting the matter had not even been discussed.[156] And with the Peronist party congress only four days off, it was apparent that if a combined slate had not been worked out on July 31, none was likely to be. On August 4, any lingering hopes were extinguished when Isabel Perón was nominated by the Peronist party.

Why did the Perón-Balbín ticket fail to become a reality? Had Perón all along been insincere in repeatedly indicating an interest in an alliance with the UCR? These questions may never be answered, for Perón died without leaving a written account of his thoughts on the matter. Judging from conversations with politicians of both parties involved in the political maneuvering at that time, however, I am convinced that Perón did in fact want an alliance and want Balbín to be his running mate. Indeed, he privately affirmed that to a number of people.

Apparently, having launched the idea, Perón quickly encountered opposition to it within his own party and his own household. Some Peronist politicians and labor leaders, having seen the vice-presidential candidacy (as well as some of the other spoils) go to a non-Peronist in the March elections, were determined that this would not happen again. The labor sector especially was determined that the executive power be "Peronized."[157] To be sure, it was Perón who finally called the shots within his party, but at the same time, he was legitimately concerned with institutional unity among his followers. He could not simply ignore resistance which might have resulted in fragmentation.

Further, additional — and perhaps decisive — pressure came from within his own "palace guard," which had demonstrated on previous occasions its ability to manipulate Perón.[158] López Rega was determined to get the candidacy for Isabel Perón, his protégée and ally, and pushed hard from the beginning for an all-Peronist ticket.[159] One must assume that Mrs. Perón herself also pressured Perón to include her on the ticket. Indeed, that may have been the deciding factor. As he was later to say to a leading Radical, "At this late stage in my life, I simply could not resist the pressure from within my own bedroom."[160] CGT leader José Rucci and others of the labor wing had hoped initially to get the vice-presidential candidacy for one of their own, but they soon gave up any such aspirations in favor of backing Mrs. Perón, who, they concluded, was their best bet to block any alliance with the UCR.[161]

Perón appears to have bowed to these pressures. A few days before the Peronist party congress on August 4, he told a ranking FREJULI leader in some disgust that he intended to wash his hands of the whole thing. He had wished to run with Balbín, believing that this was the best means of assuring the institutionalization process, but there seemed to be many within his own movement who were against it. Further, said Perón, if he gave the nod to the leader of any one sector of his movement, that would anger all the others. Hence, he had decided that the best thing to do was to leave it up to the Peronist party congress to name his wife.[162]

Whatever the considerations behind Perón's decision, the result was the same. Isabel Perón was probably as incompetent a candidate as could have been found. A year later, she would become president and lead the country to the very brink of disaster. When Perón washed his hands, Argentina paid a high price.

New Campaign Tactics: Emphasis on Consensus

As the campaign got under way, it was clear that Perón would win. But it was essential to him that he win by a larger margin than had Cámpora, thus, in a sense, legitimizing the latter's defenestration. With his unpopular wife as running mate and the danger of defections within the youth wing, Perón saw that winning by a larger margin was not so certain, and moved to meet the problem.

First, he successfully renewed his appeal to youth. In a speech on August 2, for example, he indicated that there was no place in his movement for Marxist infiltrators or terrorists, but to all others he opened his arms, expressing great confidence in youth as the hope of the nation.[163] It was a theme he was to replay frequently during the campaign. Also as part of his play to the youth wing, Perón sent their hated foe, López Rega (he of fascist tendencies), out of the country "on leave," and to some Perón even hinted that López Rega would not be back.[164] The tactic was transparent, but it worked. At a massive youth rally on August 22, the Peronist youth wing made it clear that while they had reservations concerning the candidacy of Mrs. Perón, they had full confidence in Perón himself and would support his candidacy.[165]

Having assured himself of the support of his youth wing, and thus having maintained unity within his own ranks, Perón next set about putting himself forward as Argentina's "bringer of consensus," using the one to reinforce the other. On August 31, he successfully brought off a joint labor and youth march in support of his candidacy. Only a month earlier, left and right Peronist factions had shot it out at Ezeiza. Now, on Perón's orders, many of those same elements seemed to be working hand-in-hand. As the bitterly antagonistic youth and labor columns filed peacefully by the reviewing stand together, many Argentines concluded that only Perón had the magic to unite all factions in Argentina. Political observer Heriberto Kahn, for example, emphasized a few days after the August 31 march that what the country needed more than anything else was consensus, and Perón, he concluded, offered the best hope of achieving it.[166]

This image of a nation united — with himself as the unifying factor — was one that Perón himself pushed hard. In a speech to members of Congress on August 30, for example, he stressed that no matter who won the elections, joint action would be needed if Argentina was to move ahead. "If we win," he promised, "our approach will be to listen to all ideas that may be of service to the country. . . . I ask the leaders of other political forces to be our friends and to join us in this undertaking."[167]

Perón Wins

Balbín of the UCR was Perón's principal rival in the September elections, as he had been Cámpora's in March. He had now dropped the lackluster Gammond in favor of a younger, more attractive running mate, Fernando de la Rua, whose runoff victory for a Senate seat representing the federal capital had been one of the few bright spots for the UCR in March. Manrique and Martínez Raymonda ran again as the Federalist Alliance ticket, and Juan Coral again represented the PST. The other five slates from the March elections dropped out.

Perón's three opponents in the September elections knew that he would win, but they campaigned hard to improve their March showings. Indeed, perhaps the best description of the campaign was Claudio Escribano's: it was like a golf match in which the players, having only recently been over the same course together, knew who would win, but were terribly interested in improving their individual scores over those of the previous match.[168]

As in the March elections, voting on September 23 was orderly and there were no charges of fraud. By late afternoon September 24, with all votes tabulated, it was clear that Perón had won by a landslide. He had 7,378,249 votes, or 61.85 percent of the total. As expected, Balbín came in second, with 2,905,236 votes, or 24.34 percent of those cast, more than he had won in March and thus something of a moral victory. Manrique, on the other hand, lost ground. Having won 14 percent of the vote in March, he now dropped to 12.11 percent or 1,445,981 votes. Coral came in a poor fourth, with only 188,227 votes, or 1.57 percent of those cast, thus failing to establish himself as *the* candidate of the left as he had hoped.[169]

The UCR and most other political parties immediately assured Perón of their support and cooperation.[170] Even the armed forces, which only a year before could not have stomached his candidacy, now seemed willing to give him the benefit of the doubt. And as Perón appeared on the balcony of the Casa Rosada on inauguration day dressed in the uniform of a lieutenant general of the Argentine army, he seemed to be indicating to the military that the discords of the past were forgotten and that he again considered himself one of their own. As Heriberto Kahn put it:

> To the almost 90 percent of the electorate who already were prepared to back him, Perón now wished to add—and stood an excellent chance of winning—the support of the armed forces. If so, for the first time in our modern history, a president might operate from a foundation based on a consensus of all three poles in Argentina's power structure: the Peronists, representing the working class; the UCR, representing the middle class; and the armed forces, the final guarantors of the strength and continuity of the state.[171]

As Perón stood on the balcony on October 12, 1973, the great majority of Argentines looked hopefully to him to introduce a new era in Argentine politics, one based on consensus. But a consensus which depended so much on one man was bound to be tenuous. Perhaps it would have broken down even had Perón lived. Without him, it had no chance at all, for clearly, if the largest party, the ruling party, did not hang together, there was little hope that the other parties could hold the consensus intact. To function at all, such a consensus required the gravitational pull of an intact Peronist mass. With Perón's death on July 1, 1974, that mass began to disintegrate.

After Perón's death in 1974, President Isabel Perón salutes the people while a smiling José López Rega (right) looks on. (Courtesy Juan Carlos D'Abate)

Embracing a bizarre assortment of forces from across the political spectrum — everything from old-line fascists to the "new left" — the Peronist movement had been held together by a single adhesive agent, by the certain loyalty owed to Perón himself from his disparate followers. Without Perón, the glue disappeared.

Even before Perón's death, it had become clear that he had no panaceas to offer his country. Economic ills persisted, as did left-wing terrorism. An open rupture between Perón and his youth wing took place on May 1, 1974, when he called them "stupid brats," and ordered them out of the Plaza de Mayo.

Problems there were. Even so, had Perón lived, he might have kept them within manageable limits and got through to the next elections, thus establishing a precedent for constitutional government. But his death left the Casa Rosada in the hands of his inept and inexperienced wife, who, to make matters worse, was under the influence of José López Rega, a dangerously unbalanced astrologer who tried to guide the Argentine ship of state by random star readings. A year of this duo brought Argentina to the verge of economic and political chaos. Inflation was above 400 percent and terrorism was rampant, now coming from the right as well as the left.

The civilian political leaders made some efforts to rid the country of the incompetent Isabel Perón through legal processes. An impeachment motion was launched in the Congress at the end of 1975, and moderate leaders within her own party tried to persuade her to step aside. These efforts failed. She refused to resign, and Peronists, no matter how clearly they recognized her shortcomings, could not bring themselves to participate in the impeachment of a Perón. Thus the motion never got off the ground.

With the government teetering on the brink of chaos, on March 24, 1976, the armed forces removed Isabel Perón from office and took power for the sixth time in modern Argentine history. They were cheered by the Argentine people for doing so. But the cheering stopped quickly. In terms of its political goals, the new military government was as uncertain of its directions and as divided in its purposes as had been the military regimes before it. On one point only did it appear to be united: the new leadership was determined to eradicate left-wing terrorism even if it had to wipe out half the population of Argentina in the process. In combating one extreme, the government itself went to another.

The new military government did, however, have several factors working in its favor: (1) Perón no longer loomed in the wings; (2) the Argentine people were so sick of political chaos that they appeared ready to accept, at least for a time, any government which offered a modicum of stability; and (3) the senior military leadership seemed to be sensitive to the need for dialogue with civilian political forces. That these factors will be sufficient to enable the present military government to succeed where those of the past have failed seems most unlikely.

Isabel Perón in 1974, president of Argentina, the first woman to become chief executive of an American republic. (Courtesy Juan Carlos D'Abate)

As for the Peronist movement, many speculated that with its various sectors at one another's throats, discredited by the chaos that had characterized Isabel Perón's government, and having lost its venerable leader, it was finished as a force in Argentine politics. There seemed to be only one way in which the movement might be resuscitated: that is, that the military should repeat the errors of the past and so pressure the disparate Peronist factions that they might reunite and take on new life. But whether or not the Peronist movement itself survives to play an active role in Argentine politics, the Peronist idea, or myth, most certainly will endure. Whatever his failings, Perón's egalitarian thought changed the Argentine political landscape; it will never be quite the same again.

Conclusions

How, then, are we to interpret the return of Perón to power? The military had little choice but to call for elections in 1971, for the failures of military government had swung popular opinion so strongly against the armed forces that, in Lanusse's words, they had to choose between giving up power or becoming occupation forces in their own country. And if the 1973 elections were not to be a return to the past, or a repetition of those of 1958 and 1963, they had to offer something new. These elections were to be free and unconditioned; there were to be no proscriptions. Lanusse's thinking in this was sound, for a return to constitutionalism would have appeared artificial and unworthy of confidence had over one-third of the electorate remained partially disenfranchised. The fact that the Peronists were to be allowed to participate in 1971, however, did not mean that Lanusse or anyone else in the military wished to see a resurgent Peronism. On the contrary, Lanusse was probably convinced that the Peronists could not win an open election. Certainly he intended that the process of reincorporation be carefully controlled. There was hope that Perón might be induced to throw his support to a candidate acceptable to the armed forces. Failing that, perhaps a wedge could be driven between Perón and his followers. When this also failed, Lanusse tried to place restraints on Peronist participation in the elections, and finally, to maneuver the Peronists into accepting prior guidelines for the conduct of the new government. There is some evidence to suggest that when all other efforts failed, Lanusse wished to cancel the elections. But it was too late. Too much momentum had built up and Lanusse had made too many promises with respect to free elections without proscriptions. The officer corps believed that the honor of the armed forces was committed. Hence, even though the outcome was not what they had hoped for, they insisted on completing the process Lanusse had begun.

As for the smashing Peronist victory in March, its major ingredient seemed clearly to have been the political capital that the Peronists made of the frustration and anger which had built up against the military. The latter were blamed not only for their last seven years of unsuccessful and unconstitutional government; they were also blamed for Argentina's relative decline since 1955. As Perón himself once put it, the durability of his own myth and of Peronist strength resulted "not to any perfection of ours while in office; rather, they resulted from the fact that everything after us failed."[172]

In the September elections, the strategy was quite different. The military had already been turned out. The Peronists were in power, and there was never any doubt that Perón would win. To rule effectively, he needed the military; hence it would have been not only pointless but counterproductive to have made them the targets of a new political attack. Instead, Perón built his campaign around an appeal for national unity, putting himself forward as its natural progenitor. Clearly, this touched a responsive chord in the Argentine body politic. It might be said, then, that the Peronists won the March and September elections so overwhelmingly because, in both cases, they read and capitalized on the public mood more effectively than did any other party.

NOTES

1. The military's rationale in overthrowing the Frondizi and Illia governments was extremely tenuous; even many military men admit in retrospect that the coups only complicated the country's problems. One can only speculate as to what Argentine history might have been had the armed forces left Frondizi or Illia alone.

2. General Juan Enrique Gugliamelli, "Responsabilidad de las fuerzas armadas," *Estrategia* (Buenos Aires), no. 4 (Nov. – Dec. 1969), 9. All Spanish sources have been translated by the author.

3. *Panorama* (Buenos Aires), 2–8 Aug. 1973, p. 8.

4. Alejandro A. Lanusse, *Mi testimonio* (Buenos Aires: Lasserre, 1977), pp. xviii–xix.

5. Félix Luna, *Argentina: De Perón a Lanusse* (Buenos Aires: Biblioteca Universal Planeta, 1972), p. 206.

6. Carlos Russo, "Por que los militares dieron las elecciones," *Redacción* (Buenos Aires), Mar. 1973, p. 6.

7. See "Para que sirvió la Revolución Argentina?" *Redacción*, June 1973, pp. 32–51. Some twenty leading Argentine news reporters generally agreed that the overall result of the Onganía period had been to raise public discontent with military rule to an intolerable level.

8. "Por qué se dividen los Peronistas?" *Cuarto Poder* (Buenos Aires), June 1972, p. 4.

9. Lanusse, *Mi testimonio*, pp. 43, 134.

10. "El fracaso de los frentes políticos," *Cuarto Poder*, March 1972.

11. Ibid.

12. *Confirmado* (Buenos Aires), 2 Nov. 1971, pp. 18–22.

13. *La Nación* (Buenos Aires), 24 Mar. 1971, p. 1.

14. See ibid., 27 Mar. 1971, p. 1; also *Confirmado*, Mar. 1971, pp. 9–10.

15. Arturo Mor Roig, in conversation with me, 11 June 1974. (Note: This and all other conversations cited took place in Buenos Aires. I knew most of the politicians and other key figures in the electoral process and talked to them many times. Many of these conversations had to remain in confidence. The statements cited in this work, however, were made to me with the understanding that they might eventually appear in a published work. I found that, to their credit, all were more than willing to have their views and experiences become a part of the historical record. My thanks to them.)

16. *Confirmado*, 7–13 Apr. 1971, p. 12.

17. See for example the statement of Jorge Daniel Paladino quoted elsewhere in this chapter.

18. Ricardo Balbín, in conversation with me, 26 Jan. 1976.

19. *Confirmado*, 21–27 Apr. 1971, pp. 10–16.

20. For a full account of the Perón-Cornicelli interview, see *Las Bases* (Buenos Aires), 18 July 1972, pp. 35–47; because of its confidential nature, accounts of this conversation were not released for over a year.

21. In conversation with me, 11 June 1974, Mor Roig indicated that from the time the Hora del Pueblo was organized until even after he became interior minister, consistent signals from Madrid indicated that Perón did not wish to be the candidate. Jorge Daniel Paladino, in a conversation with me, confirmed this on 19 June 1974.

22. As related to me by Ricardo Balbín in a conversation on 26 Jan. 1976.

23. According to Lieutenant Colonel Carlos Cerda, in a conversation with me on 6 Oct. 1975.

24. *La Prensa* (Buenos Aires), 21 Aug. 1971, p. 1.

25. Ibid., 8 July 1971, p. 13.

26. Ibid.

27. *Panorama*, 8 Feb. 1972, pp. 12–13.

28. *Confirmado*, 1 Sept. 1971, pp. 10–11.

29. See, for example, Rodolfo Pandolfi's analysis, *Confirmado*, 21 Sept. 1971, p. 8.

30. See also Lanusse's speech of 22 Dec. 1971, reported in *La Prensa*, 23 Dec. 1971, p. 17.

31. *Confirmado*, 7 Sept. 1971, p. 12.

32. Ibid., 19 Oct. 1971, pp. 8–9.

33. Ibid., 12 Oct. 1971, pp. 7–10; 19 Oct. 1971, pp. 11–14.

34. This conclusion is based on my conversations with Mor Roig and several other observers.

35. *La Prensa*, 31 Oct. 1971, p. 1.

36. Ibid., 25 Oct. 1971, p. 1.

37. Lanusse, *Mi testimonio*, pp. 256–57.

38. *Confirmado*, 19 Oct. 1971, pp. 8–9.

39. Another factor in Paladino's downfall was that he had come to be such a popular figure in the Peronist movement that Perón may have begun to fear him as a potential rival.

40. Paladino, in conversation with me, 19 June 1974.

41. Mor Roig, in conversation with me, 11 June 1974.

42. See, for example, Perón's editorial in *Las Bases*, 1 Feb. 1972, p. 5.

43. See Lanusse's May 31 speech at San Nicolás carried in *La Prensa*, 1 June 1972, p. 11.

44. *Panorama*, 1 June 1972, pp. 12–13.

45. Ibid.

46. Ibid., 6 July 1972, pp. 13–14.

47. *La Nación*, 7 July 1972, p. 1.

48. After my arrival in Argentina, 1 July 1972, virtually every politician and military officer to whom I spoke during the next few days expressed the view that Lanusse would soon be replaced.

49. For the text of Lanusse's speech, see *La Prensa*, 8 July 1972, p. 4.

50. Poll conducted by Instituto IPSA, S.A., in July 1972. The data from this poll may be obtained from the Roper Center, University of Connecticut, Storrs, Conn. 06268.

51. *La Prensa*, 8 July 1972, p. 4.
52. *La Opinión* (Buenos Aires), 23 July 1972, p. 9.
53. See, for example, Héctor J. Cámpora's statement carried in *La Nación*, 26 July 1972, p. 1.
54. Ibid.
55. For the text of Lanusse's speech, see *La Prensa*, 28 July 1972, pp. 1, 6.
56. See Cámpora's arrival statement upon returning from Madrid, *La Razón* (Buenos Aires), 16 Aug. 1972, p. 1.
57. In conversation with me, 12 Jan. 1973, Gelbard confirmed that he had acted as go-between for Perón and Lanusse.
58. *Las Bases*, 7 Sept. 1972, pp. 4–5.
59. For the text of the document, see *La Nación*, 5 Oct. 1972, p. 1.
60. In conversation with me, 11 June 1974, Mor Roig strongly hinted that these had been the authors.
61. *La Nación*, 5 Oct. 1972, p. 1.
62. Ibid., 7 Oct. 1972, p. 1.
63. *Las Bases*, 5 Oct. 1972, pp. 6–8.
64. Ibid., 21 Nov. 1972, p. 19.
65. For an articulation of the "golden vision," see *Panorama*, 15 Nov. 1972, pp. 12–13.
66. See *La Prensa*, 23 Nov. 1972, p. 1.
67. *Panorama*, 13 Dec. 1972, p. 13.
68. Osvaldo Pérez Pardo, in conversation with me, 2 Dec. 1972. Pérez Pardo became the Peronist undersecretary of justice following the elections.
69. *Panorama*, 20 Dec. 1972, p. 13.
70. *La Nación*, 30 Nov. 1972, p. 1.
71. *Panorama*, 6 Dec. 1972, p. 14.
72. *La Nación*, 22 Nov. 1972, p. 1.
73. Félix Luna, *El '45: Crónica de un año decisivo* (Buenos Aires: Editorial Sudamericana, 1971), p. 116.
74. Enrique Vanoli, in conversation with me, 3 Apr. 1975.
75. Ibid.
76. Ibid.
77. Independently of the offer to Hidalgo Solá, a minuscule group of Radicales led by Alberto Asseff broke party discipline and went over to the Peronist-led coalition of parties, participating in it as the Movimiento Yrigoyenista.
78. Hidalgo Solá discussed the offer with me on 29 Sept. 1975; whatever others might have thought, he was convinced that Perón's offer was serious. He had refused it, he said, not because he thought it was a tactical ploy on Perón's part, but because he felt it would be misunderstood and rejected by his own party, thus provoking dissension.
79. See, for example, *La Nación*, 5 Dec. 1972, p. 1.
80. The only party which spent more money on campaign propaganda was Nueva Fuerza, backed by wealthy businessmen.
81. In retrospect, however, Cámpora's haste was not so surprising: the government had indicated a week or so earlier that it would consider extending the deadline for the registration of alliances from December 11 to December 21, but on December 5 it was announced that there would be no extension. Perón (and Cámpora) doubtless knew about the decision the day before it was announced. Hence, with only a week to go before the deadline, some move obviously had to be made toward organizing an electoral front, and thus Cámpora raised the issue at the multiparty meeting on December 4.
82. See *La Opinión*, 6 Dec. 1972, p. 1
83. *Hipótesis de adjudicaciones en base a últimos resultados electorales*, issued by the Dirección Nacional Electoral in late 1972, chart F.

84. *La Nación*, 12 Dec. 1972, p. 16.

85. Confirmed by Alberto Fonrouge, the former FREJULI secretary, in conversation with me, 8 Sept. 1975.

86. *La Nación*, 15 Dec. 1972, pp. 1, 6.

87. Américo Grossman, a well-placed Peronist politician, related this to me in conversation, 15 Dec. 1972.

88. *La Nación*, 16 Dec. 1972, pp. 1, 5.

89. Ibid.; see also 17 Dec. 1972, p. 12.

90. Gelbard, in conversation with me, 12 Jan. 1973.

91. Lanusse, *Mi testimonio*, p. 277.

92. Solano Lima, in conversation with me, 7 June 1976.

93. *Mayoría* (Buenos Aires), 11 Jan. 1973, p. 1.

94. See, for example, ibid., 18 Feb. 1973, p. 1.

95. The rally is described in *La Nación*, 22 Jan. 1973, pp. 1, 10.

96. *La Opinión*, 9 Mar. 1973, p. 1; see also *La Nación*, 9 Mar. 1973, p. 12.

97. *La Nación*, 19 Jan. 1973, p. 1.

98. Ibid., 18 Jan. 1973, pp. 1, 6; 27 Jan. 1973, p. 8.

99. *La Opinión*, 7 Feb. 1973, p. 1.

100. *La Nación*, 22 Feb. 1973, p. 1; *Mayoría*, 17 Feb. 1973, p. 1.

101. Claudio Escribano, political observer for *La Nación*, in conversation with me, Jan. 1973.

102. *La Nación*, 24 Jan. 1973, pp. 1, 8; I also consulted with many Peronist and UCR politicians between January 21 and 25 to see what they expected Lanusse's reaction would be.

103. *Mayoría*, 25 Jan. 1973, p. 1.

104. Américo Grossman, in conversation with me, 27 Jan. 1973.

105. *La Nación*, 25 Jan. 1973, p. 18.

106. Ibid., 26 Jan. 1973, p. 1.

107. Ibid.

108. *La Opinión*, 2 Feb. 1973, p. 24.

109. *La Nación*, 4 Feb. 1973, p. 8.

110. Ibid., 6 Feb. 1973, pp. 1, 8.

111. Ibid., 8 Feb. 1973, p. 1.

112. *La Opinión*, 7 Feb. 1973, p. 24.

113. *La Nación*, 7 Feb. 1973, p. 1; confirmed by Ricardo Yofre in conversation with me, 23 Feb. 1976.

114. As related by Mor Roig, in conversation with me, 11 June 1974.

115. *La Opinión*, 6 Feb. 1973, p. 9; 17 Feb. 1973, p. 8.

116. *La Nación*, 8 Feb. 1973, p. 1.

117. Ibid., p. 18.

118. Ibid., 28 Jan. 1973, p. 8.

119. *La Opinión*, 15 Feb. 1973, p. 9.

120. UCR politician Facundo Suárez, in conversation with me immediately after the elections.

121. Balbín, in conversation with me, 26 Jan. 1976.

122. The text of the speech appears in *La Opinión*, 19 Mar. 1973, p. 1.

123. Ibid.

124. After the elections were over and he was no longer interior minister, Mor Roig told me that he also believed the Lanusse speech was a mistake and had recommended against it. "It won more votes for Cámpora than for us," he commented.

125. *La Nación*, 13 Mar. 1973, p. 7.

126. Ibid.

127. Ibid., 16 Apr. 1973, pp. 1, 12.
128. Ibid.
129. Ibid.
130. *La Opinión*, 13 Mar. 1973, p. 6.
131. See *La Nación*, 26 Apr. 1973, p. 1; 30 Apr. 1973, pp. 1, 10.
132. Ibid., 26 May 1973, p. 20; Lanusse's remarks were related to me by Ricardo Yofre, Mor Roig's assistant.
133. Ibid., 26 May 1973, p. 18.
134. *Mayoría*, 17 June 1973, p. 1.
135. For various accounts of the battle of Ezeiza, see *Mayoría*, 21 June 1973, p. 6; 22 June 1973, pp. 6, 7, 10; see also *La Opinión*, *La Nación*, and *La Prensa*, 21–22 June 1973.
136. This was an estimate agreed upon at the time by the Buenos Aires foreign press corps.
137. *Mayoría*, 22 June 1973, p. 10.
138. Vicente Solano Lima, in conversation with me, 7 June 1976.
139. *La Opinión*, 13 July 1973, p. 5.
140. As *Mayoría* put it: "A general strike was not necessary because the consensus forged by the spontaneous mobilization of the people made it unnecessary" (13 July 1973, p. 1).
141. Solano Lima, in conversation with me, 7 June 1976.
142. See *La Nación*, 13 July 1973, pp. 1, 4, 5, 8, 17.
143. Cámpora's speech is found in *Mayoría*, 14 July 1973, p. 3.
144. Ibid., p. 5.
145. Ibid., p. 20.
146. Solano Lima, in conversation with me, 7 June 1976.
147. Rodolfo Tecera del Franco, in conversation with me, 2 Apr. 1973.
148. *Mayoría*, 13 July 1973, p. 3.
149. *La Nación*, 17 July 1973, p. 1.
150. The text of Lastiri's speech is in *Mayoría*, 14 July 1973, p. 5.
151. The text of Perón's speech is in ibid., p. 20.
152. Ibid., p. 4.
153. *Mayoría*, 16 July 1973, p. 12.
154. This judgment is based on my conversations with people in Buenos Aires subways, coffee shops, and restaurants.
155. Heriberto Kahn, in conversation with me, June 1974.
156. *La Nación*, 1 Aug. 1973, pp. 1, 5.
157. As indicated to me by Américo Grossman, Enrique Osella Muñoz, and Alberto Rocamora in June–July 1975.
158. Paladino, for example, told me in late 1975 how López Rega and Isabel Perón persuaded Perón to include them on the Peronist Superior Council after he had stated flatly to Paladino that he did not want to include them.
159. *La Nación*, 12 Aug. 1973, p. 8.
160. Miguel Ángel Zavala Ortiz related this to me in April 1975.
161. *La Nación*, 1 Aug. 1973, p. 5.
162. Senator Alberto Fonrouge, secretary of FREJULI, related this to me in June 1976.
166. *La Nación*, 3 Aug. 1973, p. 5.
164. See *La Opinión*, 25 Aug. 1973, p. 3.
165. Ibid., p. 4; see also the interview with Peronist youth leader Dante Gullo, ibid., 26 Aug. 1973, p. 12.
166. Ibid., 8 Sept. 1973, p. 1.
167. *La Nación*, 1 Sept. 1973, pp. 1, 18.
168. Claudio Escribano, ibid., 20 Sept. 1973, p. 8.

WAYNE S. SMITH

169. For election results, see ibid., 25 Sept. 1973, p. 1.

170. Ibid., p. 20.

171. Heriberto Kahn, in conversation with me, Dec. 1974.

172. Taped television interview with Perón in Madrid, 16 Apr. 1972, replayed on Argentine television.

7

JOSÉ ENRIQUE MIGUENS

The Presidential Elections of 1973 and the End of an Ideology

Bitter and continuing controversy has raised the question of how much "working-class" support Juan Perón had in the election of 1946, or more recently in that of 1973, and what type of workers stood behind him. Careful evaluation of the electoral data shows vast working-class backing for Perón in these elections twenty-seven years apart, while also revealing that the most important base of support for parties of the left has been the upper middle and upper classes.[1] But what, from a more general theoretical perspective, can or should we make of these facts?

Theories about Peronism take on particular importance in the social sciences, because they demonstrate with rare clarity how ideological perspectives have distorted the creation of political theories. Rationalizations had to explain away the majoritarian, working-class backing for Perón. If not, then what could the future hold for the socialist, communist, or "democratic" parties that claimed in 1946 to be the only legitimate representatives of the working class? When Perón defeated all the traditional parties of Argentina, including the Communist party, united in what they called a "Democratic Union," the partisans of these groups — before knowing the electoral results of 1946 — uniformly rated them as honest, the first "clean" elections in fifteen years. After the fact, however, they felt compelled to represent Perón as the leader of "antidemocratic" forces, as the principal military protagonist of the "dictatorship" that called the elections in the first place.

Neither U.S. liberals nor doctrinaire Marxists have wanted to accept the realities of working-class backing for Perón, this colonel who advocated a redistribution of income and power in favor of the common people, yet who did so in keeping with the Catholic and Hispanic heritage of Latin America and who incidentally denounced both Soviet and North American imperialism.[2] Marxists and Yankee liberals alike had to contrive elaborate rationalizations for what was "really" happening in Argentina, for what the case of Perón "actually" showed. Over time, therefore, the case has become highly interesting and instructive, not only as an instance in which we must be especially careful in analyzing the class bases of politics but also as an ex-   147

JOSÉ ENRIQUE MIGUENS

ample of how social theories may arise to fit not the facts of the situation
but the ideological preconceptions and needs of the mythmakers and their
audiences.

Theoretical Interpretations of the Workers' Support
for Colonel Perón in 1946

As customarily occurs in matters that have wide repercussions and international significance, a windfall of publications on this subject has appeared
in the United States since the time of the 1946 election. While some were
fairly objective, others the work of pamphleteers, all were devoted to explaining or "explaining away" the problem of the workers' support for
Colonel Perón in the presidential elections. Principal authors of works about
Argentina published or widely read in the United States, particularly those
whose books have made the greatest impression, are Robert J. Alexander,[3]
Joseph R. Barager,[4] George I. Blanksten,[5] Tulio Halperín Donghi,[6] María
Flores (Mary [Foster] Main),[7] Gino Germani,[8] Marvin Goldwert,[9] Ruth
Greenup and Leonard Greenup,[10] David C. Jordan,[11] Ray Josephs,[12] Jeane
Kirkpatrick,[13] Seymour Martin Lipset,[14] A. F. K. Organski,[15] José Luis
Romero,[16] and Arthur P. Whitaker[17] — their works spanning the period from
1945 (Josephs) to 1978 (Germani).

The arguments and theories regarding the workers' support of Colonel
Perón adopt different tonalities, but they all try to explain that support in
terms of two fundamental ideological proposals in the liberal milieu of the
United States: first, that political progress and modernization signal the step
from militarism to civilian control of the military, as they were thought
to do more than one hundred years ago by Herbert Spencer and Auguste
Comte, and, second, that the so-called parties of the left represent the
workers and their interests.[18] Evidently, the massive support of Argentine
workers for a military man — one who originated from a "military dictatorship," who affirmed policies of a nationalist and social-Christian nature,
and who was the avowed enemy of socialists and communists — was a
phenomenon that went against a whole system of reasoning and evaluation,
creating an enormous "cognitive dissonance" that needed to be rapidly
dispelled.

Within Argentina, resentment came especially from the self-designated
"parties of the left" and from intellectual movements whose proponents considered themselves to be popular and to be the only representatives both
of the wage-earning sectors and of the whole idea of modernization and
progress. Psychologically, their frustration was reduced through what is
called the "manic negation of the frustrating object," through self-
idealization, and through total rejection of Peronism in order to make it
appear inhuman and contemptible, worthy of denigration.[19] Some Argen-

tine Marxists, like Rodolfo Puiggrós in the 1940s and John William Cooke in the late 1960s, came over to the side of Peronism, recognizing Perón's unshakable ties to labor and hoping to work with these ties rather than against them. But those who remained in the parties of the left created a literature of rejection that has shaped interpretations of Peronism in the United States and in Europe as well as in Argentina. This literature remains curious; an extraordinary effort of subtlety and theoretical refinement is required to deny the reality of events in Argentina, as is evident in the various intellectual lines that have been pursued in the literature.

Facts versus "Assumptions"

According to the utilitarian-positivist or rational-positivist models, when events do not occur according to the "rational" laws of the society established by sociologists, such aberrations are attributed to ignorance or error on the part of the actors.[20] If people knew what was truly "convenient," if they were fully rational, it is assumed, people would act as the sociologists presupposed that they were going to act, in accordance with the prevailing theory.

In narrower versions of this argument, the theory explains social action in terms of the rationality of the individual actor; in aggregative versions, the concept of social action includes mass behavior and social institutions. When social theorizing is inspired by objective idealism with Hegelian roots, the concept of rationality becomes embodied in the historical process, which is assumed to be good and rational in itself because it leads inexorably to a happy final stage in which social problems are overcome.

Within these abstract frameworks, any contradiction of theory by fact is explained away by appealing to the irrationality of the facts, never by assuming that the theory could be false in whole or in part. The starting point common to most analysts who, with these preconceptions, study the "facts" of the workers' vote in favor of Peronism in 1946, has been to state by definition that the workers must support the so-called movements of the left. If they do not do so, as in this case, the workers violate a principle of rational behavior, one that is "subjective" in the case of Western liberalism and "objective" in the case of Marxism, whereby rationality is believed to be embodied in the historical process and in those who collaborate in its development. Thus the arguments will vary among the Marxists and the liberals, but both assume that a regime like that of Perón cannot really have genuine, overwhelming support from the working class.

In these interpretations, ideology ultimately creates demonology. Actions of the workers not in agreement with the leftist movements are depicted as *anomalies* from the theoretical point of view; these anomalies come to be treated step by step as *deviations*, which, in turn, are considered to be *psychological abnormalities*, in the end seeming morally wrong or pernicious.

As a result, a "camp of the left" was established to expound this demonology. The members of this camp assumed their behavior to be rational, scientific, organized, democratic, educated, mature, progressive, and clairvoyant; they relegated the others to a lepers' colony, labeling their behavior irrational, antiscientific, manipulating/manipulated, chaotic, deceitful to the public, authoritarian, paternalistic, libidinous in the relations between the masses and a "charismatic" leader, and reactionary in their allegedly antiprogressive and obscurantist behavior. I do not know if political relationships could have been that way in the Europe of the nineteenth century, but I am sure that they are not like that in the Latin America of the twentieth century. As Edward Shils points out in analyzing the important studies of the "authoritarian personality" carried out before 1954, "The obsolete feeling that all political, social and economic philosophies can be classified on the Right-Left continuum, however, dies very hard. . . . An examination of the manner in which political principles enter into one of the most elaborate, social-psychological investigations hitherto undertaken, illuminates important problems of procedure in social research."[21]

Explanations Based on the "Irrationality" of the Behavior of the Argentine Workers

Using a dogmatic, demonological insistence on this left-right paradigm, theorists have explained away the workers' vote for Perón from various angles, each of which denies the rationality of the workers' choice. These interpretations are congruent with, and some are in part based upon, a well-known line of reasoning first published by Talcott Parsons in 1959. Without further explanation, Parsons affirms that the mechanisms by which any voter arrives at a decision "are typically nonrational" and that they operate in a "traditionalistic" form. Parsons defines the rationality of the voter very restrictively, considering only the well-being of the country and leaving out consideration of the self-interest of the voter and of the group or groups to which the voter belongs.[22] This sort of Parsonian neglect of voter self-interest is implicit in explanations of the Peronist phenomenon that stress the alleged "irrationality" of the workers and classify their political choices as traditionalist, disoriented, the product of authoritarian oppression, or as an infantile response to charismatic leadership.

Traditionalism. One way to interpret the workers' actions was a traditional type of behavior impervious to rational considerations and modern understanding. Added here is the whole debate regarding backwardness versus progress in Argentina and the voluminous recent literature about the stages of development, modernization, and Argentina's dual society.

Disorientation. According to the "available masses" theory of Raymond Aron or the "city mob" theory of Eric Hobsbawn, Argentine workers are depicted as hostile to modernization, wishing to restore a backward social and political order, impervious to rational and depersonalized political exhortations, rebellious in an archaic sense, primitive or prepolitical, as belonging to marginal groups not assimilated into modern political life and civilization. Not far from this concept is the label used by Representative Ernesto Sanmartino of the Radical party, who once referred to the supporters of Perón as a "zoological flood."

Worker authoritarianism. Connected with these ideas is the concept of *autoritarismo obrero*, or the working-class response to authoritarianism, which Seymour Lipset first advanced in 1955 and described more extensively in 1959.[23] The "sickness" that leads the workers, among other things, to vote for "Peronist fascism," was alleged to appear in a disorganized, economically insecure, and frustrated working class that had lost its psychological anchor in authoritarian families. For this type of worker, it was said, adherence to political movements reflected unconscious psychological pulsations, displacements, and anxiety projections. The politics of these people is thus seen as that of the disgruntled and psychologically homeless, the politics of irrationality and despair. As Eldon Kenworthy writes in criticizing Lipset, the image is one of a society in which "workers do not care what party they affiliate with or what ideology they adopt as long as politics provides an opportunity to vent frustrations and to repair egos."[24]

In a recent study, Walter Korpi further refutes Lipset's theory for the case of Western Europe, saying, "It is not supported by data. The correlations Lipset relies on are probably spurious. . . . The available evidence does not falsify the assumption of rational, self-interested behavior among voters basic to Lipset's theories."[25] The same can be said of the labor vote in the Argentina of 1946, where it was clearly rational for workers to vote for Colonel Perón, given the way in which the issues were stated.

Infantilism and Response to Charisma. Grafted onto a typical position of the 1950s — the urban masses are uprooted, anonymous, impersonal, and disagreeable[26] — is an explanation postulating paternalistic leadership by Perón and childishness and ignorance among his followers. This interpretation continued into the 1970s; a partisan declaration of the reactionary Partido Nueva Fuerza (the New Force party) in 1973 called Perón a "paternalistic figure," and spoke of the "elemental faith" and "mystical subjugation" of Perón's followers.[27]

This interpretation raises the issue of whether Perón was genuinely charismatic. From the 1940s through the 1970s, his leadership has been called "charismatic,"[28] by social scientists as well as by countless journalists, but if the term is taken in the true Weberian sense, it becomes a falsification and a denigration of Argentine voters. "Charismatic" comes from "charisma," an infusion of the supernatural from above which Weber accurately defined as follows: "It must be understood by charisma, the quality that passes for extraordinary, magically conditioned in its origin . . . of a personality whose virtue is considered to lie in the possession of supernatural and superhuman forces."[29] To qualify Perón as a charismatic leader in this sense automatically disqualifies his followers as rational decision makers. Perón had the *charis* or gift of inspiring fervent and emotional loyalty among his followers, as have religious leaders throughout history, but his supporters also made a rational choice in the election of 1946 and continued to support him because of the distributionist policies that he pursued which appeared to be in their interests, especially during the first presidency. There were no "supernatural" beliefs in this process.

Primary Mobilization and Predisposition to Totalitarianism

One of the best known if also most questionable interpretations of Peronism is that of the late Gino Germani, a distinguished social scientist in Argentina before he came to finish his career in the United States. He has made an informed contribution to the ideological debate regarding the sources of the labor vote for Perón which, with both its successes and errors, constitutes a permanent and positive contribution to the understanding of Argentine political processes. The problem lies in the fact that, as Germani refined his theoretical framework, creating an instructive model that cannot be ignored in any serious study of Argentina, he nevertheless darkened the hues of a false stereotype of Peronism.

Germani's interpretation has undergone major revision. In his first work on the theme, published in 1956, he referred to the real liberty that reached the workers under Peronism; he rejected the theory of Peronist demagoguery; he pointed out that the "irrationality" of the European middle classes that followed Nazi Fascism was greater than that of the popular classes in Argentina; and he affirmed both the spontaneity of the popular participation in the march of October 17, 1945, and the authentic achievements of the popular classes under Perón.[30]

In 1962, however, Germani affirmed that the masses were taken advantage of by Peronist adventurers, that Peronism was a fascist movement and a totalitarian regime offering only an ersatz political participation, an illusory participation in which the popular classes could not really express themselves.[31] Then, in an essay published in 1968, Germani concluded that Perón was a fascist leader who, in collusion with other fascist nationalists unable to support a purely military dictatorship or to establish a "classic" form of fascism, discovered that they could use the new working class. For this purpose, Perón pretended to create a "sharp separation" between himself and fascist groups, invented a "surface ideology," and manipulated the workers by infiltrating unions and building concentration camps to repress them.[32] Finally, in his last words on the subject published some twenty-two years after the 1956 essay, Germani described Perón's alleged "ideological preference for fascist solutions" and suggested in detail that Perón had tried to follow the model of Italian fascism in creating his original Labor party and in organizations to control education, culture, propaganda, and the media.[33]

With this evolution of Germani's interpretation clearly in mind, we can analyze it more intensively, uncovering not only its strengths and weaknesses but also some of the reasons for them. Germani correctly and importantly outlined the scientific problem to be solved. He defined it as an attempt "to examine more thoroughly how Peronism obtained the sincere support of vast popular sectors (and that in sharp contrast with European fascism) and what the true meaning to be given to it is."[34] With a strong hint as to what his own ultimate explanation would be, he said, "I had the principal objective of clearly distinguishing the Peronist phenomenon from the other totalitarian movements [sic] . . . to make clear its pseudo-leftist character."[35] Behind this explanation lay Germani's assumption, an unshakable if mistaken principle that did not allow for discussion. As he explained, "The general proposition that can be formulated in this respect, based on the evidence accumulated in different investigations, be it on the results, be it based on studies and public opinion surveys, is that while the popular classes tend to be oriented toward the parties and ideologies considered of the 'left,' the middle and upper classes are oriented toward the opposite pole, namely parties and ideologies considered of the 'right.' "[36] For Germani, therefore, a foundation of all theorizing was the alleged correlation between position in the social structure and the type of predominant ideology, the affirmation of a connection between ideologies of the left and the popular classes.[37]

In gradually elaborating a theory that justified this original assumption, Germani came to stress the role of the "masses." In an essay entitled "The Transition Toward a Political Regime of Total Participation in Argentina," published in 1962, he went on to discover the missing link that was needed to round out a theoretical system formulated in his previous works. This was the "discovery" of the internal migrants that he made in a section of this essay entitled "The Great Internal Migrations and the Integration of the Popular Sectors."[38] What he variously described as the "exodus of masses," as "these great masses rapidly transplanted in the cities," and as "the human base of a totalitarian movement," he found to be part of Peronism, which gave them only the appearance of political participation, "an illusory participation." Germani further explained that in order to give the masses a genuine role, Peronism "had to change its nature, really return to being an expression of the popular classes. This was impossible."[39]

Finally, in "Fascism and Class" and in his last book, Germani refines the model, incorporating the notion of *desplazamiento* (displacement) to the concept of *disponibilidad* (availability) from Raymond Aron, locating these phenomena within the context of the rapid changes of developing societies that lack channels for the integration of the masses. Therefore he utilizes the concept of mobilization, originating with Karl Deutsch, placing pre-Perón Argentina in a second stage of mobilization. This stage produces an available mass of traditional elements, who have come out of the "archaic" societies, out of the periphery of the country and its marginal elements; these people join the demobilized, lower-class sectors of the central areas.

These masses are manipulated, according to the theory. Germani claims that Perón and the Peronist leaders wanted to establish a fascist and totalitarian regime but that

> the establishment of a "classic" totalitarian régime of Spanish, Italian or German type was impossible, since there were no available masses for that purpose. . . . The change in the recruitment required a change in the surface ideology which, in turn, involved a sharp separation (at least in appearance) from the fascist groups. . . . The basis of the new political movement was provided by the organization of new unions and the penetration of the older unions by peronist elements. Labour *was* manipulated.[40]

The maximum contradiction appears when Germani makes the claim that "the surface ideology (social justice, working-class participation, extension of social rights, redistribution of national income) determined to a great extent the policy of the regime."[41] That is, a political movement expresses an ideology which is fulfilled in the action of the government, something unusual in Latin America. But Germani declares that the ideology was used only to deceive and to manipulate the workers.

To Germani's assertion of Perón's manipulative shrewdness must be added the incredible allegation of A. F. K. Organski that Perón actually *used* the workers as he "aided and protected" the industrial and agricultural elites. Organski writes, "Despite the publicity surrounding his prolabor measures, [Perón] provided a governmental framework within which Argentine industry could expand, and despite the hostility of the agricultural elite (who particularly resented his efforts to grant a semblance of humanity to the peons), Perón safeguarded the power of the agricultural elite in the agricultural world." Starting from this mistaken view of Perón as the primary defender of big business and the *estancieros*, Organski easily reaches his final conclusion that "the Perón regime was not so different from other fascist governments as is sometimes believed."[42]

Explanations Given by the "Owners" of History

In spite of the fantasy that underlies Organski's interpretation, some scientists and Argentine pamphleteers of Marxist leanings are not far behind it. For them, the System, with a capital letter, the Establishment, has completely managed all processes in Argentina. Always skillful, always omnipotent despite its apparent mistakes, its components are said to be always united despite evident conflicts of interest.[43] As an Argentine critic, Juan Pablo Feinman, has effectively said, "For them, all of Argentine history is a long monologue of the system. . . . There are never popular conquests in Argentina, only the shrewdness of the regime."[44] These interpretations, like those of Germani and Organski, deserve more detailed analysis.

When Hegel named himself "Aulic Advisor to the Spirit of the World" and "the possessor of the key of Universal History,"[45] he could not have imagined that he was giving birth to a host of assistant advisors nor could he have foreseen that, in the southern cone of a South America that he scorned so much, some of these advisors later intended to succeed the European bourgeoisie that, according to Hegel, was so powerful that "it drew up the cabinet orders of the World Spirit in its original text."[46] From their high positions as pseudo-initiates in the mysteries of history, these latter-day Hegelians and Marxists disdain the rest of us mortals for believing that things are as they seem, explaining patiently to us that all that we see is no more than a series of steps in the inevitable march toward socialism or attempts to detain its inexorable advancement.

With respect to the workers' support of Peronism, the Marxist intellectuals do no more than repeat the two compensatory rationalizations of the old, traditional left regarding the deception of the workers and their immaturity and irrationality, although the Marxists do wrap their arguments in particularly awkward and pedantic reasoning. Basically, all these explanations rely on the theory of "Bonapartism," invented by Marx to justify the failure of the communist revolutions in France[47] in which Marx and the International Workers Association actively intervened. This theory, received through European commentators, is lightheartedly applied to devalue the triumph of Peronism over Marxist-oriented movements in Argentina one hundred years later.

In brief, the explanation/justification suggests that the "bourgeoisie," threatened by the advancement of the "proletariat"[48] and feeling itself weak and incapable of managing the situation, decides to don a mask and give full power to anyone who defends it, with apparent concessions to the "proletariat" as a means of appeasement. As Engels wrote, "If the proletariat could not yet govern France, neither could the bourgeoisie continue to do so."[49] In order to solve the problem, an unscrupulous adventurer appears, capable of any disguise that leads itself to maneuvering and deceit. As Marx explained:

> Louis Bonaparte, an adventurer, took hold of all the strategic positions of power. . . . Louis Bonaparte took away the political potential of the capitalists under the pretext of protecting them [the bourgeoisie] against the workers and, on the other hand, protecting the workers against the bourgeoisie; but, in compensation for this, his government favored industrial speculation and activity: in a word, the increase and enrichment of the entire bourgeoisie, in a manner unprecedented until that time.[50]

Using these concepts within a different context, modern Marxists explain the support of Peronism by the Argentine workers as a very clever deception by either the Argentine bourgeoisie, as does Mónica Peralta Ramos,[51] or by the *lumpenbourgeoisie*, as does André Gunder Frank.[52] In the same context, Jorge Abelardo Ramos and Jorge Eneas Spilinbergo identify the period of Peronism as that of bourgeois, "democratic-national" development toward socialism.[53] Others call it "trans-class populism" and "pseudo-revolutionary reformism." Miguel Murmis and Juan Carlos Portantiero more precisely describe the shrewdness and artifices of bourgeois capitalism, of the national bourgeoisie, and of the landowning classes.[54]

Whereas the old leftist guard spoke of ignorance, error, lack of education, and the primacy of instincts, modern Marxists speak of an objective maladjustment between the true interests of the proletariat and its political convictions. When the workers do not see things as they are perceived by the Marxist intellectuals, the workers are described as a nonrevolutionary proletariat, a proletariat unaware of class. Some critics go as far as to call them a *lumpenproletariat*, unaware, I suppose, that in German (the language in which Marx and Engels wrote), *lumpen* connotes filth and garbage, that its exact meaning refers to idlers and riffraff, to penniless people and vagabonds. Ironically, for the Argentine Marxists who use that term, the word can also be used to mean *descamisados* (shirtless ones),[55] a term adopted by the Peronist workers as a title of honor just as the term *sansculotte* was used by the citizenry during the French Revolution.

Pedantic affirmations that the Argentine workers have no autonomous, proletarian consciousness also belong to this denigrating current. In other words, as Ismael Viñas and José Vazeilles affirm, the Argentine proletariat has developed quantitatively and not qualitatively. To them, it is a proletariat of large numbers but of no quality. The most elaborate degradation, as formulated by Milcíades Peña, claims that the Argentine proletariat is condemned to be the predicate and not the subject of historical action.[56] To anyone who can handle the vocabulary, these Marxist intellectuals describe the "Argentine proletariat" as a vegetative, passive entity, one which, to change the metaphor, they must redeem from ignorance just as the prince awakens the sleeping beauty.

The Real Characteristics of the Workers' Support for Perón in 1946

Scholarship based on ecological studies of electoral results — the only technique possible for use in the 1946 election — now offers a contrast to these earlier interpretations. With all the limitations and reservations that can be made in the case of Argentina, past polemics have encouraged the clarification of many points. New sociological and historical analyses can now precisely determine some characteristics of the Peronist workers.

The analytical, revisionist literature is now extensive. Peter Smith's first revisionist article in the *Hispanic American Historical Review*[57] is followed by the factual refutations of the traditional version of the old left by Floreal Forni and Pedro Weinberg in September 1972,[58] by Eldon Kenworthy in October 1973,[59] by Manuel Mora y Araujo and Tulio Halperín Donghi in May 1975,[60] by Jorge Raúl Jorrat in December 1975,[61] and finally in December 1976 by Darío Cantón, Jorge Raúl Jorrat, and Eduardo Juárez, who compared the results of the presidential elections of 1946 and 1973.[62]

Leaving aside the abstruse concepts of "working class," "labor class," and "proletariat" that do not denote concrete entities, and recognizing the risk that any simplification brings, we can arrive at the following conclusions from the collected data:

1. Peronism is a socially complex movement that cannot be explained only by the variable of social class, precisely because it is multiclass, with wide variations according to distinct ecological areas and levels of regional development. The movement has the same complexity as does Argentine society with its different subcultures.

2. The vote for Perón in 1946 was proportionally higher in the large cities than in the semiurban areas. Peter Smith has established the proportions according to those areas that he calls big cities (counties that are part of cities of 50,000 or more), townships (counties that are part of cities of 2,000 to 49,999), and rural areas (counties that are part of cities of less than 2,000) as follows:[63]

Big cities: Perón's average, 55.2 percent
Townships: Perón's average, 49.5 percent
Rural areas: Perón's average, 46.0 percent

3. The industrial workers heavily supported Peronism in the large cities, or, more precisely, in the electoral districts of cities with more than 50,000 inhabitants. In the mid-1940s, large cities were practically the only areas in which one could really speak of industrial workers, because there the industries rose above the level of the small workshops and factories that

characterized the rest of the country's industry[64] and, furthermore, because there the unions had a real effect.

4. There were, apparently, no differences in the Peronist vote between "new workers" coming from the country and "old workers" long in the cities. According to Smith, it was the presence of an industrial force in the larger urban areas rather than of internal migrants that guaranteed the Peronist success. Probably the most decisive support for Perón came from the "old" working class and not from the "new" migrants.[65] This means that the old workers voted for Perón, but that does not make them irrational and antilabor.

In the extensive discussion regarding the importance of the internal migrants, strangely, no one has mentioned the fact that a very high proportion of rural-urban migrants, already enrolled in their places of rural origin, failed to register to vote in their new locations. A high proportion of the migrants undoubtedly remained registered to vote in the country, returning there to vote in 1946 and at various times afterwards, because to re-register in the city was a complex bureaucratic procedure, because gaining assistance from a political party in re-registering made the process still more difficult, because sanctions for nonvoting were only nominal, and finally, because failure to re-register was known to be high for the country as a whole. Since the rural migrants had a lower educational and social level than those already in the cities, presumably a smaller proportion of voters still enrolled in the country or re-enrolled in their new urban areas went to the polls than did voters from other sectors of society. These factors, which ecological studies based on census data cannot detect, undoubtedly lowered the migrants' voting strength, thus suggesting once again that they were not as vital to the Peronist victory as has often been claimed.

Furthermore, when turning to the "unlettered masses" of Argentine cities, one should focus on foreign immigrants rather than internal, rural-urban migrants. The work of Halperín Donghi and Smith indicates that illiteracy levels were greater among foreigners than among migrants from the country. With major historical documentation, Halperín Donghi has demonstrated the cultural backwardness of the foreign immigrants, who spoke neither the national language nor any of its regional dialects, who rejected socialism, and who lived as small capitalists. On the other hand, he gives evidence for the lack of traditionalism among the majority of the indigenous migrants in their rural homes. He concludes that earlier literature on the topic "presents an image of Argentine reality that is both imprecise and simplified."[66]

(5) There now remains no doubt that the workers overwhelmingly supported Perón in 1946 and that they continued to show their electoral support for Peronism on every later occasion on which they were allowed to do so. Manuel Mora y Araujo concludes that "on the basis of census information, workers' support for Peronism is an indisputable and quantifiable reality."[67]

In a work using refined techniques and scarce, unpublished data from the 1947 census, Cantón, Jorrat, and Juárez show that, nationwide, 74 percent of the workers supported Perón in 1946 while only 26 percent backed all of the other parties combined. In the five most economically developed electoral districts, the proportions of worker support were, respectively, 73 percent and 27 percent, while in the ten least-developed districts they were 75 percent and 25 percent. That is, there were no appreciable differences between areas with many internal migrants and those without them.[68]

(6) Between the elections of 1946 and 1973, the workers' vote grew in favor of Peronism. In 1973, the authors cited above estimate that, nationwide, 84 percent of the workers supported the Juan and Isabel Perón ticket, while only 16 percent opted for all the other parties. This situation did not present differences among developed and underdeveloped regions.[69]

(7) For the twenty-seven-year period between the elections, if we look either at the Peronist vote in 1962 and 1965 or at the best studies available on the era, both confirm the tendencies noted above. Forni and Weinberg write of the March 1962 elections, "Peronism won in the majority of the industrial districts of the country, and if we take the election of 1965 its victory in the industrial districts was even more overwhelming."[70]

The strength of Peronism is similarly confirmed in the methodologically different election studies of Huerta Palau, Imaz, and Rowe. In an ecological study of electoral results in Córdoba, comparing citizens' occupations with the vote in each district, Huerta Palau concludes that "the only party for which workers have a clear preference is Peronism" and that "we can affirm that 41 percent of the workers voted for Peronism."[71] A sample taken by Imaz in ten voting areas of Buenos Aires showed that 46 percent of the lower class and 43 percent of the lower middle class supported Peronism in the elections of 1962, at a time when (consistent with electoral results of a decade later) another 16 percent of the voters — two-thirds of whom came from the upper middle class — declared themselves to be on the left yet nevertheless voted for Peronism.[72] James W. Rowe has made an interesting study of the election of 1962, comparing the electoral districts (precincts) of Greater Buenos Aires, and finding that the percentage of the vote given to the Peronists rose from 14.4 percent in the primarily upper-class district of Socorro, to 35.5 percent in the middle-class district of Vélez Sarsfield, and then to 57.7 percent in the lower-class and industrial working-class district of Berisso.[73]

These results are further confirmed in the data from major surveys done by Jeane Kirkpatrick in 1965 and by me in 1971. On the basis of a large sample, Kirkpatrick concludes:

The presence and importance of Argentina's lower classes within the Peronist movement are undisputed. . . . Peronists were confirmed as being disproportionately drawn from among the lower

"popular" class. . . . Lower-class Peronists demonstrated a class
consciousness unique among Argentines. . . . Occupational and
educational characteristics of core Peronists are also distinctive.
Laborers, both manual and skilled, were most numerous.[74]

Finally, in a survey of 1600 respondents that I directed in July 1971 among
the population eighteen years of age and older in the federal capital, in the
Buenos Aires suburbs, and in Rosario and Córdoba, the level of sympathy
for General Perón among the various social classes followed this pattern:[75]
11.2 percent in the upper class; 24.7 percent in the upper middle class; 40.3
percent in the lower middle class; 62.3 percent in the lower class.

Thus the majority of workers voted for Peronism in 1946 and continued
to do so for the next twenty-seven years, each time giving Peronism a higher
proportion of support up to 1973. During the course of these twenty-seven
years, the distinction between "new" and "old" workers came to be
obliterated, and the workers increased their participation in union activities
and in politics, thereby growing in experiences and maturity. It is difficult
to concede that so many people could be duped over such a long period
of time.

Are Argentine Workers Leftist?

At the end of January 1973, I directed an electoral survey (Study 31) and
in February 1973, a month before the presidential election, I carried out
two more surveys (Studies 32 and 33). Covering the federal capital, the
Buenos Aires suburbs, Rosario, and Córdoba, the surveys used different
statistical samples and a confidence level of 95 percent to represent the views
of voters over eighteen years of age, who in the areas sampled represented
5,799,166 registered voters, or 40.7 percent of the national electorate. The
final survey was closer than any of the other twelve conducted at that time
in Argentina in terms of predicting the actual results of the election.[76] In
all, the three surveys included 3,198 respondents.

Data from these surveys can importantly inform the old debate on the
social levels of support for Peronism. The comparison of electoral support
for Peronism and for the parties of the left changes many of the supposi-
tions in the sociological literature that have tended to misinform the debates
on the Argentine situation.

The Alianza Revolucionaria Popular (Popular Revolutionary Alliance,
APR) is here taken as summing up the movements and ideologies of the left
in the elections of 1973, for the following reasons: (a) because of the considerable electoral vote that it received (the vote was minimal for the other
parties on the left: the Popular Left Front, the Social Democratic party,
and the Socialist Workers party); (b) because the APR was explicitly sup-

ported by the intellectual movements on the left, by the Communist party, and by the major terrorist groups of Marxist inspiration; and (c) because the electoral program of the APR was basically a reiteration of the usual catch-phrases of the left in Latin America. It supported "the struggle against imperialism," the expropriation without compensation of large agricultural holdings, and the state takeover of foreign trade, banks, and monopolistic enterprises — creating a vast public sector, since the state already controlled public service and the distribution of energy in Argentina. This was merely a repetition of the program of the Third Communist International, adopted at the Sixth Congress in 1928, which was monotonously brought up again in Latin America forty-five years later. All of this, plus the self-classification of the APR, enables us to consider it as a political party that represents the "left."[77]

Surveys demonstrate that in this context voters for the parties and programs of the left come — not from the lower classes — but in great proportion from the upper and upper middle classes. Inversely, the lower and lower middle classes opted strongly for Peronism. Even the Radical party drew a greater proportion of what Argentines call "the popular vote" than did the left.

Data in tables 1 through 5 are taken from the three surveys referred to above conducted before the election of Héctor J. Cámpora in March 1973. Since the proportion of undecided voters was very high at the time, table 1 contains data only for those respondents who had made a party choice and were willing to express it.[78] It consolidates data from the three surveys and provides information on 1,265 voters who had made their decisions out of the 3,198 people surveyed during January and February 1973. Table 1 compares their social class with their support of the APR, the Frente Justicialista de Liberación of the Peronists, the Partido Radical, and the other parties.[79]

TABLE 1
Voting Decisions and Social Class in Argentina Before the Election of March 1973 (Percent)

	Upper Class	Upper Middle Class	Lower Middle Class	Lower Class
APR	13.5	14.3	8.0	2.2
Frente Justicialista	10.8	22.1	45.2	69.8
Radical party	32.4	29.0	24.6	15.6
Other parties	43.2	34.6	22.2	13.3
N = 1265				

Source: Studies 31, 32, 33, surveys conducted by José Enrique Miguens in Greater Buenos Aires, Córdoba, and Rosario in January 1973. Available through the Roper Center, University of Connecticut, Storrs, Conn. 06268.

If voters' uncertainty in the months before the election left voting trends still somewhat undefined, it is still possible to see in table 1 the diminution of support for the left among the lower middle and lower classes. These groups clearly gave solid backing to Peronism, and they even proved to be three times more favorable to the centrist Partido Radical than they were to the Alianza Popular Revolucionaria on the left. The two other smaller parties on the left did not receive a single backer from the lower class in any of the three surveys.

The last survey in February 1973 (Study 33) contains the highest proportion of voters who had made their decisions — 565 out of 1,030 respondents. When this survey was in the field, patterns of opinion were further clarified after what had been a highly confused campaign period. For this final survey before the March 11 elections, table 2 shows the class basis of support for Peronism and the left.

TABLE 2
Voting Decisions and Social Class in Argentina Before the Election of March 1973 (Percent)

	Upper Class	Upper Middle Class	Lower Middle Class	Lower Class
ARP	30.8	27.6	16.5	3.3
Frente Justicialista	0.0	29.3	60.4	88.3
Other parties	69.2	43.1	23.1	8.3
N = 565				

Source: Study 33, survey conducted by José Enrique Miguens in Greater Buenos Aires, Córdoba, and Rosario in February 1973. Available through the Roper Center, University of Connecticut, Storrs, Conn. 06268.

Once again, support for Peronism increases dramatically among the lower middle and lower classes. Contrariwise, while nearly a third of the upper class opts for the main party of the left, only three out of a hundred members of the lower class do the same.

In the three successive surveys, there were also questions on the sympathy that respondents felt for different political movements, such as Peronism, Radicalism, the left, conservatism, and the developmentalism of Arturo Frondizi. Nearly all respondents expressed support for one of the movements, so that these answers help to control for the voters who had not made up their minds as reported in tables 1 and 2. Out of 3,198 respondents in the three surveys, 2,062 declared themselves to favor either Peronism, the left, or radicalism. Table 3 reports these findings, leaving out the other respondents who favored other movements, did not answer, or said that they did not know what movement they favored. The results are categorized according to social class.

Table 3 shows that Peronist sympathizers, like those who voted for Perón,

TABLE 3
Social Class and Preferences for Political Movements among Argentine Voters Before the Election of March 1973 (Percent)

	Upper Class	Upper Middle Class	Lower Middle Class	Lower Class
The Left	30.3	32.1	11.6	3.6
Peronism	15.5	24.5	53.4	76.1
Radicalism	54.5	43.4	34.9	20.3
N = 2068				

Source: Studies 31, 32, 33, surveys conducted by José Enrique Miguens in Greater Buenos Aires, Córdoba, and Rosario in January and February 1973. Available from the Roper Center, University of Connecticut, Storrs, Conn. 06268.

also came especially strongly from the lower middle and lower classes that have so often been called bastions of support for the left in Latin America.

The second of the three surveys (Study 32) asked respondents whether Argentina would be better off, worse off, or about the same if it experienced a Marxist revolution like that of Salvador Allende in Chile. Table 4 compares the results of this question with the declared voting intentions of the respondents. As expected, voters on the left proved to be most sympathetic to an Allende-style revolution, with 46 percent of them saying that Argentina would be better off afterward, as compared to only 20 percent of the Peronist voters who took this position.

TABLE 4
Preferences for Argentine Political Movements and Support for a Revolution like That of Salvador Allende (Percent)

	Voters on the Left[a]	Voters for the Frente Justicialista	Voters for the Partido Radical	Voters for Other Parties and Undecided Voters
We would be better off	46.7	20.8	9.3	14.2
We would be worse off	13.3	35.7	53.4	47.6
We would be about the same	17.8	18.2	22.0	15.1
Don't know	17.8	21.4	14.4	19.5
No answer	4.4	3.9	0.8	3.5
N = 1474				

Source: Study 32, survey conducted by José Enrique Miguens in Greater Buenos Aires, Córdoba, and Rosario in February 1973. Available through the Roper Center, University of Connecticut, Storrs, Conn. 06268.

a. Includes the Alianza Popular Revolucionaria, Frente de Izquierda Popular, and Partido Socialista de los Trabajadores.

Another question probed more directly for respondents' support for revolution, asking them whether they favored a total revolution for Argentina or more gradual change within a political system where various political parties participated. Respondents were told of the two tendencies within Peronism, one favoring total revolution and the other supporting more gradual change within a system of party competition, and were then asked which tendency they thought would most help the country. For the same respondents that appeared in table 4, table 5 compares the positions on these two currents within Peronism with the voting preferences of the respondents.

TABLE 5
Preferences Among Argentine Voters for Political Movements and Support for the Two Tendencies within Peronism (Percent)

	The Left[a]	Frente Justicialista	Partido Radical	Other Parties and Undecided Voters
Centrist tendency	28.9	61.7	52.5	56.0
Revolutionary tendency	42.2	27.3	16.9	17.8
Don't know	15.6	8.4	10.2	15.9
No answer	13.3	2.6	20.3	10.3
N = 1474				

Source: Study 32, survey conducted by José Enrique Miguens in Greater Buenos Aires, Córdoba, and Rosario in February 1973. Available through the Roper Center, University of Connecticut, Storrs, Conn. 06268.

a. Includes the Alianza Popular Revolucionaria, Frente de Izquierda Popular, and Partido Socialista de los Trabajadores.

Whereas the "revolutionary tendency" found support among 27 percent of the Peronists, showing that "left-wing" Peronism did indeed have a following within the movement at this point, this position represented only about a quarter of the Peronist voters, as compared to 61 percent of the Peronists who favored the "centrist tendency." Although six out of ten Peronists supported this position, only five out of ten radical voters and three out of ten voters on the left said that they did so.

Other questions on international relations tended to confirm these differences between Peronism and the left. For the three surveys as a whole, 38.8 percent of voters on the left and 19.8 percent of the Peronists said that Argentina should move closer to the socialist countries and those of the Third World. Once again, attitudinally, the left-wing tendency within Peronism appeared to be confined to one-fifth of the membership. There was very little support for the United States within either Peronism or the non-Peronist left, and, given the rhetoric of the electoral campaign, there was surprisingly little support for "liberation" as well. Some 10.8 percent of the Peronist voters and 4.4 percent of those on the left said that Argentina should move closer to the United States, while "liberation" was named as an important objective by 7.8 percent of the Peronists and 7.8 percent of the leftists.

Finally, one other question served almost as a confession. The question asked which of three parties, in the opinion of each respondent, best represented the interests of the workers: the Frente Justicialista de Liberación (Peronists), or two parties on the left, the Alianza Popular Revolucionaria and the Frente de Izquierda Popular. Peronists knew that their movement was that of the workers, as 80.2 percent of the Peronist voters said that the Frente Justicialista best represented the workers and only 7.7 percent of the Peronists — conceivably, right-wing Peronists afraid of Marxist encroachments by the left — said that the best representative was the Alianza Popular. On the other hand, 25.5 percent — more than a quarter of the supporters of the parties on the left — admitted that Peronism was the true representative of the workers. Only half of these voters on the left believed their own movements to represent the workers, as 20.0 percent of the leftist respondents gave "don't know" or "no answer" responses to this question. In Spanish we say, *a confesión de parte relevo de prueba* (when the accused confesses, you need no further proof).

In this question too, class position operates importantly. The lower classes overwhelmingly declared that Peronism represented the workers, while in the middle classes there was a turning to the belief that the real representative was the parties of the left. Among the middle classes of the federal district, there was an almost equal split between those who thought that the workers were best represented by Peronism and by the left. It is worth noting that this belief that leftists truly represent the interests of the workers is, in Argentina at least, a bias of the middle classes of the largest cities, or if one wants to use the rather difficult vocabulary of the Marxists, "a bourgeois bias."

The data on occupation and party preferences confirm these findings on working-class support for Perón. Of all Peronist voters from the three surveys, 40.7 percent were blue-collar workers, 32.1 percent were employees, and only 27.4 percent had other occupations or, to be more precise, were not salaried people. Among voters on the left,[80] 17.3 percent were blue-collar workers, 35.5 percent were employees, and 47.1 percent — or almost half of the voters inclined toward the left — were unsalaried persons.

If we concentrate among these general occupational statistics on particular categories of workers, we can see even more striking differences. Among all Peronist and leftist voters in the three surveys, none of the leftists and 1.1 percent of the Peronists were foremen, 9.4 percent of the leftists and 21.2 percent of the Peronists were skilled workers, and 3.9 percent of the leftists and 14.1 percent of the Peronists were unskilled workers or *peones*.

Within Peronism, these working-class votes had great importance and electoral weight, as the workers who voted for Peronism made up 15.7 percent of all voters and just under half of all Peronist voters. If we add employees to the blue-collar workers, the new, larger category turns out to be 28.1 percent of all voters and 72.8 percent of all Peronist voters.

These patterns stand out even more clearly when we concentrate on the proportions of each occupational category that supported the various political movements. Peronism found backing, for example, among 45.5 percent of the foremen, 57.6 percent of the specialized workers, and 64.7 percent of the unspecialized workers. In contrast, the parties of the left garnered allegiance among none of the foremen, 7.6 percent of the specialized workers, and 4.9 percent of the unspecialized workers. These occupational data unequivocally demonstrate the crucial support for Peronism within the ranks of blue-collar workers and salaried employees in the elections of March 1973, affirming the strong working-class backing for Peronism that had also been evident in the elections of 1946, 1951, 1962, and 1963.

Conclusions

On the basis of these data, no serious scholar can maintain that, in Argentina at least, the movements and parties of the left represent the workers, or at least represent what the workers say they want. Over twenty-seven years of agitated history, Argentine workers opted for Peronism in every election in which they could do so freely, and each time they did so in greater proportions. After so many years of active participation by Argentine trade unions, during which they have received so many wage benefits and have advanced so far socially and politically, it should no longer be possible to talk — as have so many polemicists in the past, from both inside and outside Argentina — about the "immaturity" of the workers or, even less, of the "manipulation" of them or the "tricks" played upon them. It is necessary instead to look to the workers' interpretations of their own self-interest, and it is here that the debate might best focus in the future.

NOTES

This chapter was translated by Francisco Di Blasi.

1. On the ways in which the concepts of "left" and "right" are applied within the context of the Argentine political situation, see José Enrique Miguens, "¿Qué quiere decir izquierda y derecha en la Argentina?" *Cambio*, no. 5 (May 1974), p. 26.

2. On the conflict of ideologies in the Americas, see José Enrique Miguens, *The Emergence of Nationalistic Ideologies in Latin America and the Foreign Policy of the United States,* Occasional Papers Series on Latin American Problems (Amherst: University of Massachusetts, 1977).

3. Robert J. Alexander, *The Perón Era* (New York: Columbia University Press, 1951).

4. Joseph R. Barager, ed., *Why Perón Came to Power: The Background of Peronism in Argentina* (New York: Knopf, 1968).

5. George I. Blanksten, *Perón's Argentina* (Chicago: University of Chicago Press, 1953).

6. Tulio Halperín Donghi, *Argentina: La democracia de masas* (Buenos Aires: Editorial Paidós, 1972).

7. María Flores (Mary [Foster] Main), *The Woman with the Whip: Eva Perón* (Garden City, N.Y.: Doubleday, 1952).

8. Gino Germani, *Política y sociedad en una época de transición: De la sociedad tradicional a la sociedad de masas* (Buenos Aires: Editorial Paidós, 1962); "Fascism and Class," in S. J. Woolf, ed., *The Nature of Fascism* (London: Weidenfeld and Nicolson, 1968), pp. 65–95; *Authoritarianism, Fascism, and National Populism* (New Brunswick, N.J.: Transaction Books, 1978).

9. Marvin Goldwert, *Democracy, Militarism, and Nationalism in Argentina, 1930–1966: An Interpretation* (Austin: University of Texas Press, 1972).

10. Ruth Greenup and Leonard Greenup, *Revolution Before Breakfast: Argentina, 1941–1946* (Chapel Hill: University of North Carolina Press, 1947).

11. Arthur P. Whitaker and David C. Jordan, *Nationalism in Contemporary Latin America* (New York: Free Press, 1966), ch. 4, esp. pp. 66–72.

12. Ray Josephs, *Argentine Diary: The Inside Story of the Coming of Fascism* (London: Gollancz, 1945).

13. Jeane Kirkpatrick, *Leader and Vanguard in Mass Society: A Study of Peronist Argentina* (Cambridge, Mass.: MIT Press, 1971).

14. Seymour Martin Lipset, *Political Man: The Social Bases of Politics* (New York: Doubleday, 1960), esp. chs. 4 and 5.

15. A. F. K. Organski, *The Stages of Political Development* (New York: Knopf, 1965), pp. 150–55.

16. José Luis Romero, *A History of Argentine Political Thought,* trans. Thomas F. McGann (Stanford, Calif.: Stanford University Press, 1963).

17. Arthur P. Whitaker, *Argentina* (Englewood Cliffs, N.J.: Prentice-Hall, 1964); *Argentine Upheaval; Perón's Fall and the New Regime* (New York: Praeger, 1956); *The United States and Argentina* (Cambridge, Mass.: Harvard University Press, 1954); and Whitaker and Jordan, *Nationalism in Contemporary Latin America.*

18. See José Enrique Miguens, "Filicidio y guerra," *Revista de la Escuela Superior de Guerra* (Buenos Aires), July–Aug. 1973, p. 93.

19. On this process of negation, see José Enrique Miguens, "El círculo vicioso del positivismo sociológico," in *El conocimiento de lo social* (Buenos Aires: Perrot, 1953), and Instituto Luigi Sturzo, ed., *Scritti di Sociologia e Politica in omaggio di Luigi Sturzo* (Bologna: Zanichelli, 1953), vol. 2, pp. 515–41.

20. One example of this process, of many that might be cited, deals with the contrast between interpretations of mass support for Juan Perón and Fidel Castro. The ideologies of Castro's admirers and Perón's denigrators have had much to do with their interpretations of workers' support for these leaders. If we leave ideology aside, are we to believe that the masses who cheered the victories of General Perón in the Plaza de Mayo were more "irrational" and subject to "charisma" and paternalistic "dependency" than the masses who congregated in Havana to cheer Castro? Are we to believe this, when the indexes of illiteracy, level of trade union activity, duration of the democratic experience and the nation's political independence, and

JOSÉ ENRIQUE MIGUENS

many other measures that might be used, are so much greater in Argentina than they are in Cuba?

21. E. A. Shils, "Authoritarianism: Right and Left," in Richard Christie and Marie Yahoda, eds., *Continuities in Social Research: Studies in the Scope and Method of "The Authoritarian Personality"* (Glencoe, Ill.: Free Press, 1954), p. 28.

22. Talcott Parsons, "Voting and the Equilibrium of the American Political System," in *Sociological Theory and Modern Society* (Glencoe, Ill.: Free Press, 1967), p. 235.

23. Lipset, *Political Man*, ch. 4.

24. Eldon Kenworthy, "The Function of the Little Known Case in Theory Formation: Or, What Peronism Wasn't," *Comparative Politics* 6 (1973), 21.

25. Walter Korpi, "Working-class Communism in Western Europe: Rational or Nonrational," *American Sociological Review* 36 (1971), 981.

26. For a criticism of this interpretation, see José Enrique Miguens, "Un análisis del fenómeno," in Jorge A. Paita, ed., *Argentina, 1930–1960* (Buenos Aires; Editorial Sur, 1961).

27. *La Nación* (Buenos Aires), 6 Jan. 1973.

28. See David J. Butler, "Charisma, Migration, and Elite Coalescence: An Interpretation of Peronism," *Comparative Politics* 1 (1969), 423–39.

29. Max Weber, *Economía y sociedad*, trans. José Medina Echeverría (México: Fondo de Cultura Económica, 1944), p. 253.

30. Germani's essay, "La integración de las masas a la vida política y el totalitarismo" was first published in 1956 by the Colegio Libre de Estudios Superiores, and later incorporated into his classic work *Política y sociedad*, in which the quoted statements appear on pp. 244, 245, 249, 250.

31. Ibid., p. 231.

32. Germani, "Fascism and Class," pp. 94, 95. A slightly revised version of this essay, still talking about concentration camps and a "surface ideology," appeared as "Mass Society, Social Class, and the Emergence of Fascism," in Irving Louis Horowitz, ed., *Masses in Latin America* (New York: Oxford University Press, 1970).

33. Germani, *Authoritarianism*, p. 202.

34. Germani, *Política y sociedad*, p. 243.

35. Ibid., p. 231.

36. Germani, "El izquierdismo y las clases populares," in *Política y sociedad*, p. 131, emphasis in original. Initially circulated as "El autoritarismo y las clases populares" (1957).

37. Germani, *Política y sociedad*, p. 131.

38. In ibid., p. 229.

39. Ibid., p. 231.

40. Germani, "Fascism and Class," p. 95, emphasis in original.

41. Germani, "Mass Society," p. 595.

42. Organski, *The Stages of Political Development*, p. 154.

43. For a discussion and for attitudinal data on the actual conflicts between the landholding and big-business sectors in Argentina, which some Marxists have assumed to be strongly united and whose interests Organski says that Perón served, see chapter 10.

44. Juan Pablo Feinman, "Sobre el peronismo y sus intérpretes," *Envido* 2 (1972), p. 22. I am indebted to Feinman's penetrating analysis, even though I do not agree with his conclusions.

45. J. G. F. Hegel, *Lecciones sobre la filosofía de la historia universal* (Buenos Aires: Revista de Occidente Argentina, 1946), vol. 1, p. 33.

46. E. Bloch, *El pensamiento de Hegel* (México: Fondo de Cultura Económica, 1949), p. 358.

47. Karl Marx wrote, "This is communism, the 'impossible communism' " ("Discurso al Consejo General de la Asociación Internacional de Trabajadores sobre la Guerra Civil de 1871 en Francia," in *Opere* [Milan: Societé Editrice Avanti, 1914], vol. 2, p. 47). Friedrich

Engels exclaimed, "Gentlemen. Do you want to know what the dictatorship of the proletariat is like? Look at the Paris Commune. That is the dictatorship of the proletariat" (introduction to "La Guerra Civil en Francia," ibid., p. 13).

48. For those of us who conduct surveys on the actual political attitudes of the Argentine people, it has never been possible to locate or to verify the existence of these intellectual phantasms, the "bourgeoisie" and the "proletariat."

49. Engels, introduction to "La Guerra Civil en Francia," pp. 5, 6.

50. Quoted in ibid., p. 6.

51. Mónica Peralta Ramos, "La Dependence et les Alliances des Classes en Argentine" (Ph.D. diss., University of Paris, 1971).

52. André Gunder Frank says that "it is necessary to recognize that it is really the same bourgeoisie that is represented first by GetúlioVargas and then by Castello Branco and Costa e Silva; by a Justo, a Perón and now by an Onganía" (Lumpen Burguesía — Lumpen Desarrollo [Santiago de Chile: Ediciones Prensa Americana, 1970], p. 113).

53. Jorge Abelardo Ramos, Revolución y contrarevolución en la Argentina (Buenos Aires: Plus Ultra, 1965), vol. 2, p. 619; Jorge Eneas Spilinbergo, La cuestión nacional en Marx (Buenos Aires: Coyoacán, 1968), p. 18.

54. Miguel Murmis and Juan Carlos Portantiero, Estudios sobre los orígenes del peronismo, 2nd ed. (Buenos Aires: Siglo Veintiuno, 1972).

55. See the definition of lumpen in Rudolf J. Slabý and Rudolf Grossmann, Wortebuch der und spanischen deutschen sprache (Leipzig: B. Tauchnitz, 1932).

56. The concept is taken from J. G. F. Hegel, Science de la Logique (Paris: Aubier, n.d.), vol. 1, pp. 105, 130.

57. Peter H. Smith, "The Social Base of Peronism," Hispanic American Historical Review 52 (1972), 55–73; see also "Las elecciones argentinas de 1946 y las inferencias ecológicas," Desarrollo Económico 14 (1974), 385–98.

58. Floreal H. Forni and Pedro D. Weinberg, "Reflexiones sobre la relación entre clases sociales y partidos políticos en la Argentina," Desarrollo Económico 12 (1972), 421–36.

59. Kenworthy, "The Function of the Little Known Case"; see also "Interpretaciones ortodoxas y revisionistas del apoyo inicial del peronismo," Desarrollo Económico 14 (1975), 749–63; and Peter Ranis, "En respuesta a E. Kenworthy," Desarrollo Económico 15 (1975), 163–66.

60. Manuel Mora y Araujo, "La estructura social del peronismo: Un análisis electoral interprovincial," Desarrollo Económico 14 (1975), 699–718; Tulio Halperín Donghi, "Algunas observaciones sobre Germani, el surgimiento del peronismo y los migrantes internos," Desarrollo Económico 14 (1975), 765–81.

61. Jorge Raúl Jorrat, "Algunas notas sobre la correlación negativa entre voto al FREJULI y la clase obrera," Desarrollo Económico 15 (1975), 445–55.

62. Darío Cantón, Jorge Raúl Jorrat, and Eduardo Juárez, "Un intento de estimación de las celdas interiores de una tabla de contingencia basado en el análisis de regresión: El caso de las elecciones presidenciales argentinas de 1946 y marzo de 1973," Desarrollo Económico 16 (1976), 396–417; see also Elecciones y partidos políticos en la Argentina: Historia, interpretación y balance, 1910–1966 (Buenos Aires: Siglo Veintiuno, 1973). See also Peter G. Snow, "The Class Basis of Argentine Political Parties," American Political Science Review 63 (1969); "La base de clase de los partidos políticos argentinos: Crítica de una crítica," Desarrollo Económico 13 (1973), 221–26.

63. Smith, "The Social Basis of Peronism," p. 58.

64. Smith, "Las elecciones argentinas de 1946," p. 388.

65. In my twenty years of carrying out electoral surveys and studies of political attitudes and opinions in Argentina, I have noted that in urban areas, and especially in the largest cities, people tend to vote on the basis of issues, while in the interior and in rural districts people tend to vote on the basis of personal loyalty and tradition.

66. Halperín Donghi, "Algunas observaciones sobre Germani," pp. 769, 770, 772, 774–76.

67. Manuel Mora y Araujo, "Populismo, laborismo y clases medias (Política y estructura social en la Argentina)" *Criterio* 49, nos. 1755–56 (1977), p. 16.

68. Cantón, Jorrat, and Juárez, "Un intento de estimación," pp. 405–06.

69. Ibid., pp. 409–10.

70. Forni and Weinberg, "Reflexiones sobre la relación entre clases sociales y partidos políticos en la Argentina," p. 431.

71. Pedro Huerta Palau, *Análisis electoral de una ciudad en desarrollo* (Córdoba: Universidad Nacional de Córdoba, 1963), pp. 16, 17, 19.

72. José Luis de Imaz, *Motivación electoral* (Buenos Aires: Instituto de Desarrollo Económico y Social, 1962), pp. 37, 42.

73. James William Rowe, *The Argentine Election of 1963: An Analysis* (Washington: Institute for the Comparative Study of Political Systems, n.d.), pp. 31–35. In comparison to these findings for 1962, some confusion has arisen in Rowe's interpretation of the election of 1963.

74. Jeane Kirkpatrick, *Leader and Vanguard in Mass Society*, pp. 94, 96, 102.

75. The data from the 1971 and 1973 surveys are available from the Roper Center, University of Connecticut, Storrs, Conn. 06268.

76. See the electoral commentaries in *Panorama*, 1 Apr. 1973, and *Esquiú*, 6 May 1973.

77. "Vote for the left" refers to the vote for the Popular Revolutionary Alliance, unless the text explicitly says that the vote includes those for the Popular Left Front and the Socialist Workers party. "Sympathy for the left" refers to explicit answers to survey questions be the respondents. These terms must be used only with such operational definitions, because, as I have long maintained, it is not possible in Argentina to continue talking vaguely about the "left" and the "right," since these terms in the general debates have had no agreed-upon meanings and only contribute to confusing the issues. On this theme, see Miguens, "¿Qué quiere decir izquierda y derecha en la Argentina?" p. 26; and "El peronismo frente a los dos fascismos," *Panorama*, 14 June 1973, p. 6.

78. The data were processed at the Institute for Social Inquiry at the University of Connecticut and at the Banco Central de la República Argentina in Buenos Aires. I would like to thank the staffs of both institutions for their assistance.

79. The high proportion of respondents who did not express a party preference in these surveys almost certainly fell in their loyalties along the same lines as those who did. That is, tables 1–5 seem representative of the electorate as a whole, first because the findings reported here are entirely consistent with other electoral and survey information on the attitudes of the Argentine public, and secondly because, under the open campaigning that the Lanusse government allowed, people proved willing to state their electoral preferences for both Peronism and the left in the same proportion that the electoral results showed to hold true for the country as a whole.

80. These voters on the left are here measured as those who defined their electoral preference as going to the Alianza Popular Revolucionario, the Frente de Izquierda Popular, and the Partido Socialista de los Trabajadores. The Partido Socialista Democrático is not included, because it had very few supporters and because, on the Argentine political scene, it also had ties and alliances with conservative parties.

8

MANUEL MORA Y ARAUJO and PETER H. SMITH

Peronism and Economic Development: The 1973 Elections

One of the most common themes in electoral analysis concerns the relationship between the socioeconomic structures of society and the vote for political parties. Curiosity about the phenomenon of Peronism in Argentina, in particular, has prompted a series of specific studies which, despite their value, have neither exhausted the empirical possibilities for such research nor offered completely satisfactory broad explanations. Peronism, as the other chapters in this volume show, is hard to comprehend: when some of its facets appear to succumb to a given analytical scheme, others rise up to defy interpretation. Our understanding of Peronism, therefore, even of its electoral aspects alone, remains partial and fragmentary.

In this chapter we set forth some propositions about the nature of Peronism as a political movement and its social bases, and we present some empirical results on the connection between socioeconomic variables and electoral outcomes. The hypotheses emerge from some of our own current work, as well as from published studies on the Peronist vote,[1] and they yield operational predictions that fit closely with our statistical findings. At the same time, we have no desire to exaggerate the deductive qualities of our investigation. The relationship between theory and data has for us been fluid, open, and two-directional: our ideas have shaped the empirical explorations, and the data have helped to strengthen our ideas. As always, further investigation will be necessary to give more support to the ideas, and the data give rise to unsuspected problems and new questions.

On a practical level, we have worked with aggregate data on voting for the country's 479 *departamentos* (roughly equivalent to counties) in the elections of March 1973, which brought the Peronist movement back into power for the first time since 1955. We have searched out regularities between these electoral results and the few socioeconomic indicators that have been available to us for the counties. In so doing, we have used multivariate techniques appropriate to the data—correlation, stepwise regression, and path analysis.

MANUEL MORA Y ARAUJO and PETER H. SMITH

Peronism and Its Social Bases: Questions and Hypotheses

All studies of the 1946 elections, which marked the decisive triumph of Juan Perón and his new Laborista party over a coalition of previous parties, emphasize the importance of the working-class base.[2] Peronism had clearly become the predominant political expression of the urban working class. Through his control of the Laborista party, Perón managed to mobilize and organize a political force that virtually dispossessed the old Socialist, Communist, and other lesser parties of their working-class support. In 1946 this phenomenon—characteristic of urban industrial areas—occurred mainly in the city of Buenos Aires and its suburban factory zones, since the rest of the country was much less industrialized.

But the total Peronist vote was much larger than its working-class electorate, and there is no scholarly consensus about the nature of Perón's additional support. In predominantly urban middle-class areas, the Peronist coalition stood to benefit from the support of the UCR Junta Renovadora, a splinter party of the old Unión Cívica Radical, but there are no indications that Peronism gained much following among the metropolitan middle class. In many provincial cities the movement appears to have attracted votes from employees of lesser socioeconomic status and probably from other people of modest occupation in the tertiary sector. It also seems to have drawn support from manual laborers, both organized and unorganized, engaged in various economic activities. To the extent that Peronism gained a following in rural and semiurban areas, it thus appears to have been a somewhat amorphous, multiclass movement.[3] In some such districts Perón and his party did very well; in others they did not.

The relative success of the movement in rural areas and small towns of the interior can be attributed, in large part, to a spillover from old conservative provincial parties. That is, conservatism did not support Peronism in the national arena, but many of its adherents defied the central leadership and turned to Perón in various provinces.[4]

It appears, in sum, that Peronism began with massive backing from industrial workers, but that it only partially captured the vote of popular sectors in rural and semiurban areas. There was some penetration among the urban middle classes, but how much is hard to say; generally speaking, these groups were not bastions of avid support, though they furnished some votes needed for the victory.

The complexity of these patterns underlies the fact that, for the 1946 election, there is no particularly strong correlation between the Peronist vote and indicators of socioeconomic development. The notion of "development," either taken as a global concept or broken down into component parts, does not provide a convincing explanation for Peronist electoral success in 1946.[5] Since then there has been a change, however, one that became especially evident in the elections of 1973: regional variation in the Peronist vote has increased, yielding (as we shall show) a significant negative correlation between the level of development and the Peronist vote. Since Peronist electoral strength has unquestionably remained intact among the lower sectors of the population, whatever their occupational position, and since it continues to weaken progressively among the upper reaches of society, we can only conclude that this negative correlation has resulted from an increase in electoral support among the social sectors of the least developed areas.

The connection between economic development and voter behavior can be made in varied ways and through diverse mechanisms. To make analytical and substantive sense out of the correlation, we must impose an interpretive scheme and search for casual connections.

One of the possible causes behind such a relationship might be the occupational composition of the population that is associated with the different kinds of economic structure reflected in the level of development. In this situation, voting can follow divisions according to "class"; that is, it might be closely associated with the occupational stratification of the population. A second, and rather different, causal factor concerns the difference in social conditions resulting from varying degrees of economic development. In this case the vote might express a response to the prevailing conditions of life, and to consequent needs and demands, rather than reflecting occupation or class. In our interpretation of the Peronist vote in 1973 we include both of these aspects of the situation: on one hand, we believe that the vote in industrial areas was class-based, although this shows up only slightly in the aggregate statistics for *departamentos;* on the other hand, we tend to attribute the negative relationship between Peronism and economic development to disparities in social conditions.

To put these propositions in their proper historical context, it is necessary to understand the specific nature of Argentina's social, economic, and political conformation. With an economy dominated by agricultural and pastoral production, Argentine society—low in population density, with vast amounts of semiarid land—was marked by relatively early urbanization and by a strong concentration of the active population in tertiary activities. This resulted in a social pyramid or structure with a sizable bulge among the middle sectors. At the same time, a slow but sustained process of industrialization began around the start of the twentieth century, receiving a vital stimulus from the worldwide economic crisis of the 1930s and the policies designed to meet it. An industrial working class that had been gradually growing for decades suddenly expanded sharply, in the late 1930s and early 1940s, largely because of cityward migration from the countryside, from the export-producing pampas as well as from other, less dynamic areas. This proletariat was also mostly native-born, in contrast to previous periods when immigrants held sway, and it was ready to exert substantial pressure on governmental authorities. By 1945, during a political crisis following the military coup of 1943, Buenos Aires — the center of Argentina's economic, political and social life, with one-third of the nation's population — was witnessing an unprecedented concentration of working-class masses and internal migrants, and it became the scene of serious social disturbances.

Many sectors of the so-called middle classes were calling for a return to the political democracy overthrown in 1930,[6] stressing the need to remove the armed forces from the government, sometimes for reasons related to conflicts connected to World War II. Meanwhile some other groups — principally the burgeoning working class — found the antimilitaristic, antifascist clamor for a return to democratic practices to be irrelevant, especially in comparison to their own urgent demands for greater political participation and for policies designed to redistribute wealth and to protect laborers in times of economic change. Political and social concerns thus created a profound split along two apparently independent axes, leading to a polarization of Argentina's social sectors. Old working-class parties joined up with the democratic political front, but the laborers themselves responded to leaders who were beginning to speak another language, to address new themes from new perspectives. It was Juan Perón who came to represent these groups, and in 1946 he surprised many observers by winning the presidential election with a substantial majority.

Once in power, and with the new Peronist (later Justicialist) party firmly established, Perón and his collaborators managed to transform both the leadership and the rank and file of the labor unions, now augmented by thousands of new members and strengthened by new laws on labor organization. Coinciding with this development was another, equally important process in the interior — where Peronism was steadily and rapidly gaining the support of traditional caudillos, local conservative parties, and other political forces that, in combination, possessed the capacity to control provincial politics in large degree.

In the first few years of his government, Perón not only increased the bargaining power and political participation of the working class; he also went after some new electoral conquests. The masses that supported him in 1946 continued to do so afterward.[7] What changed, from the electoral point of view, was that Peronism increased its following in most of the nonindustrial provinces, especially in the least developed ones, where it soon came to be a major political force. Thus Peronism developed a characteristic that is rare among popular political movements: an ability to obtain massive electoral support both in industrial working-class areas and in the poorest rural regions.[8]

This paradox becomes even greater in view of the fact that Peronist support in the working-class districts came at the expense of the preexisting prolabor parties (though some former leaders joined up with the new union forces), while Peronist support in the least developed areas was due to the adhesion of long-standing conservative leaders and their continuing control of the local political apparatus. A curious amalgam of militant laborism and traditional conservatism, Peronism consolidated its strength by discarding old power structures over the urban working class and by preserving old power structures over the rural poor.

This tendency persisted without much modification in the eighteen years after 1955, when the movement was out of power, and it emerged once more in the elections of 1973. Electoral support for Peronism in the least developed provinces was not, therefore, a mere result of vote-getting tactics; it revealed the presence of an enduring and genuine political force. For the industrial working class and other laborers represented by the unions, Peronism constituted a vehicle for the expression of political hopes and demands; for the urban and rural lower-class sectors of the poorest provinces, and for some segments of the local middle classes too, it probably constituted a means for articulating needs and hopes for social integration. Different social conditions gave birth to different sociopolitical phenomena, which Peronism brought together under the same heading and the same leader, and partly — but only partly — under the same organization. Essentially a working-class movement in the industrial cities, essentially a multiclass movement in the least developed areas, Peronism naturally and eventually became strongest in the poorest provinces and acted as a principal agent for social integration among the diverse sectors of those areas.

We now turn to the 1973 elections. Our intent, as stated above, is to clarify our understanding of Peronism through an examination of some fragmentary but suggestive findings about the social, economic, and demographic determinants of Peronist electoral support. To place our analysis within a proper perspective, we begin by explaining our reasons for focusing on the election of March 11, 1973.

The March Elections

It is our belief that the March 1973 election returns offer a firm and reliable indication of the patterns of Peronist popular strength. To be sure, the Peronist ticket on this occasion was led by Dr. Héctor Cámpora (rather than Perón himself), and the election ushered in a brief and unique period of *camporismo*, a period characterized by the temporary ascendancy in government of sectors of the Peronist left (as shown, for example, by an amnesty law that released numerous terrorists from jail and thus permitted the reconstitution of their organizations). Such leftist influence appears to have been the result of alliances and agreements between various fragments of Peronist leadership, however, rather than an expression of the specific will of the mass electorate. Unfortunately, there are hardly any serious

MANUEL MORA Y ARAUJO and PETER H. SMITH

studies of radicalization within the Peronist movement, nor of the internal composition of its ideological sectors, so statements on this subject consist mostly of conjecture and hypothesis.

Nevertheless we argue that the March 11, 1973, election provides a usable and "representative" picture of the electoral process at large—that, in other words, it accurately depicts the social correlates of the contemporary Peronist movement. We base this stand partly on subjective first-hand observations and on the impressions of countless observers. We can furthermore offer some salient empirical considerations.

First, the national Peronist ticket (Cámpora and Vicente Solano Lima) was selected by Perón himself and clearly represented his personal will. The fact that Perón later maintained a considerable distance from them merely reflected his own strategy for controlling the political process, rather than a disagreement from the start. On the provincial level, candidacies emerged from frequently arduous negotiations between various contending groups: national Peronist authorities, led at that time by Perón and Cámpora, Peronist union leaders, and local Peronist leaders from the provinces. In many cases the resulting candidacies were challenged by other Peronist factions. In some provincial elections there was more than one Peronist candidate, meaning that rivals within the movement competed among themselves for the Perón-Cámpora vote, but this did little to affect popular preference in the national presidential balloting.

Second, the impact of leftist groups on the March 11, 1973, program is elusive and difficult to trace. Prior to the elections the principal leftist groupings produced a large number of working documents and programmatic declarations which, for the most part, did not establish effective foundations for policy. Indeed, they were generally disregarded when Cámpora was in power and were relegated to near-complete oblivion after he resigned. There is absolutely no indication that the leftist *programáticos* played a significant role in the March 11 triumph, except perhaps among statistically minuscule circles of students and intellectuals. As a matter of fact the Cámpora–Solano Lima platform did not differ markedly from Peronist platforms of the past, so the ideological content of the movement remained consistent with its mainstream and its legacy.

Third, the distribution of Peronist voting strength on March 11 corresponded closely with those in other elections. For results across *departamentos*, the correlation between Peronist votes on March 11 and September 23, 1973—when Perón ran as the candidate—comes out to + .840. (In this latter election the outcome was a foregone conclusion, however, and many diverse groupings joined the Peronist bandwagon; we therefore regard it as a less reliable opportunity for the study of Peronist voting than the March election.) The interdepartmental correlation between the March 11 results and the 1954 election is also strong and positive. Obviously, there were no great differences between the relative locations of Peronist voting strength in March 1973 and on other occasions. Now let us take up the analysis.

Peronism and Development: A Regression Analysis

The growth of Peronist strength in the least developed provinces after 1946 finds clear reflection in correlations between the Peronist vote and various indicators of development: while the correlations hovered around zero for 1946, and some were even positive, they acquired a negative sign in 1951 and have retained it ever since. Moreover, the distribution of the vote has been a stable one: from 1951 onward the correlation between Peronist votes in successive election years has been very high, meaning that the geographical base of the movement's strength has tended to remain the same.

The relationship between Peronism and development in the 1970s has been established with both county-level data and province-level data.[9] Although the latter studies suffer from the disadvantage of having only twenty-four units of analysis (this being the number of provinces), they are able to rely on a greater number and range of structural indicators. In any case, the conclusion has been categorical: the higher the level of development, the lower the Peronist vote.

It is clear, then, that an observable pattern in the distribution of Peronist electoral strength has appeared and endured. This regularity derives from:
1. the negative correlation between the Peronist vote and development, whatever the indicator one might use;
2. the surprising electoral strength of Peronism in the least developed districts, that is, in areas characterized by economic and social backwardness, by poverty, and by the lack of urbanization; and
3. the persisting electoral power of Peronism in industrial districts with large working-class populations.

Our own analysis is based on aggregate data pertaining to Argentina's 479 *departamentos* or counties. Because of the nature of the data, we attempt to avoid the pitfalls of the well-known "ecological fallacy."[10] We do not have, for instance, information on the occupational structure of the *departamentos*, so we do not have the opportunity to draw (possibly fallacious) inferences about the partisan preferences of individual members of an occupational group from patterns relating to collective communities. That is, we make no effort to speculate about the voting tendencies of certain types of people; strictly speaking, we focus only upon the environmental and structural conditions of specific political outcomes in certain types of places. So we concentrate upon the context of politics, and, as will become clear, we make a sharp and important distinction between the social and the economic dimensions of the political environment.

MANUEL MORA Y ARAUJO and PETER H. SMITH

We take, as our dependent variable, the vote for the Frente Justicialista de Liberación (FREJULI) in the presidential elections of March 11, 1973. FREJULI represented the Peronist movement, in coalition with several lesser parties, each with a meager following.[11] The FREJULI candidate for president was Héctor Cámpora, who resigned after less than two months in office. It was on September 23 that Juan Perón triumphed in a follow-up election for the presidency, bringing his wife Isabel into the vice-presidency. Upon Perón's death, of course, she would later become president.

We take, as our independent variables, a series of socioeconomic indicators for which we were able to gain satisfactory information. The paucity of data from the 1970 census, and the scarcity of statistical data in general, present severe problems for any study of this kind, and we are keenly aware of its deficiencies. In any event, we have managed to gather data for the following variables:

Urbanization, as measured by the proportion of the population living in cities with 2,000 or more inhabitants in 1970;

Population Density, as measured by the number of people per square kilometer in 1970;

Population Growth between 1960 and 1970, in extremely cautious hopes that this might furnish an indirect indicator of net migration;

Electric Energy, as measured by the per capita consumption of kilowatts in 1973;

Housing Quality, as measured by a compound index that evaluates the overall quality of housing in regard to comforts and services as of 1960;

Doctor Scarcity, as measured by the ratio between the *departamento's* population and the number of doctors in 1970 (the higher the ratio, the less the availability of medical services);

Infant Mortality, as measured by the proportion of children who die within the first year of life, as of 1970; and

City Size, as measured by the absolute size of the largest city in each department in 1970, and also as defined by seven categories (under 2,000; 2,000–4,999; 5,000–9,999; 10,000–19,999; 20,000–49,999; 50,000–99,999; 100,000 and over).

Except for *Housing Quality,* virtually all of the variables refer to 1970, and, given the relatively slow pace of aggregate change along these dimensions, we feel fairly confident in correlating them with electoral data for 1973.

All of the independent variables are taken to represent different aspects of the general concept of development. We view *Infant Mortality* and *Doctor Scarcity* as relatively accurate indicators of social deprivation and underdevelopment. *Doctor Scarcity* may also represent results of public policy, since it would vary in accordance with the existence of hospitals and medical clinics; *Infant Mortality,* on the other hand, constitutes a pure and poignant indication of the state of suffering and social backwardness. *Housing Quality* and *Urbanization* are so closely correlated (Pearson's r = + .860) that they seem to represent the same phenomenon: the presence of an urban infrastructure and demographic concentration. *Electric Energy* reflects the economic structure, and probably varies according to the level of industrial activity; in the absence of data on occupations, we construe this as an indicator of economic differentiation and development. *City Size* also reveals a special aspect of urbanization, that is, the predominant type of urban environment.

Empirically as well as conceptually, these variables represent distinct and independent dimensions of development. With the exception of *Housing Quality* and *Urbanization*, none of the independent variables correlates very highly with any other one (the next highest correlation is + .526, between *Housing* and *Electric Energy*, and most are much weaker than that). This fact is encouraging, not only because it permits the use of multivariate techniques, but more important, because it demonstrates that the data have captured separate and distinguishable aspects of the complex phenomenon that we refer to as "development."

Simple correlations between these variables and the FREJULI vote support our basic hypothesis: the higher the level of development, the lower the Peronist vote. As revealed in table 1, variables such as *Housing Quality* have negative correlations with FREJULI (in this case − .497), while indicators of underdevelopment (such as *Infant Mortality*, with + .351) show positive associations. The negative relationship between FREJULI and *Urbanization* (− .362) finds confirmation in the distribution of the Peronist vote by *City Size*, as the average FREJULI vote was largest in the rural areas (58.2 percent in counties with no city of 2,000 or more) and smallest in the metropolitan districts (46.6 percent in *departamentos* with cities of 100,000 or more).[12]

TABLE 1
Indicators of Development and the FREJULI Vote, March 1973: Simple Correlations

	No. of Counties[a]	Correlation with FREJULI (Pearson's r)
Urbanization	479	− .362
Population Density	479	− .075
Population Growth	479	+ .012
Electric Energy	477	− .231
Housing Quality	478	− .497
Doctor Scarcity	479	+ .303
Infant Mortality	473	+ .351

Source: Compiled by the authors.
a. Varies because of missing data.

MANUEL MORA Y ARAUJO and PETER H. SMITH

To interpret the correlations in table 1, we emphasize their consistency more than their magnitude. Indeed, it would be surprising to find very powerful zero-order associations between two variables in a situation as complex as this. But the consistency in these coefficients is compelling and remarkable, and it suggests a definite pattern.[13] Our hypothesis seems to be sound.

Table 2 presents the results of a multivariate regression analysis, with four independent variables: *Urbanization, Infant Mortality, Doctor Scarcity,* and *Electric Energy.* We have had to exclude *Housing Quality* because of its strong correlation with *Urbanization,* and we have omitted *Population Density* in the interests of parsimony — and because of its weakness as an indicator of development. We have employed a "stepwise" procedure, allowing a computer to construct the first equation by selecting the independent variable with the strongest correlation with FREJULI (in this case *Urbanization);* the second equation includes the independent variable, among the others, that has the strongest correlation with FREJULI, controlling for the effect of *Urbanization;* the third equation includes the variable with the strongest partial correlation, controlling for both *Urbanization* and *Infant Mortality;* the fourth includes them all. *Population Growth* did not

TABLE 2
Indicators of Development and the FREJULI Vote, March 1973: Stepwise Regression Equations (No. of counties = 472)

			R^2
Step 1	FREJULI = 59.2 − .138	*Urbanization* (− .403)	.162
Step 2	FREJULI = 52.4 − .119	*Urbanization* (− .346)	.239
	+ .081	*Infant Mortality* (+ .283)	
Step 3	FREJULI = 50.0 − .089	*Urbanization* (− .261)	.264
	+ .072	*Infant Mortality* (+ .250)	
	+ .001	*Doctor Scarcity* (+ .187)	
Step 4	FREJULI = 50.2 − .080	*Urbanization* (− .232)	.268
	+ .071	*Infant Mortality* (+ .245)	
	+ .001	*Doctor Scarcity* (+ .186)	
	− .001	*Electric Energy* (− .070)	

Source: Compiled by the authors.
Note: Figures in parentheses are beta weights.

enter any of the equations because of its consistently low partial correlations with FREJULI.

Table 2 conveys several messages. First, the explanatory power of the models increases rather substantially at each of the first three steps—but not at step 4, when *Electric Energy* enters the equation, barely edging the proportion of variance explained (R²) up from .264 to .268. Second, the indicators of social deprivation and underdevelopment have relatively strong and positive relationships to the FREJULI vote. In step 4, in fact, *Infant Mortality* has the strongest impact on FREJULI, at least as measured by the standardized regression coefficients (beta weights).[14] While the indicators of development and underdevelopment continue to bear the predicted relationship to the Peronist vote, that is, our index of economic structure has much the weakest association (note the beta weight of only − .070 for *Electric Energy* at step 4). Third, as shown by the R² value for step 4, all the variables combine to explain about 27 percent of the variance in the FREJULI vote. Though this means that most of the variation in electoral behavior correlates with forces other than the contextual factors we have been able to observe, it also means that we can account for a respectable share of that variation. Especially in view of the complexity, contradictions, and ambiguities of the contemporary Peronist movement, we accept this result with not a little satisfaction.

Towards a Causal Model: Path Analysis

The relative importance of *Infant Mortality*, with the strongest beta weight in step 4, suggests that the social consequences of development, rather than the economic structures themselves, had the greatest impact on the 1973 electoral results. To be sure, the distinction between economic structures and their social consequences is largely analytical, and economic structures normally affect social patterns through their consequences or corollaries, not by themselves. But here we have a multiple process: the economic structure generates certain social conditions, and these social conditions generate certain types of political behavior—which, in turn, have consequences for the political system as a whole. A graphic presentation of this causal scheme follows:

Economic Structure → Social → Electoral → Characteristics of
of Development   Consequences   Behavior   Political System

The central ingredient in this interpretation, especially as it affects our understanding of the 1973 elections, is the distinction between economic structure and the social aspects of development, and their differential implications for voting behavior. The phenomenon of populism—the political expression of highly mobilized but relatively unorganized popular masses—can be construed as a political reflection of the social situation which cor-

MANUEL MORA Y ARAUJO and PETER H. SMITH

responds to the conditions produced by underdevelopment. By contrast, the working-class base of many political movements whose organizational strength draws on labor unions and other such institutions can be understood as a response to substantially different socioeconomic conditions, and it is in this sense that we interpret the Peronism of the urban working class.

Our correlations and regression equations do not clearly reveal the impact of the working-class vote because (1) we do not have the necessary indicators, and (2) some of the contextual conditions affecting that vote also reflect the presence of sizable middle-class sectors whose political behavior differs from that of the industrial workers. (Thus the difficulties of aggregate data, and hence, once again, the danger of the ecological fallacy.) Here resides the class-based character, what in Spanish is more precisely termed the *carácter clasista*, of the Peronist vote in urban industrial areas: it is concentrated in the working class, rather than dispersed among all sectors of the population. This situation explains, and is explained by, the fact that Peronism is proportionally more powerful in less developed areas, a fact that contradicts a widespread assumption to the contrary.[15]

This pattern of electoral conduct undoubtedly has far-reaching implications for the political system as a whole, and in this chapter we can offer only fragmentary speculations. For instance, the sometimes overwhelming strength of Peronism in less developed areas not only assured the dominance of populist policies designed to capture and retain the "mobilized" vote; it also deprived political systems in many poor provinces of a genuine conservative alternative. Furthermore, the remarkable coexistence of an organized urban working class and of massive, unorganized, multiclass popular forces within the same political movement created an electoral majority that defies simple classification as "leftist" or "rightist." Indeed, the strength of Peronism reduced many politicians of both left and right to marginal status, thus giving Argentina's political system some of its distinctive features.

To substantiate this line of argument, at least insofar as it relates to electoral behavior, we now turn to path analysis. In contrast to stepwise regression, which chooses variables according to purely statistical criteria (see table 2), path analysis requires the a priori selection and arrangement of variables according to an explicitly causal interpretive scheme. In reflection of our reasoning, sketched out above, we have identified *Electric Energy*, our best available indicator of economic structure, as the initial causal force (in technical terminology, it is our exogenous variable, one that is not caused by any others in the model). To measure the social consequences of economic structure, we have chosen two endogenous variables, *Housing Quality* and *Infant Mortality*. Our dependent variable is, of course, FREJULI.[16]

The graphic reflection of this scheme, known as a path diagram, appears in figure 1. The arrows represen: the causal paths, here presumed to be unidirectional. The adjacent numbers are standardized regression coefficients (again, beta weights) that measure the strength and direction of each causal relationship. The calculations involve all *departamentos* (N = 471) for which we have sufficient data.

FIGURE 1
Indicators of Development and the FREJULI Vote, March 1973: Path Analysis

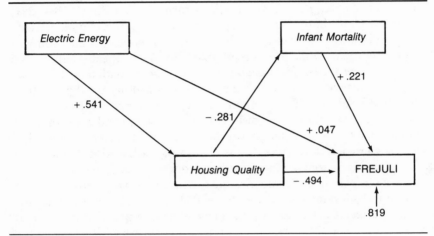

Source: Compiled by the authors.

In combination, the four independent variables explain 33 percent of the variance in the FREJULI vote (compared to the 27 percent explained by the four variables in the stepwise regression equation). As before, we regard this as substantial confirmation of the explanatory power of a relatively parsimonious model, especially in view of the imprecision of the indicators and the complexity of the social realities under observation. To be sure, the coefficient of alienation (defined as $\sqrt{1-R^2}$) comes to .819, showing that most of the variance in FREJULI obeys forces and factors outside of this scheme, but we nevertheless consider our result to be encouraging and satisfactory.

Within the model, *Housing Quality* is the variable that has the greatest *direct* effect on FREJULI, with a path coefficient of − .494: the better the housing, as we have already seen, the less the Peronist vote. *Infant Mortality* has the next strongest direct impact, with the predicted positive sign (+ .221). *Electric Energy*, however, exerts almost no direct effect at all (+ .047). Once again, it is the social conditions that result from economic development, rather than the level of development itself, that produce a significant influence on electoral results.

But *Electric Energy* does have an observable *indirect* effect on the FREJULI vote, and this is a point we want to emphasize. As shown by the path coefficient of + .541 — the strongest one in the entire model — *Electric Energy* has a real impact on *Housing Quality*, and it is through this connection that energy consumption affects the electoral patterns. (Note that there is no such connection through *Infant Mortality*, as that coefficient was so close to zero that the entire path could be eliminated from the model.) The greater the level of industrialization and economic development, the higher the standard of housing; the higher the standard of housing, the lower the Peronist vote. *Housing Quality* also has a fairly strong negative impact on *Infant Mortality* (− .281), which in turn affects FREJULI (+ .221). There exists, in short, a definite relationship between economic development and the Peronist vote, but the causal connections remain indirect.[17]

In an effort to refine these observations, we have repeated this analysis with *City Size* as a control variable, constructing one path model for counties (N = 242) with cities of 5,000 or more and another for those without cities that large (N = 229). The intent, of course, was to see if the relationships in urban contexts were different from those in rural areas (notwithstanding the crudeness of our urban-rural dichotomy). As it turned out, both models were practically identical to that in figure 1, with only one exception: *Electric Energy* had a somewhat stronger direct effect on FREJULI in the metropolitan environments, the coefficient being + .101 (in the rural communities it remained negligible, − .034, though it acquired a negative sign). Within the urban context, the moderately strong coefficient may result from the presence of working-class masses in districts with relatively high levels of industrialization — in contrast to other districts which might be equally developed but less industrialized, and where the middle classes would tend to cluster. Conditions of this kind might therefore produce, within these limits, a positive correlation between the level of development and the Peronist vote. The hypothesis seems plausible, though we cannot submit it to a rigorous test with the available data.

Conclusions

In summary, our statistical analysis of the 1973 elections has turned up the following results:

1. the higher the level of social development, the lower the relative Peronist vote;
2. the higher the level of social deprivation, the higher the Peronist vote;
3. social conditions exert a greater direct impact on the Peronist vote than do economic structures; but
4. social conditions, especially those reflected in housing, and to some extent urbanization as well, are closely dependent on the level of economic development; while
5. infant mortality appears to result not from the industrial structure or from the level of economic development, but from prevailing social conditions.

These findings probably reflect not only a persisting pattern in the structural determinants of voting behavior, but also the particular social and economic conjuncture of contemporary Argentina. It is entirely possible that, in time, processes of social and economic transformation can lead to future changes in the relationships between social and economic factors, and in the relationships between these factors and voting outcomes. Our data reveal a marked propensity for Peronism to obtain higher votes in areas of less development and greater social deprivation. And yet they also show that Peronism received substantial support in industrial working-class zones — relatively developed areas, for the most part, where syndical organizations enjoy a powerful influence over the masses and a well-known capacity for negotiation. In keeping with a well-established tradition of political and sociological thought, it could be argued that the Peronist vote, at least insofar as it corresponds to conditions of social deprivation, is a response by sizable sectors of the population to the existence of these conditions in the general context of intermediate development and the expectations it creates. On the other hand, it could also be argued that this peculiar combination of political and social possibilities creates a propitious environment for patterns of electoral behavior and political control that in turn produce a vote that is populistic but unradicalized. These two processes can take place simultaneously, in which case the Peronist vote in the less developed areas would be both a popular response to the conditions of life and a measure of elite capacity to control the mass vote through populist means that uphold the traditions — and the institutions — of conservative caudillismo. In the working-class areas, on the contrary, the Peronist vote can be attributed not so much to the prevailing conditions of social deprivation as to the legacy of the first Perón regime (1946–1955), an era marked by the strengthening of union organizations and by a notable tendency to redistribute economic resources in favor of industrial workers. The syndicates no doubt perpetuate the memories of this experience, and for them Peronism represents their major opportunity for increasing their power within society, rather than a solution to problems of social deprivation.

Our causal diagram pointed toward the nature of the "political system," a dimension that we have not been able to include in our empirical discussion. Yet our interpretation of Peronism in the less developed areas — as a multiclass phenomenon under a process of political control that depends on mobilized but scarcely organized masses, and that in turn depends on specific social and economic conditions — suggests some hypotheses about the character of the political system. In itself, populist mobilization establishes a distinctive constellation of political values, structures, and norms or rules of the game. Politics based on organized social groups establishes a substantially different constellation, the capacity to articulate interests through collective associations being perhaps its most salient feature.

MANUEL MORA Y ARAUJO and PETER H. SMITH

The coexistence of both constellations within a single political system goes a long way toward identifying the distinctive quality of Argentine politics – a quality that is clearly related to the oft-noted quality of the country's social and regional structure.[18] The fact that Peronism has managed to provide political expression for two such disparate forces is both its most notable feature and, in the end, the most singular facet of Argentine politics. Contrary to many widely accepted interpretations,[19] it is not the struggle between the interior and the coast, between underdevelopment and development, that defines the central antagonism on the political scene. Instead, the country's dominant political movement has gained its structure precisely by superseding these cleavages, rather than by exploiting them. When such a conflict takes place, if it ever does – or when urban industrial sectors align themselves against the rural sectors – it will entail a fundamental transformation in Argentine society and politics. It would also signify the end of the electoral supremacy of Peronism or of the political force that inherits the movement.

NOTES

1. Some are published in Manuel Mora y Araujo and Ignacio Llorente, eds., *El voto peronista* (Buenos Aires: Sudamericana, 1980), in which an earlier version of this chapter appeared.
2. Notwithstanding considerable controversy over the relative role of lower-class migrants, there is general agreement that the working class as a whole furnished massive support for Perón. See Gino Germani, "El surgimiento del peronismo: El rol de los obreros y de los migrantes internos," *Desarrollo Económico* 13 (1973), 435–88; and Peter H. Smith, "Las elecciones argentinas de 1946 y las inferencias ecológicas," *Desarrollo Económico* 14 (1974), 385–98.
3. On Perón's support outside the major cities, see Peter H. Smith, "The Social Base of Peronism," *Hispanic American Historical Review* 52 (1972), 55–73; E. Spencer Wellhofer, "The Mobilization of the Periphery: Perón's 1946 Triumph," *Comparative Political Studies* 7 (1974), 239–51; and "Peronism in Argentina: The Social Base of the First Regime, 1946–1955," *Journal of Developing Areas* 11 (1977), 334–56.
4. See Ignacio Llorente, "Alianzas políticas en el surgimiento del peronismo. El caso de la Provincia de Buenos Aires," *Desarrollo Económico* 17 (1977) 61–88; and Luis A. J. González Esteves, "Las elecciones de 1946 en la Provincia de Córdoba," in Mora y Araujo and Llorente, eds., *El voto peronista*, pp. 319–64.
5. See Smith, "Social Base of Peronism."
6. With the possible exception of 1938, elections between 1930 and 1946 were marked by overt political pressures and notorious government fraud.
7. As suggested by Darío Cantón, Jorge Raúl Jorrat, and Eduardo Juárez, "Un intento de estimación de las celdas interiores de una tabla de contingencia basado en el análisis de regresión: El caso de las elecciones presidenciales de 1946 y marzo de 1973," *Desarrollo Económico* 16 (1976), 395–417.
8. From 1946 on, and especially after 1955, working-class Peronism shared many characteristics of European working-class parties. What made it unique was its large-scale electoral support in rural and less-developed areas.
9. See Manuel Mora y Araujo, "La estructura social del peronismo," *Desarrollo Económico* 14 (1975), 699–718, and "Populismo, laborismo, clases medias," *Criterio* 27 Jan. 1977, pp.

9–20. Other analyses of the 1973 elections include Manuel Mora y Araujo and Ignacio Llorente, "Misiones 1973–1975: A la búsqueda de las bases sociales del comportamiento electoral," *Desarrollo Económico* 15 (1975), 459–71; Darío Cantón and Jorge R. Jorrat, "Occupation and Vote in Urban Argentina: The March 1973 Presidential Election," *Latin American Research Review* 13 (1978), 146–57; and Lars Schoultz, "The Socio-Economic Determinants of Popular-Authoritarian Electoral Behavior: The Case of Peronism," *American Political Science Review* 71 (1977), 1423–46.

10. The "ecological fallacy" refers to the erroneous assumption that relationships observed between characteristics of aggregate social *collectivities* necessarily reflect similar relationships between the characteristics of *individuals* within those collectivities. County-level data might reveal, for instance, a positive association between percent working-class in the adult population and percent literate, but this does not necessarily mean that workers tend to be more literate than other members of society. For the classic exposition of this fallacy, see W. S. Robinson, "Ecological Correlations and the Behavior of Individuals," *American Sociological Review* 15 (1950), 351–57; and Mattei Dogan and Stein Rokkan, eds., *Quantitative Ecological Analysis in the Social Sciences* (Cambridge, Mass.: MIT Press, 1969), esp. pt. 1.

11. Most important of these parties were the Conservador Popular, whose leader, Vicente Solano Lima, ran for vice-president; the Movimiento para Integración y Desarrollo (MID), led by ex-President Arturo Frondizi; the Popular Cristiano; and some Christian Democrats.

12. As a categorical variable, *City Size* explains 10.7 percent of the variance in FREJULI.

13. Scattergrams (not displayed here for reasons of space) show that these bivariate relationships are generally linear in form, so we can discard the possibility that the coefficients are disguising curvilinear associations. This also obviates the need to transform the variables or use polynomial equations.

14. Beta weights are standardized in such a way as to make it possible to compare the magnitude of slopes for different independent variables. In step 4, for instance, the slope for *Infant Mortality* (+ .071) is smaller than the one for *Urbanization* (– .080), the difference in sign being immaterial here; but when the slopes are standardized to account for the variance in the two variables, the beta weight for *Infant Mortality* is larger than that of *Urbanization* (+ .245 compared to – .232).

15. Politicians usually concentrate their attention on urban and industrial districts because that is where the greater part of the electorate lives, and developed areas have a greater impact on national elections than less-developed ones. But this does not affect our interpretation of voting and development, since our calculations (conceptually, if not always operationally) deal with the behavior of proportions of voters within the districts, not with the proportions of voters for the parties.

16. We have experimented with numerous other path analyses, using other combinations of independent variables, and have selected this one because it most closely fits our conceptual scheme.

17. The "effect coefficients" show that the entire amount of the original covariation between *Electric Energy* and FREJULI (Pearson's r for these 472 counties = – .254) can be accounted for by the direct effect (path coefficient = + .047) and the sum of the indirect effects (– .301).

18. See, for instance, Eduardo Zalduendo, *Las desigualdades económicas en las regiones de Argentina* (Buenos Aires: n.p., 1973); and *Datos comparativos de las provincias argentinas* (Bariloche: Fundación Bariloche, 1969).

19. An example is Jorge Abelardo Ramos, *Revolución y contrarevolución en la Argentina* (Buenos Aires: Plus Ultra, 1965).

9

ROBERTO P. GUIMARÃES

Understanding Support for Terrorism Through Survey Data: The Case of Argentina, 1973

Even if Rap Brown went too far in saying that "violence is necessary and it's as American as cherry pie,"[1] no one can deny the pervasiveness of political violence since the beginnings of history. In the 1960s and 1970s, one form of systematized violence—terrorist acts aimed at changing public policies or ultimately aimed at overturning governments and governmental systems—has increased sharply with acts such as bombings, kidnapings, and assassinations by the Weathermen and the Symbionese Liberation Army in the United States, the National Liberation Action in Brazil, the Tupamaros in Uruguay, and the Montoneros in Argentina. As Charles Tilly has written from a global perspective, with growing relevance for contemporary society, "The oppressed have struck in the name of justice, the privileged in the name of order, those in between in the name of fear."[2]

Why should we study terrorism, especially in its recent manifestations? How can we best do so? Answers to these two questions may be closely interrelated. As terrorism has spread over the planet, its cost in human lives, property, and social and political institutions has come to warrant a serious assessment of our knowledge about it. If for no other reason, the fact that political violence "tends to scar societies deeply and to prevent the formation of consensus indefinitely"[3] justifies considerable efforts in this direction. Perhaps it is best to approach the subject of terrorism by asking what the nature of popular support for terrorism is; only in this way can we understand terrorist strategies and the appeal of terrorism for the people. That is, instead of exclusively studying who the terrorists are and what tactics they use, we need also to investigate who supports the terrorists and why.

Why and How We Should Study Support for Terrorism

Interest in terrorism has suddenly increased. The abduction and subsequent murder of former Premier Aldo Moro of Italy during the first months   189 of 1978 took the public, including Italians, by surprise. Even though we have always been aware of the existence of terrorism and terrorists, we have never paid much attention to them. As Luigi Bonanate, an Italian expert in the emerging field of "terrorology," commented, "Terrorism, until recently and especially for Europeans, has represented a phenomenon that could be followed with the same dilettantism as, say, family relations in Polynesia, or welfare rituals in certain African tribes."[4] Yet the Moro affair occurred in the heart of Europe, calling the notice of Europeans to a growing phenomenon, of which the one-dead-every-other-day situation in Northern Ireland, the Baader-Meinhof gang in West Germany, the South Moluccans in the Netherlands, the Basques in Spain, the Croatians in Yugoslavia, and the French Canadians in Quebec, are manifestations.

Despite the fact that, except for the Red Brigades in Italy and the Red Army Faction in West Germany, all the terrorist groups mentioned above comprise a distinct type of terrorism, the nationalist-separatist variety, the overriding reality is that terrorism has many sources and has become a permanent feature of the political landscape on every continent. The message of Moro's fate is quite clear: nobody is immune. Terrorism has definitely ceased to be merely a security or police problem and has become a political problem.

According to one recent report, there are today an estimated 226 civil groups that operate in 56 countries and that openly advocate the use of violence for political purposes: 116 groups from the left (such as Trotskyites, Maoists, Castroites, and Orthodox Marxists), 30 neofascists, 34 separatists, and 12 that comprise several tendencies, from anarchists to religious groups.[5] Terrorism is now so organized and so internationalized that in 1974 the Junta de Coordinación Revolucionária (JCR) was created, with headquarters in Paris, to foster joint planning, fund raising, coordination, and logistic support among leftist groups in Latin America.[6] Innumerable reports also allege ties among the Junta de Coordinación Revolucionaria, the Palestine Liberation Organization (PLO), and the Japanese Red Army. The Italian police even claim to have found evidence that West Germany's Red Army Faction cooperated with the Red Brigades in the kidnaping and murder of Moro.[7]

Terrorism, then, seems to be here to stay. To cope with this new reality we must first question the simplistic, often propagandistic notion that terrorism is merely the outcome of deviant psychological behavior, or "aggressive tendencies" or "personal frustrations." Terrorism has become far more than this. It is also, now even more than in the past, a *political alternative* inherent in certain political situations and systems, and in order to understand it we need to appreciate the varieties of support for it that may be found in the population at large. In trying to do this, as in so many other areas, social scientists have been caught off guard.

With occasional exceptions — the works of Anthony Burton,[8] Ted Gurr,[9] Walter Laqueur,[10] Jan Schreiber,[11] and Paul Wilkinson[12] among them — the specialized literature on violence has not helped us to understand the new features of terrorism as a political alternative. Most of it concentrates either on general explanations of terrorist tactics or on the study of the social background of individual terrorists, attempting to trace the "profile of the terrorist." Among the causes of this search for the "typical" terrorist have been the desire of police officials for operational guidelines, the more general quest for certainty in the social sciences, and the equilibrium bias pervading social science today.[13] Using the all-too-familiar biological analogy, a social science that is supposed to be concerned with "healthy" social systems finds nothing more appropriate when dealing with terrorism than to attempt to identify the deviant individuals by establishing a profile, to characterize their malaise by exploring their backgrounds, and to spell out how they attempt to infect the otherwise healthy social system through terrorist tactics so that the appropriate antidote may be developed.

In the terms of an equilibrium-oriented social science, whose practitioners are necessarily disgusted with violent acts that challenge stability, a method or theory that advocates systematic violence must be treated as deviant, and all advocates of the theory must be regarded as ill or insane. This approach fits neatly with mass revulsion against specific terrorist acts, with the efforts of government officials to discredit the terrorists, and with the desire of the agencies that fund social science research to underwrite research projects that meet "national needs" and seek "peaceful solutions" to problems of violence. The assumption that terrorism results from the crazed acts of "deviant individuals" is so simple that mass publics can understand it, so appealing that public officials and the media can easily promote it, and so intriguing that foundations can further its study. This approach may greatly oversimplify, or even fundamentally misrepresent, a highly complex situation. By taking this approach, we have actually precluded more frequent journeys into the realm of empirical research.

What road map might we best use on more broadly based, and more empirically oriented, journeys? One strategy would be to compare the best data-derived interpretations of terrorism in the past with information from recent surveys on the support for terrorism in different nations. This is one approach to be used in this chapter, as I will question the utility of the concept of "relative deprivation," basing my conclusion on both elite and rank-and-file opinion data gathered in Argentina in 1973. Virtually all research on civil violence has in common the key concept of relative deprivation, an interpretation of social conflict developed by Samuel Stouffer and his associates during World War II[14] and more recently articulated through the works of Ted Gurr.[15] The concept of relative deprivation can be analyzed in light of surveys on the extent of popular support for terrorism in Argentina, such as Frederick Turner's study of six socioeconomic groups in Argentina during Juan Perón's final campaign for the presidency.[16] Surprisingly, it turns out that, when analyzed in this way, "relative deprivation" is seen to have virtually no impact on popular support for terrorism.

A second general strategy — one that turns out to have considerably more analytical value in understanding support for terrorism in Argentina during 1973 — is to investigate general surveys that include data on terrorism and then to determine which factors make respondents most sympathetic, or at least somewhat sympathetic, to terrorists. As is outlined in detail below, I have identified sixty potentially relevant explanatory variables using the Argentine data, and through regression analysis,[17] have found that five variables explain a considerable degree of popular support for terrorism in Perón's Argentina. Multiple regression, much like a telescope, helps to focus on the most important factors, after one has scanned the broad universe of possible explanations. Furthermore, it provides a very different framework of interpretation from that commonly used to study terrorism.

Virtually none of the answers offered by the literature seems to be present in the final model. Paraphrasing Eldon Kenworthy, Argentina may once more show us "the function of the little-known case in theory formation," this time underscoring "what terrorism was not."[18] The overriding dimension appears to be political rather than psychological or sociological. Charles Tilly's comment on revolutions may be equally applied to terrorism: "Despite the many recent attempts to psychologize the study of revolution by introducing ideas of anxiety, alienation, rising expectations, and the like, and to sociologize it by employing notions of disequilibrium, role conflict, structural strain, and so on, the factors which hold up under close scrutiny are, on the whole, political ones."[19]

If this interpretation of the Argentines' support for terrorism is correct, one must conclude that terrorism cannot be eliminated merely by liquidating a particular set of terrorists, as the Argentine military proved largely capable of doing in the late 1970s. The decline of political legitimacy, the reassertion of political idealism, and the rise of single-issue politics may broaden the backing that terrorists receive. From historically unlikely movements, such as environmentalism is today, challengers of established policies may increasingly turn to strategies of violence. Therefore, there are major policy implications as well as vast regions of unexplored territory when it comes to analyzing extant survey data from the standpoint of support for terrorism.

What Is Our Knowledge about Support for Terrorism?

How much do we know, then, about support for terrorism? Our present knowledge lies somewhere between speculation and complete ignorance.

To begin with, there is no such thing as a literature on terrorism. Guerrilla warfare, terrorism, rioting, and other disorders are treated somewhat indistinctly as part of the general study of revolution and violence. There are some good individual books on terrorism, but for the most part their research is historical and descriptive rather than analytical.[20]

Second, the few books specifically on terrorism do not focus on the nature of support for terrorist groups and activities. Walter Laqueur, for instance, in his latest book on terrorism has dedicated fewer than three out of several hundred pages to "popular support," and he is no exception.[21] Other writers either do not mention the issue of support or give only occasional indications of the *need* for popular support.[22] When it comes to actually studying popular support, scholars typically conclude that "it would be of great benefit for the measurement of the insurgents' public support if in-depth and systematic interviews of various elements of the . . . population were available for analysis and interpretation," but that "unfortunately these analytical aids are not at hand."[23]

Despite the scant literature on terrorism, we can identify, for the sake of simplicity, two major research traditions on the subject.[24] One group of theories can be classified under the *behavioral tradition*, emphasizing sociological and psychological explanations, and stressing the use of concepts such as "relative deprivation," "sense of powerlessness," "lack of legitimacy," "progressive degradation," "frustration," and "differential access" to explain why people resort to violence.[25] There is also a *structural tradition* that focuses not on processes but on objective conditions from which terrorism emerges. That is, violence is seen as a result of "inequality," "injustice," "social and economic bankruptcy," or "the existence of marginalized groups."[26] It should be added, however, that some researchers—such as Henry Bienen, James C. Davies, H. L. Nieburg, and Charles Tilly —notwithstanding their use of concepts that are characteristic of one tradition or the other, have in fact attempted to integrate both structural and behavioral explanations.[27] Nieburg typically states:

> The theory to be developed here gives a central place to the dynamics of social bargaining equations in which deprivation, access, structure, stress or release from stress, values in conflict, conflict management, and so on are related elements that respond to bargaining outcomes just as they provide the setting and conditions of bargaining. This theory has the advantage of permitting full integration of factors in a universal model that is of parallel significance at all levels of human action, from interpersonal to international.[28]

Bienen's conclusion also points in that direction, that violence would be prone to occur in transitional societies where modernization is occurring (that is, those characterized by rising expectations among the population but in which all wants have not yet been satisfied), where political and social integration are lacking, and where the level of institutionalization is low.[29]

The general process believed to lead to terrorism, from a behavioral point of view, centers on relative deprivation rather than on the objectification of conditions; thus the focus is on the perception of conditions. As mentioned earlier, the direct link between relative deprivation and violence was first articulated by Gurr, who based his work on the research findings of Stouffer and others during the Second World War:

> My basic premise is that the necessary precondition for violent civil conflict is relative deprivation, defined as actors' perception of discrepancy between their *value expectations* and their environment's apparent *value capabilities*. Value expectations are the goods and conditions of life to which people believe they are justifiably entitled. . . . Value capabilities . . . are the conditions that determine people's perceived chances of getting or keeping the values they legitimately expect to attain.[30]

Put another way, the higher people's expectations for material advancement, and the less likely the social and political system to deliver on its promises, the greater the probability of violent outcomes. This theory further suggests that it does not make much difference whether the economic system has *actually* not been able to fulfill expectations at large but whether individuals *perceive* this discrepancy to be real. In this context — of socioeconomic frustration being positively related to conditions of political unrest[31] — Turner's original hypothesis that "the combination of high motivation to achieve and dramatically inadequate growth points to an apparent cause for frustration and domestic violence [in Argentina]"[32] would be valid only if Argentines indeed perceived this situation to be true. As it turns out, Argentines do not generally perceive reality in this fashion, and even when they do, their perception does not explain to any extent their support for terrorism.

It is interesting to note, at this point, that even if the hypothesized relationship of relative deprivation to army morale or political violence is fairly recent (after World War II), and it is characteristic of the behavioral or sociopsychological tradition, we can nevertheless find the clear roots of the concept already (and surprisingly, in light of some structural interpretations) in Karl Marx's lectures at the German Workers' Society in Brussels in 1847.[33] For Marx, human needs and their satisfaction are socially, and not just objectively, defined, and are thus relative in nature. He suggests the following analogy: "A house may be large or small; as long as the surrounding houses are equally small it satisfies all social demands for a dwelling. But let a palace arise beside the little house, and it shrinks from a little house to a hut" (p. 32). As if this simple example were not enough, he went on to explain the process in more articulated terms:

> A noticeable increase in wages presupposes a rapid growth of productive capital. The rapid growth of productive capital brings about an equally rapid growth of wealth, luxury, social wants, social enjoyments. Thus, although the enjoyments of the worker have risen, the social satisfaction that they give him has fallen in comparison with the increased enjoyments of the capitalist, which are inaccessible to the worker, in comparison with the state of development of society in general. (P. 33)

For those more difficult to persuade, Marx unmistakably concludes that "our desires and pleasures spring from society; we measure them, therefore, by society and not by the objects which serve for their satisfaction. Because they are of a social nature, they are of a relative nature" (p. 33).

As far as the Argentine data can tell us, one of the few instances in which current theories come close to explaining support for terrorism is the notion of differential access to power. This concept is mostly used to qualify the idea of relative deprivation, in the sense that lack of access to power is thought to make frustrated people more violent in demanding access to the center of economic and political decisions. As Nieburg says:

> The access theory admits a general congruence between power and deprivation, but dwells upon factors of social organization as more significant in stabilizing or upsetting public peace and tranquility. Social disorganization and the rise of subcultures of violence are viewed more as results of differential access and unequal social power than as inevitable results of relative deprivation.[34]

Strictly structural explanations, in their turn, place a special emphasis solely on the objective conditions that not only lead to terrorism itself but also justify popular support for terrorist activities. Unequal participation in decision making, that is, political inequality itself and not just an aggravation of perceptions of deprivation, is one such general condition. Social chaos and economic bankruptcy would be another.[35] Social class and group antagonisms are still another, especially used by advocates of violence to justify their undertakings. A common statement is that "the proletariat and poor peasantry are the exploited classes and it is they who are the progressive elements in society; their emancipation both justifies and demands a battle."[36]

But social and political relationships are not as simple as that, at least in Argentina. Only through careful analysis of hard data on Argentine attitudes does one clearly understand these realities.

Analysis of the Argentine Data: What Terrorism Was Not

Argentine data show in the first instance what terrorism was not. *Absolute* deprivation, if by that we describe the poverty and powerlessness of the lower strata in the socioeconomic ladder, as well as *subjective* perceptions of economic frustration, are not the major factors explaining support for terrorism in Argentina during 1973. On the other hand, the *political marginalization* of a particular movement, Peronism — which is multiclass in nature[37] — seems to be the sole significant explanation.

The present analysis is based on data gathered in survey research conducted by Frederick C. Turner in Argentina in 1973.[38] The final data set comprises 429 variables and 890 cases, from which 61 variables have been chosen for analysis. (See appendix 2 for selected variables and respective frequency distributions.[39]) Like any research project, the present analysis developed through several steps. The first task was to select from Turner's questionnaire those questions that appeared to tap relevant dimensions to explain the degree of support for terrorism in Argentina. Appendix 1 lists all questions selected, followed by the variable numbers to which they correspond.

The second step was to group these variables in regression equations, according to the basic ideas to be tested here, and to perform the simple regression of V68, *Civil Groups*, on each explanatory variable.[40] The results appear in appendix 4. The first five equations represent, roughly, the main hypothesis of the structural tradition: equations 1 and 2 group social class and group antagonism variables; equation 3, general objective conditions such as education, socioeconomic level, and so forth; and equations 4 and 5 represent one aspect of the often-voiced argument of social and political bankruptcy, the encapsulation of the state apparatus by specific groups to the detriment of the nation as a whole. In the remaining five equations are grouped the so-called behavioral variables: equations 6, 7, and 8 represent relative deprivation viewed from different perspectives; equation 9, the perceptions of Argentines as to the legitimacy of the government's decisions in general, as well as that of specific regimes; and, finally, equation 10 summarizes the overall attitude of Argentines toward violence.

One point can be made on the basis of the simple correlation coefficients: all variables grouped in equations 1, 4, 5, 6, 7, and 8 (the social and political identification of the respondent, the perception of groups or individuals influencing the government for their own gain, as well as the respondent's overall expectations and perception of economic conditions, and his or her unwillingness to sacrifice) are not at all related to support or lack of support for terrorist activities in Argentina.

Furthermore, if we decide to accept only correlations of .15 or higher —

which still is a very weak correlation — it turns out that from the original sixty explanatory variables only eight meet the above criteria:

from equation 2	V59,	*Univ. Students*	(r =	.300)
	V65,	*Workers*	(r =	.222)
from equation 9	V71,	*J. Perón — 1st Pres.*	(r =	.124)
	V72,	*Aramburu*	(r =	−.177)
	V74,	*J. Perón — 2nd Pres.*	(r =	.155)
	V88,	*Institutional Legality*	(r =	−.176)
from equation 10	V122,	*How Change*	(r =	.155)
	V124,	*Violence — Necessary*	(r =	−.185)

Even at first glance, these numbers give us an accurate preview of what more sophisticated techniques such as multiple regression and path analysis will underscore: that relative deprivation does not play any role at all in explaining support for terrorism in Argentina. What does seem to matter is whether one feels closely associated with workers (V65), whether one regards Peronist regimes as legitimate (V74), and whether one strongly respects the legality of institutions (V88). Variable 59, *Univ. Students*, has to be understood as associated with V65, *Workers* (r = .357), but since it is well known that a good proportion of terrorists comes from the university population, the fact that these variables have the highest correlation coefficient does not add much to our knowledge about terrorism.

The next stage in the analysis was to perform a multiple regression analysis of V68, *Civil Groups*, on each of the ten equations. The results appear in appendix 5. Here, what the zero-order correlations have already demonstrated becomes even more clear as equations 1, 3, 4, 5, 6, 7, 8, and 10 do not contribute anything to explain support for terrorism. The remaining two equations explain over one-third (36 percent) of the variance on V68, *Civil Groups*. Once more it becomes clear that relative deprivation can be entirely neglected (equations 6, 7, and 8). Structural explanations seem to have also been severely weakened (equations 1, 3, 4, and 5).

Multiple regression did not, in fact, tell us anything that we did not know already through the zero-order correlations. Its main contribution was that, unlike simple regression, its results accounted simultaneously for all variables in each equation. What we thus see in appendix 5 are those variables that, among all variables in each equation, contributed most to the total multiple correlation coefficient.

On the basis of the information provided in appendix 5, I decided to group all eight best explanatory variables (in terms of the proportion of the variance explained) in a single equation. Appendix 6 displays the results of this final equation showing those variables that contributed most to the final solution and the matrix of intercorrelations for those variables.

Through this process of successively selecting the most important variables, through the analysis (1) of the direct effect of all sixty relevant variables, (2) of the combined effect of all relevant variables, according to ten regression equations, and finally (3) of the combined effect of the eight "best" variables in one single equation, I arrived at the next and final stage: path analysis.

In filtering down the most important factors, I found it possible not only to identify a dozen or so critical variables but also to attain a more realistic picture about the degree to which these variables describe support for terrorism in Argentina during 1973. From an initial situation of explaining over one-third of the total variance in V68, *Civil Groups*, we have been reduced to one-fourth. It is, however, more realistic, because through this process we have been able to eliminate some "noise" caused by intercorrelations among certain variables. In other words, the former figure is true, but only to the extent that it summarizes the *independent* contribution of each regression equation, whereas the latter, smaller (and less charming, from the point of view of reporting results) figure accurately describes the *combined* effect of all involved variables.

Using the information produced during the last step (appendix 6), I selected six variables for inclusion in the path analysis. The main criterion

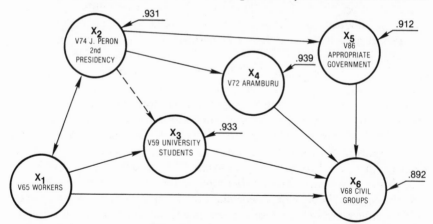

Note: Assuming no reciprocal causation, a six-variable recursive model allows for fifteen possible arrows (n!/2(n-2)!, where n is the number of variables). No arrow between variables indicates that the path coefficient for that linkage is less than .100 (six linkages are not shown here). All path coefficients shown in this model (solid arrows) are statistically significant at the .001 level.

for selection was the magnitude of their correlation coefficients with other explanatory variables, and their contribution to the variance explained. The results appear in appendix 7. The advantage of using this mode of analysis, as we shall see in a moment, is that it allows us to assign a specific weight to each path, and that is what makes the whole difference in substantive terms.

The first conclusion underscored by path analysis is that those survey respondents who expressed the most support for terrorist groups in Argentina (V68) felt closely associated with workers (V65), and gave a high degree of legitimacy to Peronist regimes (V74). This does not, however, put the question of support for terrorism to rest. We are not explaining all the variance in V68, *Civil Groups*, and even within that proportion that we do explain, the situation is not as straightforward as it seems.

It is crucial, but also potentially deceptive, to recognize the fact that the model arrived at through path analysis does not contain any variable to lend credibility to theories of "relative deprivation" (or behavioral theories in general) but instead has as its critical variables those that could be labeled structural variables. That relative deprivation is out of the question there can be no doubt. But to conclude in support of Marxist interpretations that terrorism is indeed a result of the economic exploitation of the working classes (urban proletariat and rural peasantry alike) is open to argument.

A closer look at table 1 reveals that, after the direct effect of feelings toward workers and the degree of belief in the legitimacy of Peronist regimes on support for terrorism, the most important paths among the variables

TABLE 1
Two Explanations of Popular Support for Terrorism in Argentina in 1973 (Percent)

	Feelings Toward Workers (V65)	Degree of Legitimacy of Peronist Regimes (V74)
Direct link to support for terrorism (V68)	44	39
Paths through degree of group antagonisms (V59)	51	25
Paths through degree of legitimacy of Argentine governments (V72, V86)	20	17
Paths through group antagonisms only	0	21
Paths through legitimacy only	−11	0
Total	104	102
Correlation between explanatory variables 65 and 74 and support for terrorism (V68)	.271	.205

Source: Path coefficients (beta weights) from appendix 6.

Note: The correlation between V65 and V68 (.271), as well as that between V74 and V68 (.205) is equal to the sum of all pathways from explanatory to explained variable. Pathways are computed by multiplying all path coefficients along the given path (see Norman H. Nie et al., "Social Structure and Political Participation, Part I," *American Political Science Review* 63 [1969], 812). Percentages do not add up to 100 because of rounding procedures.

used in the analysis run through the degree of group antagonism in Argentine society, as well as through feelings toward government decisions in general. Feelings toward workers contributed positively to popular support for terrorism only if they were linked to feelings toward government decisions. This means that we can attempt an interpretation that emphasizes political marginalization as an explanation for terrorism (especially in Argentina, where in 1973 many felt that there was virtually no alternative left for action) rather than explaining it as the result of class struggle alone.

Conclusions

What, then, does detailed analysis of the Argentine case indicate? First, and above anything else, it shows that in 1973 terrorism did not enjoy a high degree of support among the diverse social groups studied by Turner, as attested by the 68 percent of respondents who gave no approval whatsoever to civil groups seeking armed struggle (see note 40). Unfortunately, the 1973 survey results (see appendix 4) do not allow precise identification of the remaining 32 percent—that is, those who revealed any degree of support for terrorism: neither group membership (equation 1) nor the respondent's age, sex, education, housing, or socioeconomic level (equation 3) offered any clue as to his or her degree of support for terrorism. The only conclusion that can be drawn from this survey is that those who supported terrorist groups felt closely associated with workers and assigned high marks to Perón's regime. What has to be stressed is that these supporters are not necessarily workers, nor Peronists, since the variables which measured group affiliation and political identification did not show significant correlations with support for terrorism. This may, on the other hand, strengthen the argument that Peronism was a multiclass movement.

In what is related to the main focus of this chapter—the assessment, through survey data analysis, of the current knowledge about the *nature* of popular support for terrorist groups—two main conclusions can be drawn. First, support for terrorism among Argentines cannot be fully explained either by structural interpretations or behavioral interpretatons of this attitude; the notion of relative deprivation is especially unhelpful. People, or at least Argentines, seem to choose terrorism as a result of a rational and conscious decision regarding the possibilities for action within their political system. It should not be surprising, by now, that "in Argentina, urban terror developed in the period preceding Perón's second coming (1973),"[41] for from 1955, when Perón was expelled from office, to 1970, when the first publicized operation of the Montoneros took place—the kidnaping and murder of former President Pedro Aramburu—the political space for radical Peronism was reduced to zero. The banning of Peronism by the Argentine political and military elite was centrally responsible for the "dark age" under which Argentina, once the most prosperous nation in South America, lived before Perón's return in 1973 and after Isabelita's downfall in 1976. Closing the doors of power to dissent, even radical dissent, provided fertile ground for the flourishing of political violence from all directions.

The present situation in West Germany and Italy can be viewed from the same perspective. What makes the two nations comparable is that, despite their frequent differences in economic practices, their political systems have reached a dead end. The incorporation of the Italian Communist party in the government (or giving it tacit support, which, for all practical purposes, amounts to the same thing) represents in fact the closing of the political system. The state becomes so solid and so strong, and the political system so closed, that those citizens left outside the system cannot do anything, but they cannot have any hope for change either. The results of this type of configuration are manifest. When *Time* magazine asks, "Why should [West Germany] — its political system stable and democratic, its wealth distributed reasonably well, its society open and obsessively moderate — have produced the murderous young of the Baader-Meinhof gang and the Red Army Faction?"[42] we should look for part of the answer in the very question being posed. Could it not be that precisely because West Germany is so obsessively committed to moderation, to the point of overreacting to the slightest manifestation of radical dissent, we are now witnessing the escalation in terrorist activities?

The situation in Italy also lends credence to the conclusion that political marginalization is the most important single explanation of popular support for terrorist activities. The Red Brigades are made up of people who had believed that a revolution could be made with the Communist party. Disillusioned with the PCI, which turned toward the right, the *brigatisti* took the radical road. In their own words: "We waited for our own Communist Party to throw its weight behind the revolution, but as you know, it went the other way, to compromise with the forces of reaction."[43]

The second conclusion that can be inferred from the Argentine case is that terrorism, because its techniques and weapons are easily within reach of even the smaller groups, and because it has proved to be a viable strategy from a military standpoint, may indeed become a common alternative to action for many groups. As Jan Schreiber has indicated, "We need not deceive ourselves: we know the techniques and have already found them useful, on past occasions, ourselves. When the time comes when they are perceived to be necessary, our politicians will have ready justifications for their use. We are the terrorists of tomorrow."[44]

One example is the growing debate among environmental groups throughout the world, especially antinuclear advocates, that violence may indeed be the only alternative to counter the financial and organizational capabilities of both big business and big government. Are the demonstrations at the new Tokyo International Airport or the incidents at the Seabrook nuclear plant in New Hampshire in 1977, 1978, and 1979 an indication of things to come?[45] We shall see. At any rate, when thinking about political terrorism, we had better restrain our profound repugnance and horror, and learn instead how to cope with situations such as that which recently took place in Bologna, Italy, where

> Participants debated for two days in a stadium whether they should resort to violence. The opponents of violence won, and not a shot was fired.
>
> When one of the advocates of violence was asked why his group had bowed meekly to the nonviolent majority, he gave a revealing answer: "What we wanted to do was to raise the issue of violence publicly. We will keep doing so in rallies until the public gets used to the idea that violence is a legitimate means of reaching one's political goal. Then we will have won."[46]

Above and beyond any immediate interpretations, what the present study seems to indicate is that we have only touched the tip of a huge iceberg: we still know little about support for terrorism. The fact that even by using virtually all extant concepts on the subject we have not been able to explain half of the variance in support for terrorism in Argentina in 1973 is highly suggestive. New excursions into empirical research seem to be in order. The challenge lying ahead is overwhelming, and success or failure depend entirely upon ourselves.

APPENDIX 1
Questions from the Turner Survey of 1973 Selected for Analysis

Q1. Could you name for me a figure (or some figures) whom you especially admire? (V232 recoded, also Q3)

Q3. Still within the field of political figures, I would like you to tell me who is (or are) the most important leader(s), the best leader(s), whom you remember. (V232 recoded, also Q1)

Q4. Many times it is said that there are some groups or persons who have a lot of influence on government and take advantage of their position for personal gains, putting aside the well-being of the common people. Would you say that this is true or that it doesn't correspond to reality? (V234)

Q4A.   (For those who said "It is true" or "It is true in part"): What persons, or groups, would you say are in this situation? (V235, V236 recoded, V237, V238 recoded, V239, V240, V241 recoded)

Q5.   You probably feel, as everyone else does, that you agree more with some groups of people than with others; in other words, you feel that some people represent you better, that they think more like you do. If once again we use our portions scale, with the same criterion (0 to 49 for those groups who think less like you, 50 parts for lukewarm agreement, and from 51 to 100 parts if they think as you do), how many parts would you give to:
University students (V59)
Politicians (V60)
Peasants, farmers (V61)
Big businessmen/industrialists (V62)
Large landowners (V63)
Labor union leaders (V64)
Workers (V65)
The clergy (V66)
The armed forces (V67)
Civil groups who seek a solution through armed struggle (V68)

Q6.   Turning to another subject, some people say that all governmental decisions — whatever they are — should be respected, even those that harm us or those with which we disagree, understanding by this that the government deserves respect because it is the government, because of the respect that the institution merits. Would you say that you agree or disagree with this idea? (V69)

Q7.   Following this idea, thinking now of the different governments that the country has had, I would like you to tell me for each one of them — using our positions scale — in what proportion their decisions deserved respect. Remember that from 0 to 49 positions, it would mean that these decisions deserved to be little respected, 50 is the middle term, and from 51 to 100 the decisions deserved to be very respected. For example, the decisions taken by [the following]; in what proportion do you think that they were deserving of respect?
Juan D. Perón (first presidency) (V71)
Pedro Aramburu (V72)
Arturo Illia (V73)
Juan D. Perón (second presidency) (V74)
Alejandro Lanusse (V75)
Arturo Frondizi (V76)
Juan Carlos Onganía (V77)

Q7A.   (For those who make distinctions and assign different portions between one government and another): According to your judgment, I understand that decisions made by certain governments were more deserving of respect than those of others. Could you tell me which is the most important reason for this difference in evaluation? (V85)

Q8.   Would you say that Argentina has had in the past thirty years a type of government that has been appropriate to the needs of the country? (V86)

Q9.   In our country we have had different periods, some of more consitutional legality than others. As you know, according to different ideologies or positions, there are those who say that institutional legality is best for the country and others who think that there are other paths that are more effective. With which of these positions do you agree more? (V88 recoded)

Q11.   Some people say that in the past thirty years Argentina's prestige has decreased, while others are of the opposite opinion. To your way of thinking, would you say that it increased or decreased, in comparison with that of other countries, for example? (V95)

Q12.   Considering the revolutions the country has suffered since 1930, which of the following events would you consider as being really justifiable? And which were not?
        1930 (Fall of Irigoyen)
        1943 (Coming to power of Perón)
        1955 (Fall of Perón)
        1962 (Fall of Frondizi)
        1966 (Fall of Illia)
        1970 (Fall of Onganía) (V500)

Q13B.   There are people who feel totally proud of their country and, although they know that there are problems, try to find justification for them; on the other hand, others do not seem to see anything good. Following the rule that we have been using, thinking that the closer we get to 100 the more pride and the greater optimism is felt toward country, and the closer to 0 the less pride is felt, where would you place yourself? (V104)

Q14.   As you know, the problem of Argentina's sovereignty over the Falkland Islands has always been a basis for discussion with England. Suppose for a moment that the majority of the people who live in the Falkland Islands voted, in a free election, not to accept Argentina's dominion. Which of the following actions do you think that Argentina should follow? (V105 recoded)
        Try to convince the islands' inhabitants, stressing the advantages
            (education, medical services) they receive [from Argentina]
        Send the army and the navy to take over the islands
        Take the case to the United Nations
        Do nothing
        Other (specify)
        Don't know
        No answer

Q18A.   Do you think that these changes [in our country] should be carried out gradually or done at once, using even the power and violence of special groups? (V122)

Q19.   If you could evaluate the use of violence in Argentina up to now, violence

with the purpose of producing changes, would you say that it was used:
A lot, always
Quite frequently
Sometimes
Very infrequently
None, never
Don't know
No answer

Q19A. Do you feel that this amount of violence (that you mentioned in question 19) was necessary to bring the country to elections? (V124)

Q19B. And the use of violence in the *world in general* for the purpose of changes, would you say it was used:
A lot, always
Quite frequently
Sometimes
Very infrequently
None, never
Don't know
No answer

Q21. Turning to a different subject, you probably agree with the idea that what is good for one person may not be good for others. Suppose that *you personally* had the chance of earning much more money but this increase of income would affect the price of basic, necessary articles. In what proportion would you say that you would be willing to give up your income increase if by doing so you contributed to reducing inflation and aiding the economic development of the country? (V127)

Q22. Suppose — now on a personal level — that you are offered a much better job (better pay) but in a different country. But by leaving you know that you stop helping Argentina's growth and well-being. What would you do? (V128)

Q23. If you had been offered the same thing before, with the same conditions and results, when Argentina had a military government, what would you have done then? (V129)

Q24. Suppose now that Argentina was at war, as, for example, in the War of the Triple Alliance with Paraguay. If you had a son or brother, would you encourage him to volunteer? (V130)

Q25. We go now to a different type of question. In comparison with the way other people live in Argentina, do you think you have your just share of the good things of life, less than what is just, or more than what is just? (V131)

Q26. If we think now in a more general sense, how would you say wealth is distributed in our country? (V135)

Q27. In personal terms, would you say that your present income is [better, about the same, or worse] than ten years ago? (V136)

Q28.   And in relation to the future, for example, thinking of the next five years, do you believe that your personal situation will improve, will continue the same, or will get worse? (V137)

Q29.   Let's think now of the last thirty years; if we go over what has happened in the country in this time, would you say that there was a more favorable moment in which Argentina could have become a prosperous and strong nation in a *much faster* manner than actually occurred? (V138)

Q34.   I would like you to tell me now what education you have. (V182 to V184 recoded)

Q35.   Could you tell me now what is your occupation? (V233)

Q37A. What was or is your specific job? (This corresponds to): Housing level (V202); Socioeconomic level (V203)

Q40A. That is, you are now _____ (years old). (V210)

Q41.   Sex. (V211)

APPENDIX 2

Variables Used in the Analysis: Codes and Frequency Distribution
(DK = don't know; NA = no answer; MD = missing data)

V59, *Univ. Students* (Q5)			V63, *Large Landowners* (Q5)		
0–100	feelings	(709)	0–100	feelings	(700)
998	DK	(156)	998	DK	(161)
999	NA	(25)	999	NA	(29)
V60, *Politicians* (Q5)			V64, *Labor Union Heads* (Q5)		
0–100	feelings	(714)	0–100	feelings	(722)
998	DK	(144)	998	DK	(136)
999	NA	(32)	999	NA	(32)
V61, *Peasants/Farmers* (Q5)			V65, *Workers* (Q5)		
0–100	feelings	(752)	0–100	feelings	(804)
998	DK	(116)	998	DK	(64)
999	NA	(22)	999	NA	(22)
V62, *Big Business* (Q5)			V66, *Clergy* (Q5)		
0–100	feelings	(724)	0–100	feelings	(718)
998	DK	(138)	998	DK	(144)
999	NA	(28)	999	NA	(28)

APPENDIX 2 (continued)

V67, *Armed Forces* (Q5)

0–100	feelings	(709)
998	DK	(141)
999	NA	(40)

V68, *Civil Groups* (Q5)

0–100	feelings	(737)
998	DK	(123)
999	NA	(30)

V69, *Govt. Respect* (Q6)

1	Yes	(435)
3	It depends	(151)
5	No	(251)
8	DK	(46)
9	NA	(7)

V71, *J. Perón — 1st Pres.* (Q7)

0–100	feelings	(750)
998	DK	(107)
999	NA	(33)

V72, *Aramburu* (Q7)

0–100	feelings	(650)
998	DK	(191)
999	NA	(49)

V73, *Illia* (Q7)

0–100	feelings	(706)
998	DK	(145)
999	NA	(39)

V74, *J. Perón — 2nd Pres.* (Q7)

0–100	feelings	(759)
998	DK	(94)
999	NA	(37)

V75, *Lanusse* (Q7)

0–100	feelings	(762)
998	DK	(90)
999	NA	(38)

V76, *Frondizi* (Q7)

0–100	feelings	(728)
998	DK	(118)
999	NA	(44)

V77, *Onganía* (Q7)

0–100	feelings	(733)
998	DK	(114)
999	NA	(43)

V85, *Pos/Neg Response* (Q7A)

1	All positive	(223)
3	Positive and negative	(466)
5	All negative	(45)
8	DK	(7)
9	NA	(114)

V86, *Appropriate Govt.* (Q8)

1	Yes	(296)
3	It depends	(40)
5	No	(435)
8	DK	(110)
9	NA	(9)

V88, *Institutional Legality* (Q9)

recoded		
0	No	(82)
1	Yes	(734)
9	MD	(74)

V95, *Prestige Decreased* (Q11)

1	Increased	(194)
3	The same	(103)
5	Decreased	(517)
8	DK	(61)
9	NA	(15)

V104, *Pride in Country* (Q13B)

0–100	feelings	(769)
998	DK	(12)
999	NA	(9)

V105, *Falkland Islands* (Q14)

recoded		
0	No force	(617)
1	Force	(70)
9	MD	(203)

APPENDIX 2 (continued)

V122, *How Change* (Q18A)

1	Gradually	(653)
3	Using force, if necessary	(79)
5	Only force	(6)
8	DK	(43)
9	NA	(101)

V123, *Violence* (Q19)

1	A lot, always	(324)
2	Quite frequently	(305)
3	Sometimes	(129)
4	Very little	(70)
5	None, never	(14)
8	DK	(41)
9	NA	(7)

V124, *Violence — Necessary* (Q19A)

1	Yes	(269)
5	No	(527)
8	DK	(85)
9	NA	(9)

V125, *Violence — World* (Q19B)

1	A lot, always	(473)
2	Quite frequently	(256)
3	Sometimes	(59)
4	Very little	(15)
5	None, never	(4)
8	DK	(73)
9	NA	(10)

V127, *Income/Inflation* (Q21)

1	In good part	(489)
2	Only a little	(200)
3	Very little	(44)
4	Almost nothing	(19)
5	Nothing	(49)
8	DK	(44)
9	NA	(23)

V128, *Leave Argentina* (Q22)

1	Would go	(99)
5	Would not go	(737)
8	DK	(42)
9	NA	(12)

V129, *Leave Before* (Q23)

1	Would have gone	(155)
5	Would not have gone	(675)
8	DK	(48)
9	NA	(12)

V130, *Volunteer/War* (Q24)

1	Would encourage	(350)
5	Would not encourage	(431)
8	DK	(93)
9	NA	(16)

V131, *You — Good Life* (Q25)

1	More than just	(78)
3	What is just	(471)
5	Less than just	(295)
8	DK	(27)
9	NA	(19)

V135, *Wealth Distributed* (Q26)

1	Very unequally	(341)
2	Fairly unequally	(305)
3	Somewhat unequally	(132)
4	Quite acceptably	(67)
5	Very acceptably	(7)
8	DK	(25)
9	NA	(13)

V136, *Income Now* (Q27)

1	Much better	(80)
2	Better	(310)
3	Almost the same	(226)
4	Worse	(209)
5	Much worse	(16)
8	DK	(32)
9	NA	(17)

V137, *Income Improve* (Q28)

1	Will get much better	(208)
2	Will get somewhat better	(449)
3	Will continue the same	(95)
4	Will get somewhat worse	(33)
5	Will get much worse	(2)
8	DK	(95)
9	NA	(8)

APPENDIX 2 (continued)

V138, *Argentina Grow Faster* (Q29)

1	Yes	(558)
3	It depends	(3)
5	No	(145)
8	DK	(173)
9	NA	(10)

V182, *Education* (Q34)

recoded
0	No	(9)
1	Yes	(881)

V183, *Secondary* (Q34)

recoded
0	No	(224)
1	Yes	(666)

V184, *University* (Q34)

recoded
0	No	(651)
1	Yes	(239)

V202, *Housing Level* (Q37A)

1	High	(22)
2		(50)
3		(255)
4		(317)
5	Low	(9)
9	NA	(237)

V203, *Socioeconomic Level* (Q37A)

1	High	(287)
2		(53)
3		(250)
4		(234)
5	Low	(64)

V210, *How Old* (Q40A)

18–92	(890)

V211, *Sex* (Q41)

1	Male	(682)
2	Female	(204)

V232, *Peronists* (Q1, Q3)

recoded
0	No	(262)
1	Yes	(628)

V233, *Military* (Q35)

1	No	(860)
2	Yes	(30)

V234, *Influence on Government:* (Q4)
Persons or Groups

0	No	(270)
1	Yes	(620)

V235, *Persons: J. D. Perón* (Q4A)

0	No	(881)
1	Yes	(9)

V236, *Persons: Peronists* (Q4A)

recoded
0	No	(871)
1	Yes	(19)

V237, *Persons: Trade Unionists* (Q4A)

0	No	(879)
1	Yes	(11)

V238, *Persons: Non-Peronists* (Q4A)

recoded
0	No	(735)
1	Yes	(155)

V239, *Groups: Peronists* (Q4A)

0	No	(874)
1	Yes	(16)

V240, *Groups: Trade Unionists* (Q4A)

0	No	(833)
1	Yes	(57)

APPENDIX 2 (continued)

V241, *Groups: Non-Peronists* (Q4A)

recoded
0	No	(617)
1	Yes	(273)

V500, *Support for Revolutions* (Q12)

0	Low	(14)
1		(27)
2		(66)
3		(77)
4		(92)
5		(60)
6	High	(30)
9	MD	(524)

V501, *Businessmen* (Var 2)

0	No	(770)
1	Yes	(120)

V502, *Urban Workers* (Var 2)

0	No	(691)
1	Yes	(199)

V503, *Landowners* (Var 2)

0	No	(790)
1	Yes	(100)

V504, *Rural Workers* (Var 2)

0	No	(790)
1	Yes	(100)

V505, *Middle Class* (Var 2)

0	No	(592)
1	Yes	(298)

V506, *Retired Military Officers* (Var 2)

0	No	(817)
1	Yes	(73)

APPENDIX 3
Two-Group Discriminant Analysis of All Sixty Explanatory Variables on the Explained Variable (V68, *Civil Groups*)

Equation	Univ. "F" Test	"F" Prob.	Stand. Disc. Function	Mult. "F" Test	"F" Prob.
1. Social and Political Identification					
V232, *Peronists*	10.91	.001	− .180		
V233, *Military*	3.53	.050	− .137		
V501, *Businessmen*	10.03	.001	.533		
V502, *Urban Workers*	20.92	.001	− .125	79.59	.000
V503, *Landowners*	19.74	.001	.641		
V504, *Rural Workers*	10.17	.001	− .121		
V505, *Middle Class*	5.67	.010	.137		
V506, *Retired Military*	20.77	.001	.724		

APPENDIX 3 (continued)

Equation	Univ. "F" Test	"F" Prob.	Stand. Disc. Function	Mult. "F" Test	"F" Prob.
2. Group Antagonisms					
V59, *Univ. Students*	32.40	.001	− .527		
V60, *Politicians*	18.86	.001	− .341		
V61, *Peasants/Farmers*	2.54	NS	.304		
V62, *Big Business*	1.16	NS	.482		
V63, *Large Landowners*	0.09	NS	− .007	63.10	.000
V64, *Labor Union Heads*	21.00	.001	− .317		
V65, *Workers*	18.09	.001	− .369		
V66, *Clergy*	5.92	.010	− .156		
V67, *Armed Forces*	0.51	NS	.017		
3. Demographics (Objective Measures)					
V182, *Education*	0.01	NS	.106		
V183, *Secondary*	0.10	NS	.101		
V184, *University*	5.87	.01	− .075		
V202, *Housing Level*	20.86	.001	.084	35.26	.000
V203, *Socioeconomic Level*	27.18	.001	.678		
V210, *Age*	8.57	.01	− .307		
V211, *Sex*	6.74	.01	− .390		
4. Influence on Government — Persons					
V234, *Influence on Government*	1.42	NS	.233		
V235, *J. D. Perón*	0.19	NS	.100		
V236, *Peronists*	3.40	.05	− .465	10.43	.06
V237, *Trade Unionists*	2.25	NS	− .417		
V238, *Non-Peronists*	4.97	.05	.637		
5. Influence on Government — Groups					
V234, *Influence on Government*	1.42	NS	.039		
V239, *Peronists*	1.05	NS	.394		
V240, *Trade Unionists*	0.90	NS	.224	6.99	.03
V241, *Non-Peronists*	5.60	.05	.837		
6. Overall Expectations					
V95, *Prestige Decreased*	4.06	.05	− .973		
V104, *Pride in Country*	0.02	NS	− .127	4.29	.02
V138, *Argentina Grow Faster*	0.22	NS	.205		

ROBERTO PEREIRA GUIMARÃES

APPENDIX 3 (continued)

Equation	Univ. "F" Test	"F" Prob.	Stand. Disc. Function	Mult. "F" Test	"F" Prob.
7. Perception of Economic Conditions					
V131, *You—Good Life*	6.09	.010	.372		
V135, *Wealth Distributed*	7.95	.010	−.512	19.62	.001
V136, *Income Now*	0.14	NS	−.098		
V137, *Income Improve*	10.96	.001	.636		
8. Willingness to Sacrifice					
V127, *Income/Inflation*	1.21	NS	.338		
V128, *Leave Argentina*	3.78	.050	−.011	9.82	.04
V129, *Leave Before*	8.71	.010	−.919		
V130, *Volunteer/War*	0.07	NS	−.127		
9. Legitimacy/Legality					
V69, *Govt. Respect*	0.01	NS	.126		
V71, *J. Perón—1st Pres.*	25.33	.001	.249		
V72, *Aramburu*	2.70	NS	.062		
V73, *Illia*	0.54	NS	.000		
V74, *J. Perón—2nd Pres.*	40.23	.001	.721		
V75, *Lanusse*	0.11	NS	.060	47.34	.000
V76, *Frondizi*	1.58	NS	−.162		
V77, *Onganía*	1.30	NS	.088		
V85, *Pos/Neg Response*	0.00	NS	.109		
V86, *Appropriate Govt.*	13.84	.001	−.277		
V88, *Institutional Legality*	0.30	NS	−.137		
10. Overall Attitude Toward Violence					
V105, *Falkland Islands*	0.72	NS	−.018		
V122, *How Change*	6.05	.01	−.570		
V123, *Violence*	1.88	NS	−.227	15.81	.01
V124, *Violence—Necessary*	8.28	.01	.645		
V125, *Violence—World*	0.49	NS	−.118		
V500, *Support for Revolution*	1.64	NS	−.245		

APPENDIX 4

Simple Regression of All Sixty Explanatory Variables on the Explained Variable (V68, *Civil Groups*)

Equation	$\bar{X}$	SD	r	N	P
1. Social and Political Identification					
V232, *Peronists*	.705	.456	.080	238	.10
V233, *Military*	1.033	.180	− .081	238	.10
V501, *Businessmen*	.134	.341	− .067	238	.14
V502, *Urban Workers*	.223	.416	.076	238	.12
V503, *Landowners*	.112	.316	− .018	238	.38
V504, *Rural Workers*	.112	.316	− .001	238	.49
V505, *Middle Class*	.334	.472	.009	238	.44
V506, *Retired Military Officers*	.082	.274	− .111	238	.04
2. Group Antagonisms					
V59, *Univ. Students*	52.670	31.824	.300	208	.001
V60, *Politicians*	36.983	28.025	.096	212	.080
V61, *Peasants/Farmers*	70.545	30.604	.103	224	.060
V62, *Big Business*	43.888	30.689	− .051	217	.220
V63, *Large Landowners*	32.188	31.124	.000	212	.490
V64, *Labor Union Heads*	38.216	30.846	.046	217	.240
V65, *Workers*	74.298	28.479	.222	236	.001
V66, *Clergy*	46.210	33.374	.015	217	.410
V67, *Armed Forces*	35.524	32.102	.058	221	.190
3. Demographics (Objective Measures)					
V182, *Education*	.989	.100	.057	238	.19
V183, *Secondary*	.748	.434	− .063	238	.16
V184, *University*	.265	.441	− .040	236	.27
V202, *Housing Level*	3.369	.785	.096	198	.08
V203, *Socioeconomic Level*	2.701	1.348	.127	238	.02
V210, *Age*	41.928	13.022	− .135	238	.01
V211, *Sex*	1.230	.421	− .058	238	.18

ROBERTO PEREIRA GUIMARÃES

APPENDIX 4 (continued)

Equation	$\overline{X}$	SD	r	N	P
4. Influence on Government— Persons					
V234, *Influence on* *Government*	.696	.460	.058	238	.18
V235, *J. D. Perón*	.010	.100	−.061	238	.17
V236, *Peronists*	.021	.144	.030	238	.32
V237, *Trade Unionists*	.012	.110	.051	238	.21
V238, *Non-Peronists*	.174	.379	.011	238	.43
5. Influence on Government— Groups					
V234, *Influence on* *Government*	.696	.460	.058	238	.18
V239, *Peronists*	.018	.132	−.027	238	.33
V240, *Trade Unionists*	.064	.245	.022	238	.36
V241, *Non-Peronists*	.306	.461	−.001	238	.49
6. Overall Expectations					
V95, *Prestige Decreased*	3.793	1.693	−.055	223	.20
V104, *Pride in Country*	99.589	107.442	−.022	237	.36
V138, *Argentina Grow Faster*	1.831	1.617	.068	193	.17
7. Perception of Economic Conditions					
V131, *You—Good Life*	3.514	1.226	−.031	230	.31
V135, *Wealth Distributed*	1.936	.969	−.111	231	.04
V136, *Income Now*	2.727	1.000	.045	224	.24
V137, *Income Improve*	1.947	.757	−.057	213	.20
8. Willingness to Sacrifice					
V127, *Income/Inflation*	1.745	1.237	−.110	226	.04
V128, *Leave Argentina*	4.526	1.293	.026	221	.34
V129, *Leave Before*	4.253	1.559	−.045	218	.25
V130, *Volunteer/War*	3.207	1.990	−.123	219	.03

APPENDIX 4 (continued)

Equation	$\overline{X}$	SD	r	N	P
9. Legitimacy/Legality					
V69, *Govt. Respect*	2.560	1.757	.091	225	.080
V71, *J. Perón — 1st Pres.*	75.592	27.127	.124	216	.030
V72, *Aramburu*	36.972	31.307	− .177	191	.007
V73, *Illia*	38.611	28.909	− .113	205	.050
V74, *J. Perón — 2nd Pres.*	52.971	34.784	.155	216	.010
V75, *Lanusse*	35.326	29.547	− .009	215	.440
V76, *Frondizi*	36.571	28.984	.079	207	.120
V77, *Onganía*	28.828	28.942	− .138	210	.020
V85, *Pos/Neg Response*	2.667	1.396	− .128	216	.030
V86, *Appropriate Govt.*	3.360	1.915	.035	211	.300
V88, *Institutional Legality*	.899	.300	− .176	222	.004
10. Overall Attitude Toward Violence					
V105, *Falkland Islands*	.101	.302	− .006	185	.460
V122, *How Change*	1.233	.713	.155	194	.010
V123, *Violence*	1.984	1.010	.062	230	.170
V124, *Violence — Necessary*	3.648	1.893	− .183	219	.003
V125, *Violence — World*	1.539	.752	.122	218	.030
V500, *Support for Revolutions*	3.382	1.524	.074	102	.220

Note: $\overline{X}$ = mean
SD = standard deviation
r = correlation coefficient (zero-order)
N = number of cases for correlation
P = level of statistical significance

216

ROBERTO PEREIRA GUIMARÃES

APPENDIX 5
Multiple Regression of All Sixty Explanatory Variables
on the Explained Variable (V68, *Civil Groups*)

Equation	R	VE(%)	F	DF	P
		Summary			
1. Social and Political Identification	.156	2.4	0.82	7/230	NS
2. Group Antagonisms[a]	.469	22.0	4.86	9/155	.001
3. Demographics (Objective Measures)	.204	4.1	1.67	7/188	NS
4. Influence on Government— Persons	.099	0.9	0.46	5/232	NS
5. Influence on Government— Groups	.072	0.5	0.30	4/233	NS
6. Overall Expectations	.124	1.5	0.95	3/181	NS
7. Perception of Economic Conditions	.150	2.2	1.09	4/189	NS
8. Willingness to Sacrifice	.195	3.8	1.80	4/181	NS
9. Legitimacy/Legality[b]	.373	13.9	2.26	10/140	.01
10. Overall Attitude Toward Violence	.310	9.6	1.08	6/610	NS

a. Most important variables for equation 2:

	r	R	R²	R²Ch	B	F	P
V59, *Univ. Students*	.344	.344	.118	.118	.323	16.41	.001
V62, *Big Business*	−.140	.396	.156	.038	−.323	13.97	.001
V65, *Workers*	.249	.429	.184	.027	.149	2.41	.010
V63, *Large Land-owners*	.021	.457	.209	.025	.147	2.88	.010

b. Most important variables for equation 9:

	r	R	R²	R²Ch	B	F	P
V72, *Aramburu*	−.265	.265	.070	.070	−.220	3.86	.001
V75, *Lanusse*	.014	.311	.097	.026	.213	4.21	.001
V74, *J. Perón—2nd Pres.*	.236	.332	.110	.013	.134	1.60	.050
V86, *Appropriate Govt.*	.006	.351	.123	.012	.107	1.53	NS

Note: R = multiple correlation coefficient
VE = variance explained
F = "F" test
DF = degrees of freedom
P = level of statistical significance
r = simple correlation coefficient (zero order)
R² = multiple correlation coefficient squared (= VE)
R²Ch = change in R²
B = standardized regression coefficient (beta weight)

APPENDIX 6
Multiple Regression of the Overall Eight Best Explanatory Variables, in Terms of the Proportion of the Variance Explained on the Explained Variable (V68, *Civil Groups*)

		Regression Equation Summary			
	R	VE(%)	F	DF	P
	.502	25.3	5.63	8/133	.001

Most important variables

	r	R	R^2	R^2Ch	B	F	P
V65, *Workers*	.271	.271	.073	.073	.116	1.67	.050
V59, *Univ. Students*	.339	.375	.141	.067	.343	17.49	.001
V74, *J. Perón —*							
2nd Pres.	.205	.394	.155	.014	.084	0.82	NS
V72, *Aramburu*	− .239	.433	.188	.033	− .182	3.51	.010
V86, *Appropriate*							
Govt.	.057	.462	.214	.025	.137	2.76	.010

Note: R = multiple correlation coefficient
VE = variance explained
F = "F" test
DF = degrees of freedom
P = level of statistical significance
r = simple correlation coefficient (zero order)
R^2 = multiple correlation coefficient squared (= VE)
R^2Ch = change in R^2
B = standardized regression coefficient (beta weight)

Matrix of Intercorrelations	V68	V65	V59	V74	V72
V68, *Civil Groups*	1.000				
V65, *Workers*	.271	1.000			
V59, *Univ. Students*	.339	.357	1.000		
V74, *J. Perón — 2nd Pres.*	.205	.474	.091	1.000	
V72, *Aramburu*	− .239	− .183	− .023	− .295	1.000
V86, *Appropriate Govt.*	.057	− .117	− .092	− .356	.128

APPENDIX 7
Path Analysis (Beta Weights) of the Overall Five Best Explanatory Variables in Terms of the Proportion of the Variance Explained

Recursive Equations:

$$X_3 = .384\ x_1 - .106\ x_2 + e_3$$
$$X_4 = -.099\ x_1 - .297\ x_2 + .075\ x_3 + e_4$$
$$X_5 = .077\ x_1 - .406\ x_2 - .077\ x_3 + .054\ x_4 + e_5$$
$$X_6 = .120\ x_1 + .080\ x_2 + .318\ x_3 - .190\ x_4 + .170\ x_5 + e_6$$

Note: $X_1 = $ V65, *Workers*
$X_2 = $ V74, *J. Perón–2nd Pres.*
$X_3 = $ V59, *Univ. Students*
$X_4 = $ V72, *Aramburu*
$X_5 = $ V86, *Appropriate Govt.*
$X_6 = $ V68, *Civil Groups*

NOTES

I want to thank Frederick C. Turner for his friendly advice and encouragement and for the use of his survey data on Argentina. All I know about data analysis I owe to David E. RePass, Fred Kort, and Frank M. Andrews; needless to say, I am the only one to be blamed for any misinterpretation of Turner's data, or for any pitfalls in this analysis. I am grateful to Gary Grandon for his help in data processing, and to Betty G. Seaver, who typed the first version, especially for her editorial comments, and Waleska Iara, loyal secretary, for her expeditious typing of the final version.

1. Quoted in Henry Bienen, *Violence and Social Change: A Review of Current Literature* (Chicago: University of Chicago Press, 1972), p. 13.

2. Charles Tilly, "Collective Violence in European Perspective," in Hugh Davis Graham and Ted Robert Gurr, eds., *The History of Violence in America: Historical and Comparative Perspectives* (New York: Praeger, 1969), p. 4.

3. Clifford Payton and Robert Blackey, eds., *Why Revolution: Theory and Analyses* (Cambridge, Mass.: Schencken, 1971), p. 124.

4. Luigi Bonanate, "Um Ensaio de Terrología," *Veja* (Rio de Janeiro), 31 May 1978, p. 3.

5. "Os 226 braços da violência," *Jornal do Brasil* (Rio de Janeiro), 23 Mar. 1978, p. 12.

6. Such groups have included the People's Revolutionary Army (ERP) of Argentina, the National Liberation Army (ELN) of Bolivia, the Movement of the Revolutionary Left (MIR) of Chile, the National Liberation Front (FLN) of Paraguay, and the National Liberation Movement (MLN/Tupamaros) of Uruguay.

7. For the international links of terrorism, see Yonah Alexander, ed., *International Terrorism: National, Regional, and Global Perspectives* (New York: Praeger, 1976); J. Bowyer Bell, *Transnational Terror* (Washington, D.C.: American Enterprise Institute for Public Policy Research, 1975), pp. 72–77; Walter Z. Laqueur, *Terrorism* (Boston: Little, Brown, 1977), pp. 112–16; Albert Parry, *Terrorism: From Robespierre to Arafat* (New York: Vanguard, 1976), pp. 537–76; Paul Wilkinson, *Terrorism and the Liberal State* (Somerset, N.J.: Wiley Interscience, 1978), pp. 173–234; and Edward F. Mickolus, *Transnational Terrorism: A Chronology of Events, 1968–1979* (Westport, Conn.: Greenwood Press, 1980).

8. Anthony Burton, *Urban Terrorism: Theory, Practice, and Response* (New York: Free Press, 1975).

9. Ted Robert Gurr, "The Revolution–Social-Change Nexus: Some Old Theories and New Hypotheses," *Comparative Politics* 5 (1973), 359–92; *Why Men Rebel* (Princeton, N.J.: Princeton University Press, 1970); "Psychological Factors in Civil Violence," *World Politics* 20 (1968), 245–78.

10. Walter Z. Laqueur, *Guerrilla: A Historical and Critical Study* (Boston: Little, Brown, 1976); and *Terrorism*.

11. Jan Schreiber, *The Ultimate Weapon: Terrorists and World Order* (New York: William Morrow, 1978).

12. Paul Wilkinson, *Political Terrorism* (New York: John Wiley, 1974); "Three Questions on Terrorism," *Government and Opposition* 8 (1973), 290–312; and *Terrorism and the Liberal State*.

13. See Roberto P. Guimarães, "Science or Wishful Thinking? The Concept of Equilibrium in Human Ecology," unpublished, Department of Political Science, University of Connecticut, 1978.

14. Samuel A. Stouffer et al., *The American Soldier: Adjustment During Army Life*, vol. 1 (Princeton, N.J.: Princeton University Press, 1949).

15. See note 9.

16. See Frederick C. Turner, "The Study of Argentine Politics Through Survey Research," *Latin American Research Review* 10 (1975), 73–116.

17. For a general overview of regression, see Norman H. Nie et al., *SPSS: Statistical Package for the Social Sciences* (New York: McGraw-Hill, 1975). For a more technical explanation, refer to Hubert M. Blalock, Jr., *Social Statistics* (New York: McGraw-Hill, 1972); or Edward R. Tufte, *Data Analysis for Politics and Policy* (Englewood Cliffs, N.J.: Prentice-Hall, 1974).

18. Eldon Kenworthy, "The Function of the Little-Known Case in Theory Formation or What Peronism Wasn't," *Comparative Politics* 6 (1973), 17–45.

19. Charles Tilly, "Does Modernization Breed Revolution?" *Comparative Politics* 5 (1973), 447.

20. See notes 7–12.

21. Laqueur, *Terrorism*, pp. 110–12.

22. For example, J. Bowyer Bell, *The Myth of the Guerrilla: Revolutionary Theory and Malpractice* (New York: Alfred Knopf, 1971), pp. 52–58; and Carlos Nuñez, *The Tupamaros: Urban Guerrillas of Uruguay* (New York: Time Change Press, 1972), pp. 25–30.

23. Richard Maullin, *Soldiers, Guerrillas, and Politics in Colombia* (Lexington, Mass.: Lexington Books, 1973), p. 49.

24. See Gurr, "The Revolution–Social-Change Nexus."

25. In addition to works already cited by Bienen, Payton and Blackey, Gurr, Laqueur, and Wilkinson, this tradition is represented by Monica Blumenthal et al., *Justifying Violence: Attitudes of American Men* (Ann Arbor, Mich.: Institute for Social Research, 1972); Harry Eckstein, ed., *Internal War: Problems and Approaches* (New York: Free Press, 1964); Ivo K. Feierabend et al., "The Comparative Study of Revolution and Violence," *Comparative Politics* 5 (1973), 393–424; James C. Davies, ed., *When Men Revolt and Why: A Reader in Political Violence and Revolution* (New York: Free Press, 1971); Ernst Halperin, *Terrorism in Latin America* (Beverly Hills, Calif.: Sage, 1976); Eric Hoffer, *The True Believer: Thoughts on the Nature of Mass Movements* (New York: Harper and Row, 1951); Carl Leiden and Karl M. Schmitt, *The Politics of Violence: Revolution in the Modern World* (Englewood Cliffs, N.J.: Prentice-Hall, 1968); H. L. Nieburg, *Political Violence and the Behavioral Process* (New York: St. Martin's Press, 1969); and Joseph S. Roucek, "Sociological Elements of a Theory of Terror and Violence," *American Journal of Economics and Sociology* 21 (1962), 165–72. For further studies, see Edward F. Mickolus, comp., *The Literature on Terrorism: A Selectively Annotated Bibliography* (Westport, Conn.: Greenwood Press, 1980).

ROBERTO PEREIRA GUIMARÃES

26. Four representative works are: James Kohl and John Litt, *Urban Guerrilla Warfare in Latin America* (Cambridge, Mass.: MIT Press, 1974); Z. Martin Kowalewski and Miguel Sobrado, *Antropología de la guerrilla: Hacia la ciencia social del Tercer Mundo* (Caracas: Editorial Nueva Izquierda, 1971); Nuñez, *The Tupamaros;* and Luis Mercier Vega, *Guerrillas in Latin America: The Technique of the Counter-State* (New York: Praeger, 1969).

27. An excellent review can be found in Bienen, *Violence and Social Change.*

28. Nieburg, *Political Violence,* p. 45.

29. Bienen, *Violence and Social Change,* pp. 48–58.

30. Gurr, "Psychological Factors in Civil Violence," pp. 252–53.

31. Wilkinson, *Political Terrorism,* p. 218.

32. Turner, "The Study of Argentine Politics," pp. 74–75.

33. Karl Marx, *Wage Labour and Capital* (Moscow: Progress Publishers, 1976). Subsequent page references are given in the text in parentheses.

34. Nieburg, *Political Violence,* p. 40.

35. This is true of Nuñez, *The Tupamaros,* and, interestingly enough, may be found in virtually all newspaper reports of the Italian Red Brigade but in none on the West German Baader-Meinhof gang.

36. Mercier Vega, *Guerrillas in Latin America,* p. 67.

37. See chapters 7 and 8.

38. See Turner, "The Study of Argentine Politics Through Survey Research," which contains the original questionnaire in Spanish; the English version and the complete data set are on file at the Roper Center, University of Connecticut, Storrs, Conn. 06268.

39. I have maintained original variable numbers and names. The codes in each variable are also the same unless otherwise noted. The explained variable that measured the degree of support for terrorism in Argentina was originally V68, *Civil Groups,* and it will be thus referred to throughout the analysis. The only exception to this rule is related to social class, originally V2, *Group Membership,* and here numbered V501–V506. This was done because regression analysis assumes at least ordinal data (strictly speaking, ordinal data still violate the assumptions for regression), and *Group Membership* is a nominal scale. The way to avoid this difficulty (see, for example, Blalock, *Social Statistics,* pp. 498–502) was to create six dichotomous variables, each corresponding to one category under *Group Membership.* The only addition was V500, *Support for Revolution,* which represents an index measuring in how many instances the respondent considered revolution to have been justifiable in Argentine history.

40. Note that V68, *Civil Groups,* was recoded after a preliminary examination showed that V68 was highly skewed: of 737 respondents who expressed their feelings, on a scale from zero to 100, toward civil groups who seek armed struggle, 499 answered zero. I faced two alternatives: to log V68 or to limit the analysis to those assigning answers 1–100. I chose the latter after examining the results of discriminant analysis (appendix 3), which clearly indicated a difference between respondents answering zero from those answering 1–100; zero answers have been excluded.

41. Laqueur, *Terrorism,* p. 182.

42. Lance Morrow, "Terrorism: Why West Germany?" *Time,* 19 Dec. 1977, p. 37.

43. Quoted in Raymond Carroll, "Inside The Red Brigades," *Newsweek,* 15 May 1978, p. 44.

44. Schreiber, *The Ultimate Weapon,* p. 207.

45. Numerous acts of terrorism have reportedly been carried out by environmental groups. In September 1978 the FBI discovered an ex-navy diver, James R. Rose, a submarine, several photographs of Russian and Japanese whaling ships, and enough C-4 plastic explosive to blow up a whole whaling fleet. An environmental organization was apparently involved ("A Whale of a Tale," *Newsweek,* 18 Sept. 1978, p. 15). In April 1979 the French Ecologists Group claimed responsibility for several bombings at Seyne-sur-Mer, near Toulon (*Jornal do Brasil,* 11 Apr.

1979). In May 1979 the Surry, Virginia, nuclear reactor was sabotaged with a corrosive substance in its fuel deposit *(O Globo*, 10 May 1979). Also in May 1979 Dr. Giuseppe Ghetti,
health officer for Seveso, Italy, was shot; he had been accused of failing to protect the region's
workers from occupational carcinogens and local residents from industrial pollution. Poison
gases, especially dioxin, had accidentally escaped from the Hoffman–La Roche factory at Seveso
in 1978; a factory executive's home was bombed on the anniversary of the event in 1979. In
what has come to be termed "environmental terrorism," activists in 1981 took a bucket of
earth infected with anthrax bacilli to the British Chemical Defense Establishment in Wiltshire
and another one to the annual conference of the Conservative party in Blackpool. The soil
came from an uninhabited island off the Scottish coast where the British government, fear-
ing the Nazis were about to launch biological warfare, had authorized anthrax tests in 1941
(Time, 9 Nov. 1981, pp. 55–56). Whereas the Nazi threat is long over, political leaders and
researchers are now being threatened with the dangerous product of British tests performed
forty years ago.

46. Henry Tanner, "With Moro Abduction, Italian Terrorists Achieve Goal of Shaking the
State," *New York Times*, 19 Mar. 1978, p. 3.

10

FREDERICK C. TURNER

Entrepreneurs and *Estancieros* in Perón's Argentina: Cohesion and Conflict Within the Elite

In the Third World nations of Latin America, large landowners and executives of the biggest firms are often perceived as the backbone of the private-sector elite, unified in their political interests and demands. But how homogeneous are their interests in fact? If majorities in each sector have come together to demand military intervention against populist governments that promise income redistribution and fail to maintain strong economic growth, is there a series of less grandiose issues on which these elites still differ? Do their perceptions of each other, as well as differences in background and work habits, separate them more than is commonly supposed?

Argentina is a country where these issues can be especially well investigated. Given the fundamental importance of agriculture to the nation's trade and wealth, landowners there retain considerable status, while the industrial push since the 1940s has created a group of national business executives with increasing economic clout and political concern. In the context of the great expectations created by Juan Domingo Perón, one of the most significant populists and rallying leaders of the twentieth century, we can analyze the plethora of contrasting elite support patterns for the more than a dozen governments to rule the country since Perón's first rise to power in 1945. Since a wide range of elite and mass survey research has been conducted in Argentina, we can specify far more about political attitudes and self-perceptions among citizens of this country than we can for most others. By comparing the behavior and the views of the business and landowning elites, we can better understand the degree to which their interests and positions have actually been compatible, and on what issues.

The Presumption of Closeness

From a variety of past studies, representing vastly different ideological perspectives, it has been easy to conclude that large landowners (*estancieros,*   223 who typically produce cattle or grain or both) and business executives from the largest corporations *(empresarios)* form one closely interconnected elite. In the finest study that we have of these groups, for example, José Luis de Imaz points to accommodation between the landholding and the business sectors. Once business executives acquire wealth, he says, they buy land and seek status; "they seek to identify themselves with the criteria, the points of view, and the arguments of the rural sector."[1] Another study of the Argentine elite lumps both large ranchers and urban *empresarios* into a single "business sector," concluding that, while the former part of this "sector" has more independence and status, both parts of it "are becoming increasingly articulate politically."[2] Closeness of interests also appears in the 1965–1966 survey of Argentine entrepreneurs by Fernando Henrique Cardoso; when they were asked whether important divergences existed between the interests of the rural and the industrial sectors, 51 percent said "no," with only 20 percent saying "yes," and another 20 percent saying "sometimes."[3] In Brazil as well as in Argentina, Cardoso found that both the "nationalist-populist" entrepreneurs who are in low-technology, mass-consumption industries, and those he defines as the "internationalizing bourgeoisie" in the most modern, high-technology areas, find it in their interest to follow "accommodationist" policies, to try to go as far as possible to meet the demands of whatever vigorous political group is in power. This finding — or the fact that the business executives perceive little divergence of interest with the rural sector — does not mean, however, that deeply seated antagonisms are impossible, because political interests and strategies often converge.

Both general textbooks and specialized monographs frequently agree with these conclusions. A popular history written by one of the most respected North American scholars of Argentine affairs thus talks of "the neo-oligarchs . . . of the landowning-commercial class."[4] The interests of less prominent and powerful sectors are often seen as distinct from those of the privileged and affluent *estancieros* and *empresarios*. Students of Argentine business, for instance, contend that nationalism arose among those employed in small and medium-sized businesses of the interior, partly because their economic survival and prosperity depended upon expanding and integrating the national market, and partly because they felt excluded from the rich world of those in the import and export trade, the world of both the agriculturalists and the foreign-oriented industrialists whose lives revolved around the trading center of Buenos Aires.[5]

With even more intellectual depth, revisionist historians have recently come to stress an unexpectedly high level of agreement between landowners and industrialists on public policies and socioeconomic orientations. Boris Fausto's reinterpretation of the revolution of 1930 in Brazil, for example, has deflated the old interpretation that an emerging industrial bourgeoisie brought Getúlio Vargas to the presidency over the opposition of rural power brokers.[6] Basing his thesis on both extensive interviewing of the elites and on a detailed appraisal of their policy preferences at the time, Fausto shows that the industrial sector was then too small to impose a new leader on the country. Instead, industrialists went along with the positions of the "coffee elite," which was not in fact opposed to Vargas's general orientation. Brazilian experience did not necessarily mirror Argentina's; more fundamentally, the confrontations of the 1930s do not mean that considerable antagonism cannot exist in the 1970s between these groups. But this revisionist historiography at least calls into question some earlier assumptions of differences between these sectors of the elite.

Survey Findings on Group Distinctions

In the face of the assumptions of homogeneity of attitudes between the landholding and the business elites, considerable evidence — historical and contemporary — points in the opposite direction. Not only are there major differences between them, but also, splits within each group on vital issues reduce the level of consensus still further. Historically, the most central struggle of the nineteenth century was that between Buenos Aires–based *unitarios*, who profited from international trade and a form of "democracy" that they could control, and the *federales* of the interior, whose domestic industries and political interests met defeat in the long struggle after independence.[7] Today, major conflicts of interest remain among those aggregations of business executives who are primarily oriented to the international economy, either through their ties to multinational corporations or through their primary activity in importing or exporting, and those who are more narrowly national or local in their markets and concerns. Institutionally, the split appears between the internationalist Unión Industrial Argentina, representing the largest firms, and the more nationalistic Confederación General Económica, with its base in small and medium-sized enterprises.

Even when we turn to the attitudes and self-perceptions of executives of the largest Argentine and foreign firms, whose orientation to foreign markets is most like that of the *estancieros*, we observe a degree of differentiation that we could not anticipate on the basis of the assumptions outlined above. If landowners and industrialists are asked how close they feel to various groups in Argentine society, including their own, the truly striking difference is in the business elite's alienation from the landowners.

This orientation emerged very clearly in a survey that I directed in Argentina in 1973. Supported by the National Science Foundation and the National Endowment for the Humanities, the survey focused upon six groups: urban workers, rural workers, the middle class, military officers of the rank of colonel and above, *estancieros*, and business executives. The executives interviewed were drawn from those in the top three positions in the 120 largest firms in the country, while the hundred *estancieros* interviewed came from a representative sample of the members of the Sociedad Rural Argentina, the association of the most powerful landowners.[8] The survey was conducted in August and September, 1973, during Juan Perón's final campaign for the presidency, and it covered greater Buenos Aires, Córdoba, Rosario, and a series of small towns in the interior of the country. The interviews were done by Instituto IPSA, a leading survey research firm in Argentina.[9]

The survey contained a large number of open questions, and these frequently provided answers that were both interesting and revealing. For example, many industrialists gave their occupations as *empleado gerente* (employee director), revealing in their own perceptions the classic difference between early and late capitalism, that is, between the earlier era when business executives (like contemporary *estancieros*) could own their companies, and later times in which they have become merely chief administrators.

One objective of the survey was to measure the subjective sense of closeness and loyalty that members of each group had for people in the other groups, and the responses to open questions on this issue were sometimes quite significant. While we would expect many *peones* (rural workers) to be emotionally tied to the landowners for whom they toiled, the survey demonstrated that the landowners often had a surprisingly high level of admiration for the *peones*. The ties of loyalty and admiration were more mutual than one-sided. Thus *peones* frequently named their boss as the figure they admired most, but, while it was less common, this was also true of what some *estancieros* said of their *peones*. One of the owners — a full-time rather than an absentee rancher who had taken over ranch operations from his father — spoke of one of his workers as the person he most respected, saying, "I admire him for being conscientious in his work, for leading a life of sacrifice for the good of his family."[10]

In the coding stage of the research project, differences in social class sometimes made for amusing contrasts in this "personal loyalty" response. The majority of those giving this response in several open questions were workers who felt a personal attachment to Juan Perón. They said, for instance: "My family is fanatically for him"; "It is as though he lived in my house"; "The first shoes that I put on my feet were a present from him"; "He is like a father to me." These workers saw Perón as a *padrino*, a godfather; curiously, it proved necessary to place in the same category the response of a well-to-do *estanciero*, whose actual godfather was one of the famous Argentines often mentioned in the survey.

In addition to answering open questions, respondents were also asked to give their feelings of warmth toward a variety of groups in Argentine society, using a scale of 0 to 100, with the higher numbers reflecting greater warmth and attachment. Representing mean scores, table 1 indicates the results of this question for the *estancieros* and business executives. These two groups proved to be strikingly close in their feelings about university students, politicians, labor union chiefs, and guerrillas, described in the survey as "civil groups who seek a solution through armed struggle."

TABLE 1

Argentine Business Executives' and Landowners' Identification with Major Social Groups, 1973 (mean scores on a 100-point scale)

Question: You probably feel, as everyone else does, that you agree more with some groups of people than with others; in other words, you feel that some people represent you better, that they think more like you do. If once again we use our portions scale, with the same criterion (0 to 49 for those groups who think less like you, 50 parts for lukewarm agreement, and from 51 to 100 parts if they think as you do), how many parts would you give to:

	Business Executives (N = 120)	Landowners (N = 100)
University students	49.6	45.5
Politicians	37.9	40.7
Peasants, farmers	51.5	68.9
Big businessmen/industrialists	57.6	58.9
Large landowners	36.8	67.7
Labor union leaders	41.0	38.7
Workers	57.9	64.2
The clergy	42.8	55.9
The armed forces	34.7	49.0
Civil groups who seek a solution through armed struggle	29.0	33.3

Source: Question 5, survey conducted by Frederick C. Turner in greater Buenos Aires, Córdoba, Rosario, and small towns of rural Argentina, in August and September 1973; more complete data available from the Roper Center, the University of Connecticut, Storrs, Conn. 06268.

As might be expected, the landowners felt far closer than did the business executives toward rural laborers (who work for the landowners), urban blue-collar workers (who in the more impersonal industrial work situation are not so close to their bosses), the clergy (the rural elite being more traditionally religious), and the military (who seemed the best hope of aiding agricultural exporting interests). In general, the *estancieros* were more empathetic than the *empresarios*, with notably higher mean scores on the 100-point scale. In a rather striking case in point, the *estancieros* even reported that they felt slightly closer to the business group than the latter reported feeling toward themselves.

This was decidedly not so in the obverse situation. The mean score for the landowners' feelings of closeness to their own group was 67.7, while that of the business executives toward this group was only 36.8. Table 2 presents the F measure from discriminant analysis of the difference between these two elites' professed identification of interests and outlook with each group mentioned in the question. Although discriminant analysis has been more used in educational psychology than in political science, in this case it powerfully indicates to what extent we could predict whether respondents belonged to the landowning or business elites from their responses to the question on identification with various groups.[11] As table 2 reveals, in responses toward most groups we could not differentiate between them at all. The 3.58 F figure for attitudes toward rural workers allows some discrimination, but the real giveaway comes in the 13.66 F for attitudes toward large landowners. With statistical significance at the .003 level, we could correctly predict whether the respondent was in business or in agriculture some 87.5 percent of the time.

TABLE 2

Differences in the Identification of Business Executives and Landowners with Various Groups in Argentina, 1973

Question: You probably feel, as everyone else does, that you agree more with some groups of people than with others; in other words, you feel that some people represent you better, that they think more like you do. If once again we use our portions scale, with the same criterion (0 to 49 for those groups who think less like you, 50 parts for lukewarm agreement, and from 51 to 100 parts if they think as you do), how many parts would you give to:

	F
Large landowners	13.66
Peasants, farmers	3.58
Civil groups who seek a solution through armed struggle	2.79
The armed forces	2.45
Labor union leaders	1.82
Workers	0.24
University students	0.20
Politicians	0.12
Big businessmen/industrialists	0.08
The clergy	0.01

Source: Taken from question 5, survey conducted by Frederick C. Turner in greater Buenos Aires, Córdoba, Rosario, and small towns of rural Argentina, in August and September 1973; more complete data available from the Roper Center, the University of Connecticut, Storrs, Conn. 06268.

Why do business executives perceive so much distance between themselves and the landowners? Hypothetical interpretations, to be tested with other data in other contexts, include: (1) historical displacement, (2) competition, (3) jealousy, and (4) meritocratic orientations.[11] First, in a Marxist sense, these two segments of the Argentine elite may have developed opposing attitudes from their separate relationships to very different productive processes, those of the countryside and of the factory, so that the urban elite of modern capitalism naturally resents the old, landed elite whose power it has come to challenge. In *The German Ideology*, Marx and Engels wrote:

> The first premise of all human history is, of course, the existence of living human individuals. . . . What they are, therefore, coincides with their production, both with *what* they produce and with *how* they produce. Hence what individuals are depends on the material conditions of their production. . . . Morality, religion, metaphysics, and all the rest of ideology as well as the forms of consciousness corresponding to these, thus no longer retain the semblance of independence. They have no history, no development; but men, developing their material production and their material intercourse, alter, along with this their actual world, also their thinking and the products of their thinking. It is not consciousness that determines life, but life that determines consciousness.[12]

The working conditions and life situations of the *estancieros* and *empresarios* differ greatly, and their contrasting "consciousness" — including their perceptions of each other — may derive significantly from this.

Under a second interpretation, one stressing the competition between these groups, those in business may feel that the landowners get more out of the Argentine system than they deserve, that their material reward is out of proportion to their contribution. In contrast, with the economic and psychological security that comes from owning property, the *estancieros* themselves may feel less competition and distance from those in business. Third, the business community may jealously resent the high social status of the landed elite. While *estancieros* often live in Buenos Aires and frequently take a hand in business, a fact which helps to explain their close feeling for the business elite, business executives cannot so easily gain the land and status of the traditional Argentine elite. Finally, as a group whose members have worked hard to earn and maintain their positions, the business elite in the sample may resent the land and wealth that is the birthright for so many members of the Sociedad Rural. These four interrelated interpretations would, if true, help to explain a considerable degree of antagonism between the two groups.

Not only these summary statistics, but also the richness of individual responses to the open questions in the survey, prove the conventional stereotypes of the groups to be highly inadequate. There were, of course, a few members of each group who fit a familiar stereotype. One *estanciero*, for example, attacked Juan Perón as a demagogue who divided the great Argentine family, denounced Arturo Frondizi as a "leftist," and even claimed that General Pedro Aramburu's weakness had allowed dangerous leftist infiltration.[13] In contrast to this image of the right-wing oligarch, however, several other *estancieros* were of an unequivocal Marxist orientation, admiring Lenin and Mao Tse-tung, denouncing patriotism and religion, and calling for a revolution that would undercut the position of their own social group. One young woman who had inherited lands from her father was of this persuasion; perhaps because she had studied social science, she vehemently denounced Yankee imperialism and "the right-wing group around Perón." Interestingly, she felt personally aggrieved economically, saying that her economic condition was worse than it had been ten years before and that she had less than her fair share of the good things of life "because of those who have more."[14] In partial contrast to this respondent, women of higher educational attainment — the university-educated — tended to be not only more cynical regarding the legitimacy of Argentine political institutions but also more politically conservative, apparently as a result of both their higher class status and the more critical attitudes developed by their education.[15]

Some Areas of Agreement

The *empresarios* and *estancieros* in the survey agreed in four significant ways: in their attitudes toward political leaders, their nationalist orienta-

TABLE 3
Argentines' Admiration for Prominent Figures in 1973 (Percent)

Question: Could you name for me a figure (or some figures) whom you especially admire?

	Juan Perón	World-famous Argentine Physicians	Foreign World-famous Scientists	No One
Business executives (N = 120)	3.5	9.6	7.8	15.7
Landowners (N = 100)	7.1	12.1	5.1	11.1
Military officers (N = 73)	9.9	12.7	1.4	5.6
Middle-class persons (N = 298)	19.1	3.7	2.3	8.4
Rural workers (N = 100)	22.0	0	0	21.0
Urban workers (N = 199)	40.6	0.5	0	8.1

Source: Question 1, survey conducted by Frederick C. Turner in greater Buenos Aires, Córdoba, Rosario, and small towns of rural Argentina, in August and September 1973; more complete data available from the Roper Center, the University of Connecticut, Storrs, Conn. 06268.

tions, their class background, and their clear tendency to interpret reality in terms of self-interest. The landowners and business executives were, as expected, less favorable toward Juan Perón than were urban and rural workers, the middle class, or even high-ranking military officers, but in general the *estancieros* and *empresarios* also turned out to be more alienated from possible hero figures than were members of the latter groups. As table 3 illustrates, high proportions of respondents in both groups said voluntarily that they admired no one at all, either historical or contemporary. Curiously, rural workers also recorded a high negative response on this question, suggesting little consideration of the issues; however, more than one in ten of the highly educated business executives and landowners also simply found few persons to admire.

What relationship does the evident cosmopolitanism of these two elites have to their views of foreigners and foreign investment, to their perception of their own self-interest? It has often been assumed, as Frank Brandenburg put it in the era of the Alliance for Progress, that "foreigners are welcomed by the most progressive Latin American industrialists," although the latter might be "temporarily engulfed in the tide of excessive nationalism."[16] Data from the 1973 survey, summed up in table 4, reveal several ways in which this view should be modified. The proportion of business executives interviewed who espoused a form of nationalism that welcomed foreigners was higher than for any group save the large landowners, and it was three times higher than for urban or rural workers. But still, only about one-third of the people in business took this position, com-

TABLE 4
Argentines' Attitudes Toward Foreigners as a Measure of Nationalistic Feelings (Percent)

Question: Also, there are different ideas on whether it helps the country more to have a nationalism with a favorable predisposition toward what is foreign, for example in the investment of capital, or whether it is better to have a more closed nationalism. With which of these postures do you agree most?

	Well Disposed to Foreigners	Tolerant of Foreigners	Hostile to All Foreigners
Business executives (N = 120)	35.0	61.7	0.8
Landowners (N = 100)	42.0	52.0	2.0
Military officers (N = 73)	31.5	64.4	0
Middle-class persons (N = 298)	17.8	64.6	5.7
Rural workers (N = 100)	11.0	31.0	19.0
Urban workers (N = 199)	12.1	56.3	10.6

Source: Question 16, survey conducted by Frederick C. Turner in greater Buenos Aires, Córdoba, Rosario, and small towns of rural Argentina, in August and September 1973; more complete data available from the Roper Center, the University of Connecticut, Storrs, Conn. 06268.

pared to nearly two-thirds who merely tolerated foreigners. Social class standing turned out to be a major determinant of attitudes toward foreigners, as all three elite groups were far more accepting of foreigners than were the workers, with the middle class far less disposed toward foreigners than the elite, yet not as hostile toward them as urban or rural workers.

Concern over foreign business interests did not uniformly coincide with a leftist stance in politics, as some of those who were preoccupied over appearances of foreign exploitation were conservative citizens who in other ways did not appear radical at all. One such was a middle-class daughter of a truck driver, herself employed in a candy factory, whose values stood out clearly when she said that she most admired her fiancé, "because he is a responsible boy, considering his age." Nevertheless, given her view of foreign firms, she said that the most important change for Argentina would be "that the bosses of factories and plants be Argentine, not the foreigners who fill their pockets and then skip the country."[17]

These findings are confirmed in a 1971 survey of 112 leading Argentine business executives. As James Petras reports, many of his respondents advocated that Argentines rather than foreigners should hold key executive positions, but they widely accepted both heavy foreign investment in Argentina and U.S. political leadership in the Western Hemisphere. Petras concluded that "in the multitude of day-to-day policy choices confronting Argentine industrial executives, there need be no person or group representing U.S. interests on the premises to keep watch. Rather, the imperial presence is incorporated into the political culture of a dependent Argentina."[18]

Given the nature of the Petras sample, we must be cautious in interpreting the results. Like my own survey, it concentrated on top executives in the leading firms, seeking to interview the presidents or top executives available in the largest 150 firms in terms of the number of employees and sales in the year before the survey was conducted. Reflecting the views of Unión Industrial members, it thus says nothing about executives in smaller firms, those of the Confederación General Económica. But, since 45 out of the 150 executives targeted refused to answer sensitive questions on economic dependency, it can be assumed that the sample is biased, if at all, in the direction of those executives in larger firms who are less critical of foreign investment.

In the 1973 survey, the top executives and landowners interviewed also proved to be similar in their class backgrounds. Because it is virtually impossible to gather accurate personal income statistics in Argentina, table 5 gauges occupational status and intergenerational mobility without reference to income data. Instead, respondents' occupations are compared with those of their fathers. While it is more natural for landowners to have inherited their means of livelihood than it is for business executives, and while a disproportionate number (nearly a third) of the major industrialists in my survey came from urban white-collar or blue-collar families, most members of each group came from elite backgrounds other than the military. The inherited status of the *estancieros* is somewhat higher, with some 55 percent of them being the children of *estancieros* or major business executives. Substantial proportions of each group came from upper-middle-class professional families and the independently employed bourgeoisie.

TABLE 5
Occupations of the Fathers of Business Executives and Landowners (Percent)

Question: "What is or was the occupation of your father?"

	Business Executives (N = 120)	Landowners (N = 100)
Military service	3	2
Business	14	18
Landowning	5	37
White-collar work	20	6
Independent employment	32	19
Government employment	6	3
Blue-collar work	9	1
Rural labor	1	2
Professional employment	9	12

Source: Question 36, survey conducted by Frederick C. Turner in greater Buenos Aires, Córdoba, Rosario, and small towns of rural Argentina, in August and September 1973; more complete data available from the Roper Center, the University of Connecticut, Storrs, Conn. 06268.

Like the members of other social classes and occupational groupings, those under study here interpreted national problems and needs in terms of their own self-interest. When Argentine industrialists proclaim their sense of public responsibility, for example, they often do so in terms of the successful fulfillment of their entrepreneurial activities. As Elvio Coelho, the president of the Unión Industrial Argentina, declared during the campaign for the elections of September 23, 1973, "Businessmen are conscious of their social responsibility, and because of that responsibility they must give priority to efficiency, in order to offer more and better jobs and an optimum wage."[19] In contrast, blue-collar workers seldom call for harder work, new attitudes, or coordinated economic policies. Instead, like the taxi driver who was the son of a petty officer in the navy, they demand more *benefits* from government; as he said, so "that there be more work for everyone, that things cost less so the money is enough, and that everyone have a house."[20] Even more fancifully, a retired factory worker asked government "to improve the situation of the worker, give him welfare, so that everyone can own a ranch and nobody has to pay rent."[21]

Similarly, *estancieros* as a group were more concerned for the personal profits that would allow the maintenance of their life style than they were with raising production for the nation as a whole. Their responses showed them to be thoughtful and cultured, with time for reading, music, and reflection. Many listed novelists as admired figures, with high ratings also going to Mozart, Beethoven, and Wagner. Under Argentina's system of export taxation that discourages greater production, *estancieros* have remained more interested in maintaining steady profits for themselves and indulging their cultural tastes than in instituting costly measures to increase productivity, measures that would substantially increase the number of cattle in Argentina, thus aiding the country by providing more beef for the domestic market and for export while also eventually repaying ranchers for the costs of innovation. As one of their most sympathetic critics wrote after the presidential victory of Héctor Cámpora in 1973, "The beef barons of Argentina have always been considered a privileged class, shut away in their own little world and completely out of touch with reality. The situation today shows this to be true, since the average livestock breeder is as inefficient as he was 15 years ago and except in very isolated cases, has made no effort to avoid the impending debacle."[22] Because self-interest is so basic to the perceptions of *estancieros*, it shapes their attitudes toward such nationalist leaders as Juan Perón and such issues as foreign investment. It also underscores the reasons why perceptions should vary according to social class.

Conclusions

What implications are raised by these findings in Argentina? In part, they confirm the historical, leftist interpretations that stress differences between the "feudal" and the capitalist elites, the rural landowners who continue the traditions of the precapitalist era and the industrial leaders of modern capitalism.[23] While the landowners may adopt an urban life style and feel close to the business sector, the leading members of the business community feel a great distance between themselves and the rural elite with traditional power and status. However, the survey also points to a number of areas of agreement. Similar in their backgrounds, in their attitudes toward Perón and other figures, in their view of foreigners, and in a fundamental stance based upon self-interest, landowners and business executives are far more like one another than they are like other groups in Argentine society. Thus their policy differences are likely to remain less than one would expect from looking merely at the entrepreneurs' antipathy toward the *estancieros*.

NOTES

A shorter version of this chapter appeared as "La élite empresarial y la terrateniente de Argentina: ¿ Coincidencias o divergencias de intereses?" *América Latina* 42, no. 6 (1981), 41–53. It is reprinted with permission.

1. José Luis de Imaz, *Los que mandan* (Buenos Aires: Editorial Universitaria de Buenos Aires, 1967), p. 160.

2. Julio A. Fernández, *The Political Elite of Argentina* (New York: New York University Press, 1970), p. 27.

3. Fernando Henrique Cardoso, *Ideologías de la burguesía industrial en sociedades dependientes (Argentina y Brasil)*, 2nd ed. (Buenos Aires: Siglo Vientiuno Argentina Editores, 1972), p. 146. See also Fernando Henrique Cardoso, *Política e desenvolvimento em sociedades dependentes: Ideologías do empresariado industrial argentino e brasileiro* (Rio de Janeiro: Zahar Editores, 1971); Julio Broner and Daniel E. Larriqueta, *La revolución industrial argentina* (Buenos Aires: Editorial Sudamericana, 1969); Carlos Ramil Cepeda, *Crisis de una burguesía dependiente: Balance económico de la "Revolución Argentina," 1966–1971* (Buenos Aires: Ediciones La Rosa Blindada, 1972); Esteban Rey, *Frigerio y la traición de la burguesía industrial* (Buenos Aires: A. Peña Lillo, Editor, 1959); and Oscar Braun, ed., *El capitalismo argentino en crisis* (Buenos Aires: Siglo Vientiuno Argentina Editores, 1973).

4. Thomas F. McGann, *Argentina: The Divided Land* (New York: Van Nostrand, 1966), p. 40.

5. Dardo Cúneo, *Comportamiento y crisis de la clase empresaria*, 2nd ed. (Buenos Aires: Editorial Pleamar, 1967), p. 281.

6. Boris Fausto, *A revolução de 1930: Historiografia e história* (São Paulo: Editora Brasiliense, 1970).

7. See Guillermo A. O'Donnell, *Modernization and Bureaucratic-Authoritarianism: Studies in South American Politics* (Berkeley: Institute of International Studies, University of California, 1973), pp. 118–24.

8. An excellent discussion of the position of the Sociedad Rural in Argentine politics may be found in Imaz, *Los que mandan*, ch. 5.

9. For a detailed description of the survey, a statement of the preliminary results, and a copy of the questionnaire, see Frederick C. Turner, "The Study of Argentine Politics Through Survey Research," *Latin American Research Review* 10, no. 2 (Summer, 1975), 73–116.

10. Respondent 3068, question 1a, Turner survey.

11. In the generation of these explanations, the thoughtful assistance of Elizabeth Wingate Turner proved to be most useful.

12. From Karl Marx and Frederick Engels, *Collected Works* (New York: International Publishers, 1976), vol. 5, pp. 31–32, 36–37.

13. Respondent 3064, question 7a, Turner survey.

14. Respondent 3073, questions 4a, 25, 25a, 27, and 44, Turner survey.

15. See David G. Roger, "Variations of Political Opinion by Sex, Social Class, and Education: A Study of Argentina" (unpublished, University of Connecticut, 1979).

16. Frank Brandenburg, *The Development of Latin American Private Enterprise* (Washington, D.C.: National Planning Association, 1964), p. 46.

17. Respondent 5131, questions 1 and 17, Turner survey.

18. James Petras and Thomas Cook, "Dependency and the Industrial Bourgeoisie: Attitudes of Argentine Executives Toward Foreign Economic Investments and U.S. Policy," in James Petras, ed., *Latin America: From Dependence to Revolution* (New York: John Wiley, 1973), p. 163.

FREDERICK C. TURNER

19. *La Nación* (Buenos Aires), 18 Aug. 1973.

20. Respondent 2014, question 17, Turner survey.

21. Respondent 2023, question 17, Turner survey.

22. Clifford Potter, "Camp Comments: Beef Barons Still Out of Touch," *Buenos Aires Herald*, 19 June 1973.

23. As Boris Fausto puts it, "At the heart of the thinking of the left, with deep roots that have been shaken today, Brazilian society is characterized as having two sectors: one precapitalist, located in the country, with relationships that are predominantly feudal or semifeudal, whose typical expression is the *latifundia;* [and] the capitalist and urban, which has formed an industrial bourgeoisie in the great cities" *(A revolução de 1930,* p. 12).

FREDERICK C. TURNER

Epilogue

At the opening of *The Eighteenth Brumaire of Louis Bonaparte,* Karl Marx
wrote:

> Hegel remarks somewhere that all facts and personages of great
> importance in world history occur, as it were, twice. He forgot to
> add: the first time as tragedy, the second as farce. . . . Men make
> their own history, but they do not make it just as they please;
> they do not make it under circumstances chosen by themselves,
> but under circumstances directly encountered, given and
> transmitted from the past.[1]

In various ways, these thoughts apply to the public career of Juan Perón,
who was just beginning his second term as president of Argentina on the
hundredth anniversary of the publication of *The Eighteenth Brumaire.*

There is, in retrospect, both greatness and tragedy in the career of Perón.
He enjoyed the charisma that touched such other leaders of our century
as Charles De Gaulle or John F. Kennedy. Like De Gaulle, Perón wanted
to reshape the political parameters of his nation, to resist the forces of the
extreme left by undercutting them, as a general of the army might be expected to do. Like Jack Kennedy, Perón enjoyed "the good life" — affluence,
deference, the company of beautiful women — but, even more than Kennedy, Perón tied his political fortunes to making "the good life" more
available to all citizens, spreading the benefits of the natural wealth of
Argentina beyond the elites that had traditionally enjoyed its greatest
benefits. Perón was not an ideologue; he set down no blueprint for achieving
his objectives. But he was genuinely committed to them, and others took
heart from his commitment. Furthermore, he tried to achieve reform
through democratic norms and electoral support. He was scrupulously
careful to follow the letter of the law in altering the Constitution, even
though he demonstrated less concern with democratic procedures in his
second presidency after 1952 and even though he encouraged those who
risked and gave their lives fighting for his return to Argentina in 1973.

If the tragedy of Perón came in his failure to realize "the good life" for
underprivileged Argentines during his first two terms as president from 1946

to 1955, then the farce came at the conclusion of his third term, beginning after eighteen years of exile in 1973 and cut short by his death in 1974. He attempted, in the third term, to avoid the failures of the first: not merely to distribute the national wealth, as he had done in the 1940s, but to enlarge it for the benefit of all; to create a consensus on national goals including both labor and management, one upheld by the military. Unfortunately, he was not able to withstand what Wayne Smith has called "the pressures from within his own household," that is, was unable to keep his third wife, Isabel, from succeeding him, to be counseled by her mentor, José López Rega. Profound economic deterioration under the government of Isabel Perón from 1974 to 1976 led to a military coup and governments by a series of generals: General Jorge Videla from 1976 until 1981, General Roberto Viola from March until December 1981, followed by General Leopoldo Galtieri. In June 1982, after the conclusion of the short but tragic Falklands/Malvinas war with Great Britain, Galtieri was replaced by a retired army general, Reynaldo Bignone.

Military rule brought stiff repression of Peronists but no great amelioration of the economic situation. Between 1976 and 1981, Amnesty International has declared that security forces and paramilitary death squads abducted at least 6,800 persons, the so-called *desaparecidos*. Responding to the violence of the terrorist underground, the actions of the government forces were designed not only to break up the Montonero guerrilla groups, but also to deprive the labor movement and the country as a whole of its Peronist leaders.[2] Most of the persons who "disappeared" were killed, although some are said to have slipped into exile abroad. While Major General Luciano Menéndez once remarked ironically that the *desaparecidos* included "five thousand mistakes,"[3] most of them represented those most willing to take action against military rule. Over time, the kidnapings eliminated the most vocal opponents of the government, and the number of "disappearances" fell from more than four hundred per month in 1977 to one per month in 1980 and 1981. In July, 1981, the Viola government even felt secure enough to allow Isabel Perón to leave the house arrest under which she had been held for five years and to return unobtrusively to Madrid, where she had lived so long in exile with Perón.

The economic failures of the military governments since 1976 underscore structural conflicts within Argentina. In contrast to Perón's orientation, which was to increase the real purchasing power of the working class, the strategy after 1976 was to hold down wages and raise output, to encourage profits and — it was hoped — reinvestment from those who controlled the agricultural and industrial wealth of the nation. Yet this strategy failed: inflation, which had dropped dramatically from the 600 percent annual rate of the Isabel Perón presidency, nevertheless rose to about 150 percent for most of 1981; Argentina suffered from 13 percent unemployment; and some 1,800 firms fell into bankruptcy in the first nine months of 1981 alone.

Whereas many Argentines had welcomed a change in government in 1976, hoping for economic stability and growth, five years later they had become greatly disillusioned with the inability of the military governments to achieve these goals.

This pattern of hopes and frustrations has occurred over and over again in recent Argentine history, as in the ascension of Perón in 1946, his political demise in 1955, the rise of Frondizi in 1958, Onganía's takeover in 1966, and the return of Perón in 1973. Labor is pitted against management, and neither wins in the long run. Unlike the situation in Japan, where labor and management work closely together, where they increase productivity and raise wages through technological innovation, labor and management in Argentina — and those governments that try mainly to uphold one or the other — assume that one must win out, and eventually they both lose in the process of confrontation. This conflict takes place in the context of highly inflated popular expectations, which have been heightened both by the Argentines' traditional view of themselves and of their country as an especially prosperous nation and also by Perón's emphasis upon sharing the national bounty among all economic groups. Confrontations among groups of Argentines, which prevent the greater consensus and growth from which all would benefit, defeat the possibility of achieving the wide national consensus that Perón tried to construct in the last years of his life.

Peronism, however, remains a vital political force, still central to Argentine politics nearly a decade after the death of General Perón. *World Business Weekly*, although far from sympathetic to the Peronists, notes quite rightly that "Peronism remains Argentina's most vital political force."[4] The movement has always enjoyed multiclass support, and it continues to do so today. As the analyses of the 1973 elections reveal, the largest numbers of Peronist supporters are still found among the least privileged members of Argentine society. Groups on the left and on the right continue to conjure in the general's name, although, given his actions each time he held the presidency, the latter have more genuine cause to do so than the former.

In diverse ways, the Falklands/Malvinas war of 1982 also reveals the continuing strength of Peronism. General Galtieri, whose government initiated the invasion of the islands on April 2, not only resembled Perón as a highly magnetic public speaker. More fundamentally, Galtieri, like Perón, felt that Argentina had an urge to greatness, a need to realize the potential that it had always possessed. The taking of the Malvinas Islands, as the Argentines call the Falklands, and the initially successful expulsion of the British marines achieved one of Perón's oldest objectives. At least verbally, the other Latin American nations sided with Argentina in meetings of the Organization of American States and the United Nations, creating a firm stance against the European countries and the United States that supported the British. Perón always stressed the need for Latin American unity, and this was a special concern of the last year of his life.

Furthermore, the invasion of the Falklands united Argentines behind their government. Anglo-Argentines were especially vocal in their support of the repatriation of the Malvinas. If, indeed, they had been able to show the eighteen hundred islanders of British descent how very well Anglo-Argentines live on the mainland — as an historically prosperous and prestigious ethnic group within the Argentine community, enjoying their own schools, clubs, and traditions — the islanders might well have opted for closer ties to Argentina and eventual Argentine sovereignty, thus solving the central British concern for "self-determination." As Argentine leaders have frequently pointed out, it would also have changed the situation greatly if Britain had allowed Argentines to immigrate to the islands; it is self-serving of the British to stress "self-determination" when loyal Britishers are the only ones who have ever been allowed to settle there. With such considerations in mind, other Argentines also firmly backed the invasion. From exile in Cuba and Mexico, members of the Montoneros, whose comrades had been cut down by Argentine military and police forces in the 1970s, even offered to return to fight alongside the military in order to keep control of the Malvinas. Such an outpouring of unity, patriotic pride, and willingness to sacrifice would have pleased Perón.

On the darker side, however, among the precipitate causes of the 1982 invasion were continuing economic failures and the growing manifestation of political dissent. Argentina had claimed sovereignty of the Malvinas for a century and a half; the decline of British military power relative to Argentina's after World War II made an invasion seem comparatively feasible by the 1980s. With offshore fishing and mineral exploration rights having recently been extended to two hundred miles, the islands had taken on far greater significance, especially as a source of petroleum and natural gas; moreover, claiming the islands became a means of strengthening the Argentine claim to South Georgia, the South Sandwich Islands, and a large slice of the Antarctic continent. Also, in 1981 and early 1982, the administration of President Ronald Reagan moved far closer than the Carter administration had been, with its focus on human rights, to Argentina's military government. With Reagan's opposition to leftist insurgency in Central America, Argentines naturally assumed that, since Washington was now courting their favor, it might remain neutral rather than providing support for the British.

Even when these underlying causes of the invasion are weighed in the balance, however, failures of Argentina's military governments since 1976 must be weighed as well. In early 1982, Argentine unemployment continued at 13 percent, while inflation stood at about 120 percent a year. The economy was stagnant, and the foreign debt was very high, even before the huge military expenditures of the confrontation with Britain. Although many CGT militants had been killed or exiled in the past six years, the CGT thus launched a major march in Buenos Aires to protest economic failures and political repression. Less than three days later, the invasion of the Malvinas began. After the first rush of nationalistic euphoria and unity, and especially after the British retook South Georgia island eight hundred miles to the east of the Malvinas, Argentines became more openly critical of government decisions. Crowds in the Plaza de Mayo began to sing old Peronist songs, to shout "yes" for the repatriation of the Malvinas but "no" for the military junta. In this sense too, the old antagonisms between Peronism and one side of the Argentine military are also playing themselves out in the 1980s.[5]

Scholarly interpretations of Peronism help us to understand the reasons for this continuing importance in Argentine politics and, without any dogmatic forecasting of the future, to gauge its likely impact in the years ahead. Wayne Smith has meticulously detailed how much the return of Peronism in 1973 was the result of increasing popular dissatisfaction with the military governments of the late 1960s and early 1970s. If Isabel Perón and other leaders of the movement are regaining stature today, a major reason is once again the failure of military leaders to achieve economic growth as well as stability. The controversy over incomes policies analyzed by Gary Wynia remains central in the conflict of labor and management, while investigation of the status insecurities of industrialists vis-à-vis large landowners indicates one reason why the groups dominant in recent years are by no means as cohesive as their enemies sometimes caricature them to be. In studying the extent of popular support for guerrilla attacks on the military in 1973, Roberto Guimarães has shown that guerrilla activities were essentially a political option; since 1976 the military has dealt with it ruthlessly, eliminating groups of guerrilla opponents by killing off their members and sympathizers, so that, at least for the moment, the semiofficial terror of the government-supporting death squads has replaced the antigovernment terror of the Montoneros and the other guerrilla groups.

Both quantitative and historical descriptions of Peronism also help us to understand its continuing appeal. Marysa Navarro emphasizes the sincerity of Perón and the crucial role of Evita in advancing his career and promoting his popularity; this continuing commitment is also described in the work of such Peronist labor leaders as Juan Carlos D'Abate. The electoral analysis of Manuel Mora y Araujo and Peter Smith reveals how strongly Perón was supported by the least advantaged sectors of Argentine society in 1973; one can only expect an attachment to the memory of Perón to continue and intensify when these sectors are, comparatively, put at an even greater disadvantage by the economic strategies of the military governments since 1976. Quite in contrast to the exotic and rather self-serving interpretations of foreign scholars, José Miguens has shown Perón to be consistently a Catholic nationalist, one who drew his commitment to the less privileged and to the nation from some of the deepest historical and religious roots of Argentine culture. Nevertheless, as Antonio Donini points out, present cleavages within the Argentine Catholic church reflect divisions in the society as a whole, so that the church in Argentina has not been easily able to champion the reforms of Perón, as, for instance, the church in Chile has done, in administering social welfare policies initiated by the late Salvador Allende.

How does Perón contrast with Allende, Fidel Castro, and the other major leaders of Latin America in this century? A faithful husband, unlike Allende, he differed considerably from both Allende and Castro in his politics. In his public career he remained far more supportive of private enterprise than they were. In the 1940s and 1950s, Perón was frequently compared to Getúlio Vargas, the "populist" president of Brazil, but the contrasts between Brazil and Argentina remain striking. Despite the legacy of Vargas, the Brazilian economy as led by Juscelino Kubitschek in the late 1950s and by a series of military presidents since 1964 has produced striking (if unevenly distributed) economic growth, with sophisticated technology used to spur higher and higher levels of both industrial and agricultural production and exports. Vargas never gave Brazilian labor the stake in the system that Perón did in Argentina; the co-optation and repression of labor have proved far more successful in Brazil than in Argentina. Finally, perhaps the most revealing contrast to Perón in twentieth-century Latin America is Lázaro Cárdenas, the Mexican president from 1934 to 1940. Firmly committed to leaving office after one term, Cárdenas led the revolutionary party to be organized around groups representing the major occupational sectors of society; this reform has helped to allow the presidency to rotate to a new leader of the party every six years since 1934. While Mexico's economic growth was not as pronounced under Cárdenas as it was later to become, Cárdenas distributed massive amounts of land to give practical assistance to the poor, revived belief in the best ideals of the 1910 Revolution, engineered a political party to carry on his reforms, and thus laid the foundation of political stability upon which the Mexican economy could grow. Cárdenas's ideals were not so different from Perón's, but the ways in which he was able to alter the political and economic system of his nation differed greatly.

With these contrasts among leaders in mind, one might be tempted to speculate as to whether the "Argentine experience" is a portent for other nations, in Latin America or in other parts of the world. Generally, this remains rather unlikely. Just as Argentina has been shaped in recent decades by the appeals and the limitations of Juan Perón, so each nation is shaped by its own leaders, its natural resources, its culture, and its historical inheritance. The potential benefits of Mexican economic growth remain curtailed by heavy population increases and a level of political corruption and venality that is high by any standards. Brazil continues its pattern of exceptional industrial and agricultural growth; its problems result from the cost of foreign petroleum more than from inadequacies of leadership. Cuba enjoys a more even distribution of goods but is far slower in producing them than Brazil, as Castro sends his troops into Africa and remains dependent on massive subsidies from the Soviet Union. The Bolivian elite becomes wealthy from trade in cocaine, while generals replace each other in the presidential chair more often than once a year. In Uruguay, the utopian days of high wages, advanced social legislation, and the welfare state are gone, as the military takeover of the early 1970s was in part the result of a stagnating economy and years of neglected productivity. It would be difficult to argue convincingly that the "Argentine experience" is a portent for Latin America any more than is the experience of Mexico, Brazil, Cuba, Bolivia, or Uruguay.

Yet the experience of Argentina in the years of Perón may teach a sobering lesson, one of general relevance to many countries. At the very least, it demonstrates that good intentions are insufficient in the political world. Redistributing income in favor of the poor, even giving them an emotional and political stake in decision making at the national level, may not be the surest way to increase the people's welfare in the long run. The fall of socialist governments in Norway and in Sweden, the rise of Margaret Thatcher in Britain and of Ronald Reagan in the United States, suggest a turning away from the egalitarian, often distributionist policies associated with Perón and other "populists." Perón himself found that redistribution of the national wealth alone was no solution. It remains to be seen whether the economic strategies of the neoconservatives who have replaced socialists and populists in so many countries will in fact bring more rapid economic advancement, and, *if* they do, whether in the long run the lower classes will enjoy more economic or psychological security as a result. The Argentine case does demonstrate the difficulties and the confrontations that may result when leaders greatly encourage expectations. But, when the expectations of the poor are held down decade after decade, can this genuinely produce an economic system in which they (or their descendants) materially benefit?

Whatever the impact of rising expectations in other nations, General Perón profoundly stimulated them in Argentina, and in doing so he lastingly reshaped his country. Unlike the ephemeral military caudillos who preceded and succeeded him, in Argentina and in so many nations of Latin America, Perón created attitudes, expectations, and a political movement that were to survive him. Perón did this not under circumstances chosen by himself, but, in Marx's words, "under circumstances directly encountered, given and transmitted from the past." Through the efforts of Perón and Evita, members of the working class and Argentine women — who had known only marginal political effect in the past — came to experience political participation to an extent that assured their participation in the future. Perón's own failure to engineer self-sustaining economic growth, or a broad national consensus on growth and distribution, or a unified party that could function without him — none of these failures would terminate the impact of Peronism. Neither would the economic "farce" of the government of Isabel Perón, nor would the killing or kidnaping of thousands of Argentines by military governments between 1976 and 1981. Those who are longest remembered in history — Christ or Lincoln, Marx or Sarmiento — are known, not so much for parties or movements that they founded, but for the quality of their ideas, for the force of their dreams, the appeal of their ideals. So too, perhaps, should Perón be remembered, not for what he was able to achieve, but for what he wanted for others, what he foresaw in the future and tried to bring closer to fruition.

NOTES

1. Karl Marx, *The Eighteenth Brumaire of Louis Bonaparte*, in Karl Marx and Frederick Engels, *Collected Works* (New York: International Publishers, 1979), vol. 11, p. 103.

2. *Amnesty International Report 1981* (London: Amnesty International Publications, 1981), p. 108. Other estimates of the total number of *desaparecidos* since 1976 range from a low of 6,000 to a high of about 24,000, with many estimates falling at about 15,000.

3. Quoted in "Córdoba: Argentina's Second City," *Atlantic*, Nov. 1981, p. 16.

4. "Argentina: Rising Impatience with the Military," *World Business Weekly*, 12 Oct. 1981, p. 11.

5. For more detailed analysis of Argentina after the Falklands/Malvinas war, see Frederick C. Turner, "The Aftermath of Defeat in Argentina," *Current History* 82 (1983), 58–61, 85–87.

Appendix

MARISABEL BRÁS CASTRO

A Chronology
of the Public Career of Perón

1895
October 8. Juan Domingo Perón is born in Lobos, a small town in the Province of Buenos Aires, Argentina.

1911
March 1. Perón enters the Colegio Militar, the national military academy, at the age of fifteen.

1913
December 13. Perón graduates from the Colegio Militar with the rank of *subteniente* in the infantry.

1915
December 31. Perón is promoted to lieutenant.

1916
June 12. Dr. Hipólito Yrigoyen is elected president of Argentina.
October 12. Yrigoyen assumes office as president.

1919
May 7. Eva Duarte is born to a poverty-stricken family in the small pampa town of Los Toldos.
December 31. Perón is promoted to first lieutenant.

1924
December 31. Perón is promoted to captain.

1926
September 21. Perón meets his first wife, Aurelia Tizón.

1929
January 5. Perón marries Aurelia Tizón in the Iglesia Nuestra Señora de Luján.

1930
September 6. Yrigoyen is removed from office by a coup. General José F. Uriburu assumes control.
December 1. Perón becomes a professor of military history in the Escuela Superior de Guerra.

1931

February 4. "Isabel" Perón, née María Estela Martínez Cartas, is born in La Rioja, a provincial capital in Argentina.

December 31. Perón is promoted to major.

1936

December 31. Perón is promoted to lieutenant colonel while serving as military attaché in Chile.

1937

September 22. Dr. Roberto M. Ortiz is elected president, receiving 248 electoral votes out of 376 in the electoral college. His leading opponent, Marcelo T. de Alvear, Radical party leader, receives 128 electoral votes.

1938

February 20. Ortiz assumes office as president.

September 10. Perón's first wife, Aurelia Tizón de Perón, dies of cancer.

1939

February 17. Perón becomes an observer in the Italian army.

1940

July 3. President Ortiz delegates his power to Ramón S. Castillo, his vice-president, due to illness.

August 22. President Ortiz resigns.

1941

January 8. Perón returns from Italy; he is assigned to command mountain troops in Mendoza.

October 14. Argentina signs an agreement with the United States to resolve shortages caused by World War II.

1942

March 21. Perón is reassigned to the federal capital; he promotes the organization of the Grupo de Oficiales Unidos (GOU), a secret military lodge.

1943

June 4. A coup encouraged by the Grupo de Oficiales Unidos (GOU) overthrows the Castillo government. Heading the insurrection are General Pedro Pablo Ramírez, the minister of war under Castillo, and General Arturo Rawson. The Constitution is suspended.

June 5. General Rawson dissolves Congress and names a mixture of pro-Axis and pro-Allied ministers to the cabinet.

June 6. General Ramírez replaces General Rawson as chief of state and appoints a new cabinet.

June 8. Perón is named undersecretary of war.

October 27. Strikes break out all over the country, indicating labor opposition to Ramírez. Perón is appointed head of the National Labor Department.

November 27. The Secretaría de Trabajo y Previsión (the Secretariat of Labor and Social Security) is created.

December 3. Perón is named head of the Secretariat of Labor and Social Security. Perón requires employers to give employees one month's salary bonus each year (the *aguinaldo*).

December 10. Perón is appointed director general of civil aeronautics.

December 31. All political parties are dissolved.

1944

January 26. President Ramírez severs Argentine relations with the Axis.

February 24. The GOU expels Ramírez in a bloodless coup and replaces him with the vice-president, General Edelmiro Farrell.

February 26. Perón is named provisional minister of war in the new government.

May 1. Perón holds the first of the great May Day rallies.

May 4. Perón is named minister of war.

June 7. Perón is named vice-president of Argentina.

1945

March 27. Argentina declares war on Germany and Japan.

September 19. Demonstrators in Buenos Aires support freedom and a restoration of the Constitution.

October 9. The Campo de Mayo garrison applies pressure on the Farrell administration to force Perón to resign his three governmental posts: vice-president, minister of war, and secretary of labor and social welfare.

October 10. Perón in a last public appearance makes a nationwide radio address to workers.

October 13. Perón is detained and confined on the Isla de Martín García; his friends begin organizing a labor protest.

October 16. Labor demonstrations begin in Greater Buenos Aires; workers concentrate in the Plaza de Mayo.

October 17. Perón emerges from five days' detention after mass demonstrations in the Plaza de Mayo by his supporters, the *descamisados*, the "shirtless ones." He declines reinstatement to his government posts in order to become a presidential candidate. October 17 henceforth is known as the Día de la Lealtad (Day of Loyalty); the clear, sunny weather in Buenos Aires on each subsequent celebration while Perón is in office adds to the aura and myth that surround Perón.

October 21. Perón marries Eva Duarte in Buenos Aires.

October 23. One hundred fifty-three labor leaders found the Partido Laborista, which with the Junta Renovadora of the Unión Cívica Radical nominate Perón as a presidential candidate for the February 24, 1946, election.

1946

February 24. The first honest presidential election since 1928 is held. Perón is elected president, receiving 1,487,886 votes (52.40 percent) out of 2,839,507 ballots cast. The other candidate, Dr. José Tamborini, receives 1,207,080 votes (42.51 percent).

June 4. Perón assumes office as president.

October 21. Perón presents in Congress the outline of a vast five-year plan for industrialization and development.

Appendix

1947

March 1. British-owned railways are nationalized.

July 9. Perón presents the Act of Economic Independence.

October 15. Women obtain the right to vote, gaining full equality with men in the franchise.

1948

September 20. Noncommissioned officers receive the right to vote.

1949

March 11. Congress approves the new Constitution, permitting Perón's reelection.

July 25. The Peronist party is officially founded. It is the first party in Argentine history officially named for one person.

July 26. The Feminist Peronist party is founded.

December 27. Perón is promoted to major general at a special session of the Senate.

1950

October 17. Perón presents the Twenty Truths of Justicialism, a series of slogans for his movement.

1951

February 27. The Perón government expropriates *La Prensa,* a conservative newspaper highly critical of the government.

August 22. *Descamisados* demand that Eva Perón accept the nomination to run for vice-president of Argentina. She does, but then withdraws allegedly because of military pressure, giving as the official reason her being under the necessary age limit stated in the Constitution.

September 28. A segment of the army revolts against the government, but is suppressed.

November 11. Perón is reelected to a second term as president of Argentina, receiving 4,745,168 votes (62.49 percent) out of a total of 7,593,948 ballots. His major opponent, Ricardo Balbín of the Radical party, receives 2,415,750 votes (31.81 percent). Peronists control both houses of Congress and all provincial governments.

1952

February 3. A plot to assassinate Perón is uncovered. Over one hundred are arrested.

May 7. Congress confers on Perón the title of Liberator of the Republic.

May 21. In an attempt to reduce the army budget, Perón grants the Ministry of War full authority and resources to achieve economic self-sufficiency.

June 4. Perón is inaugurated for his second term as president. Eva Perón makes a last public appearance.

July 26. Eva Perón dies of cancer.

1953

August 26. The Perón government passes a law to attract foreign investment in industry, mining, and petroleum development.

1954

November 10. Perón becomes openly critical of the Catholic church with a speech in which he charges the church with interfering in labor relations and trying to build up a separate party.

1955

March 29. Perón signs an agreement with the Standard Oil Company of California to exploit petroleum reserves in Patagonia.

May 1. Supporters of Perón call for the separation of church and state.

June 16. The pope excommunicates Perón. Elements of the air force and navy revolt against the government, but the army suppresses them. Several hundred civilians are killed in the fighting. Several historic Catholic churches and the offices of the archbishop are deliberately set afire.

July 5. Perón calls for the cessation of political strife.

July 15. Perón resigns his leadership of the Peronist party, and announces an end to his twelve-year revolution.

July 28. In a radio broadcast replying to Perón, Arturo Frondizi, a leader of the Radical party and critic of the government, says that there can be no peace without freedom.

August 31. Perón offers his resignation as president, but then withdraws it and makes an incendiary speech when members of the General Confederation of Labor (CGT) stage another mass rally reminiscent of that on October 17, 1945.

September 16. General Eduardo Lonardi in Córdoba proclaims a Liberating Revolution and gains some support from all branches of the armed forces.

September 17. The Cuyo garrison rebels in support of Lonardi.

September 18. Ships of the Argentine navy appear at the entrance of the Río de la Plata, threatening to blow up oil tanks and refineries if the Peronists fail to concede.

September 19–22. A military junta in Buenos Aires takes over from Perón, who takes refuge on a Paraguayan gunboat.

September 23. General Lonardi is installed as provisional president of Argentina, promising a speedy return to constitutional, democratic government.

November 7. Perón arrives in Panama from Paraguay.

November 13. Leaders of the armed forces depose Lonardi on the grounds that he has reactionary advisors. General Pedro E. Aramburu replaces him as provisional president.

November 30. President Aramburu declares the abolition of the Peronist party and the release of *La Prensa* from control by the CGT; it is returned to its original owners.

1956

March 6. Peronist union leaders are banned from holding union offices by official decree.

May 1. Perón's Constitution of 1949 is annulled, and the 1853 Constitution is restored.

June 9. When Peronists in the army move against the Aramburu government, the coup is aborted and Peronist leaders are executed.

July 19. Perón moves from Panama to Managua, Nicaragua.

August 8. Perón moves to Caracas, Venezuela.

1958

January 27. Perón moves to Ciudad Trujillo, Dominican Republic.

February 5. Perón exhorts his followers to vote for Arturo Frondizi, in the February 23 presidential elections.

February 11. Perón is asked to leave the Dominican Republic "without delay" because he violated the asylum given him there by using the Dominican mails to send instructions to his Argentine followers.

February 23. Dr. Arturo Frondizi, candidate of the Radical party, is elected president with Peronist support, gaining 2,128,523 votes (46.65 percent) out of 4,562,676 ballots cast. His opponent, Ricardo Balbín, receives 1,273,086 votes (27.90 percent).

May 1. Frondizi is inaugurated as president.

November 11. President Frondizi dismisses those advisors who favor integration with the Peronists.

1959

January 1. In economic policy shifts, most government subsidies and price controls are dropped, restrictions are placed on imports, and it is announced that wage hikes must be limited to increases in productivity.

September 2. General Carlos Severo Toranzo leads an unsuccessful army rebellion against the Frondizi administration.

1960

January 25. Perón leaves Ciudad Trujillo for Spain aboard a Brazilian airliner.

March 13. A state of siege is declared.

December 24. The platform of the Intransigent Radicals is adjusted to policies followed by the Frondizi administration since 1958, becoming more conservative and less appealing to the Peronists, as it drops references to agrarian reform, government ownership of industry, and state planning for the economy.

1961

December 27. Perón secretly marries María Estela ("Isabel") Martínez in Spain.

1962

March 18. Peronists are allowed to present their own candidates in state elections for the first time since 1955, but when the election results are favorable to them, President Frondizi, in agreement with the armed forces, suspends the consequences of the elections.

April 20–21. Divisions erupt in the army; a clash is averted by the retirement of rival chiefs.

August 8–12. A new confrontation emerges between the *colorados* and the *azules*, two factions in the Argentine army.

September 18–23. Armed conflict occurs between the *colorados* and the *azules*.

1963

April 2. The navy stages an unsuccessful revolt.

April. 16. The number of admirals is reduced from twenty-seven to two.

July 3. From Madrid, Perón orders his followers to cast blank ballots in the upcoming Argentine elections.

July 5. Dr. Arturo Illía, candidate of the Popular Radical party, wins the presidential election, gaining 2,441,064 votes (25.14 percent) out of a total of 9,710,116 ballots. The runner-up, Oscar Alende, receives 1,593,002 votes (16.41 percent). With Peronist candidates banned, 1,884,435 votes (19.41 percent) are cast blank.

October 12. Illía is inaugurated as president.

1964

December 2. Perón attempts to reenter Argentina through Brazil without being detected, but his plane is turned back in Rio de Janeiro. He returns to Spain.

December 17–18. The CGT stages a general strike after the public announcement of Perón's attempted return.

1965

March 1. Peronist political activity is once again permitted in elections.

June 7. Overt evidence appears of a break between the Illía administration and the military.

October 11. Perón's third wife, María Estela ("Isabel") Martínez de Perón, arrives in Buenos Aires to bring about a common front among Peronist factions. She becomes a center of speculation and political intrigue.

November 23. General Juan Carlos Onganía resigns as commander-in-chief of the Argentine army and retires from the service, reflecting an open breach between the military and the Illía government.

1966

June 28. A military junta ousts Illía, removes all provincial governors, dissolves Congress, and proclaims the Argentine Revolution.

June 29. General Onganía is selected by the junta as president. Police and troops close the University of Buenos Aires.

November 8. President Onganía announces the removal of controls from the peso and from exports.

1967

March 1. When railway workers strike, President Onganía reacts strongly, further antagonizing labor.

April 23. Onganía issues a decree revoking the right of university students, both graduate and undergraduate, to participate in the determination of university policies.

1969

May 29. The important Cordobazo takes place, as students and workers in the city of Córdoba take up arms against the military, causing the government to abandon the wage-freezing, anti-inflationary policies of the economic minister Adalbert Krieger Vasena. This proves a turning point for the Onganía government, making it far more short-lived than it had promised to be.

May 30. A state of siege is declared.

June 30. Terrorists murder Augusto Vandor, head of the Metal Workers' Union and a leader of the moderates in the labor movement.

1970

May 29. On the first anniversary of the Cordobazo, former provisional President Aramburu is kidnaped by Montonero guerrillas who later kill him.

June 8. The commanders in chief of the armed forces depose President Onganía and replace him with General Roberto Marcelo Levingston, then serving as the Argentine delegate to the Inter-American Defense Board in Washington.

July 16. The body of Pedro Aramburu is found in the cellar of an old farmhouse near Buenos Aires.

1971

March 23. Army leaders depose President Levingston.

March 26. General Alejandro Agustín Lanusse, the commander in chief of the army, is sworn in as president.

April 1. Political parties, which had been outlawed in 1966 following the military coup, are legalized.

August 11. Long lines of Perón followers register, for the first time in sixteen years, for membership in his Justicialist party.

1972

July 7. Lanusse announces the adoption of a residential clause prohibiting anyone not establishing residence in Argentina prior to August 25, 1972, from running for public office.

November 17. Perón returns to Argentina.

December 14. Perón departs for Paraguay, Peru, and Europe. Héctor José Cámpora, a long-time Perón spokesman, is nominated as the Peronist presidential candidate due to Perón's failure to meet the residence requirement.

1973

February 6. The Lanusse government bars Perón from returning to Argentina.

February 24. Lanusse goes to Spain for an official visit of four days.

March 11. Cámpora wins the presidential election, receiving 5,908,414 votes (49.56 percent) out of a total of 11,920,925 ballots cast. Other major candidates were Ricardo Balbín, with 2,537,605 votes (21.29 percent), Francisco Manrique, with 1,775,867 votes (14.90 percent), and Oscar Alende, with 885,201 votes (7.43 percent).

March 25. Cámpora flies to Rome for consultation with Perón.

April 30. When left-wing guerrillas assassinate Rear Admiral Hermes Guijada, the government declares a state of emergency and tensions increase greatly.

May 25. Cámpora is inaugurated, pledging complete loyalty to Perón. Congress enacts broad amnesty for those confined or hunted for political crimes including acts of terrorism.

June 15. Cámpora arrives in Spain for a four-day conference with Perón.

June 20. Perón returns to Argentina with Cámpora; massive demonstrations greet him. Gunfire erupts at Ezeiza airport between rival Peronist factions, killing and wounding hundreds of people.

July 13. Cámpora resigns as president, to be succeeded by Raúl Lastiri, president of the National Chamber of Deputies.

July 20. The government sets new presidential elections for September 23, and the inauguration for October 12.

August 4. The Justicialist party nominates Perón for president and his third wife, Isabel, for vice-president.

September 23. Perón is elected president of Argentina for the third time in a free election, winning 7,378,249 votes (61.85 percent). The other major candidate, Ricardo Balbín, wins 2,905,236 votes (24.34 percent).

October 12. Perón is inaugurated as president.

1974

June 29. Isabel Martínez de Perón becomes acting president with full executive powers, while Perón remains under intense medical care.

July 1. Perón dies of a heart attack.

August 1. Montoneros resume guerrilla warfare, seriously threatening the ability of President Isabel Perón to govern.

September 19. Political violence continues in Buenos Aires and other cities as a right-wing group, the Argentine Anticommunist Alliance (AAA), steps up its campaign to murder several dozen prominent leftists.

November 6. President Isabel Perón places the nation under a state of siege as political assassinations and other terrorist attacks continue.

1976

February 16. Isabel Perón closes a special session of Congress as political, labor, and management leaders urge her to resign to avert a military coup.

February 18. Mrs. Perón announces that she will not run for a full term later in 1976 but that she will complete her current term scheduled to end in May, 1977.

February 20. Mrs. Perón's government announces that the elections will take place on December 12.

March 24. A coup overthrows Isabel Perón, replacing her with army commander Jorge Videla as president.

March 29. General Videla and his cabinet formally assume power.

Sources: Most of the facts in the chronology were taken from *The New York Times* and *Facts on File.* Other sources consulted were Carlos S. Fayt, ed., *La naturaleza del peronismo* (Buenos Aires: Viracocha Editores-Distribuidores, 1967); Enrique Pavón Pereyra, *Vida de Perón* (Buenos Aires: Editorial Justicialista, 1965) and *Perón, preparación de una vida para el mundo* (Buenos Aires: Ediciones Espiño, 1952); Bernardo Rabinovitz, *Sucedió en la Argentina (1943-1956): Lo que no se dijo* (Buenos Aires: Ediciones Gure, 1956); Román J. Lombille, *Eva Perón: Su verdadera vida* (Buenos Aires: Ediciones Gure, 1955); Robert A. Potash, *The Army and Politics in Argentina, 1928-1945* (Stanford, Calif.: Stanford University Press, 1969); Ernesto Palacio, *Historia de la Argentina,* vol. 5 (Buenos Aires: Editorial Revisión, 1976); and Russell H. Fitzgibbon, *Argentina: A Chronology and Fact Book, 1516-1973* (New York: Oceana Publications, 1974). The results of the elections were taken from Darío Cantón, *Materiales para el estudio de la sociología política en la Argentina* (Buenos Aires: Centro de Investigaciones Sociales, Instituto Torcuato Di Tella, 1968). The dates used in all chapters of this book are fully congruent with this chronology. Robert A. Potash of the University of Massachusetts, Marysa Navarro of Darmouth College, and José Enrique Miguens made especially helpful comments on an earlier draft of this chronology.

Notes on Contributors

MARISABEL BRÁS CASTRO, a candidate for the Ph.D. at the University of Connecticut, is an instructor in the Departamento de Ciencias Sociales at the University of Puerto Rico, Mayagüez Campus. She has served on the executive commitee of the New England Council on Latin American Studies, and has published in the *Revista Cayey*.

JUAN CARLOS D'ABATE, who graduated in law from the University of Buenos Aires, is a Peronist politician of long standing. A former consultant to the Confederación General de la República Argentina, Empleados de Comercio, one of the largest and most responsible trade unions in Argentina, he also directed its Escuela Sindical from 1970 to 1976. During the 1962 elections, he served as a campaign manager for the Peronists in the Province of Buenos Aires. He has recently published *El antipoder sindical* and articles in various journals, including *Derecho del Trabajo*.

ANTONIO O. DONINI has been a professor for the last sixteen years and chair of the Department of Sociology at California State College, Stanislaus. Both before and after he received the Ph.D. from the Università Gregoriana in 1960, his research and writing have focused upon the sociology of religion, especially in Argentina. Currently, he is teaching at the Universidad Nacional de Rosario.

ROBERTO P. GUIMARÃES is deputy secretary for modernization and administrative reform of the Secretariat of Planning of the presidency of Brazil, and a lecturer at the Escola Interamericana de Administração Pública of the Fundação Getúlio Vargas. He is currently completing his doctoral dissertation in political science at the University of Connecticut and has contributed to the recent volume, *Qualidade de vida en áreas urbanas*, edited by Amaury de Souza.

JOSÉ ENRIQUE MIGUENS has chaired the Department of Sociology at the Catholic University of Argentina and directed the Institute of Motivational and Social Research in Buenos Aires, as well as working in the presidency under both Peronist and non-Peronist governments, carrying out research at the Instituto Torcuato di Tella, and serving on the board of directors of the Bariloche Foundation. After receiving the Ph.D. from the University of Buenos Aires in 1946, he has directed thirty-three major surveys in Argentina and written a wide variety of books and articles on social and political topics.

MANUEL MORA Y ARAUJO was director of the Centro de Investigaciones Sociales at the Instituto Torcuato di Tella in Buenos Aires, and is at present the head of the graduate training program at that institute. He is the author of numerous articles in *Desarrollo Económico*, *Criterio*, and other journals; with Ignacio Llorente, he has edited a book entitled *El voto peronista*. He received his degree in sociology from the Latin American Faculty of Social Sciences in Santiago in 1963.

MARYSA NAVARRO, professor of history and chair of women's studies at Dartmouth College, has published *Los nacionalistas* and, with Nicholas Fraser, a biography entitled *Eva Perón*. Her articles have appeared in *Studies in International Development, SIGNS: Journal of Women in Culture and Society, Les Temps Modernes,* and the *Journal of Latin American Studies.* She is president of the New England Council on Latin American Studies, and received the Ph.D. from Columbia University in 1964.

FREDERICK C. TURNER is professor of political science at the University of Connecticut, where he also serves on the executive committee of the board of directors of the Roper Center. A past president of the New England Council on Latin American Studies, he has received fellowships from the National Science Foundation and the National Endowment for the Humanities. His work includes books on *The Dynamic of Mexican Nationalism, Catholicism and Political Development in Latin America,* and *Responsible Parenthood: The Politics of Mexico's New Population Policies,* and articles in *Science,* the *American Behavioral Scientist,* and the *Journal of Politics.* He obtained the Ph.D. from the Fletcher School of Law and Diplomacy in 1965.

PETER H. SMITH is professor of history and political science at the Massachusetts Institute of Technology and past president of the Latin American Studies Association. He has also taught at Dartmouth College and, from 1968 to 1980, at the University of Wisconsin, where he was professor of history, chair of the Department of History, and associate dean of the graduate school. His books include *Politics and Beef in Argentina: Patterns of Conflict and Change; Argentina and the Failure of Democracy: Conflict Among Political Elites, 1904–1955; Labyrinths of Power: Political Recruitment in Twentieth-Century Mexico;* and *Mexico: The Quest for a U.S. Policy.* He has received a Guggenheim fellowship and served on the national review boards of the Social Science Research Council and the Tinker Foundation. He obtained the Ph.D. from Columbia University in 1966.

WAYNE S. SMITH, now a senior associate at the Carnegie Endowment for International Peace, was chief of the U.S. Interests Section in Havana from 1979 until he left the foreign service in 1982. He was political officer at the American embassy in Buenos Aires from July 1972 until May 1977. During that time, he wrote his doctoral dissertation on the political process leading up to the Argentine elections of 1973. He received the Ph.D. from George Washington University in 1980, and has published articles in *Foreign Policy, Intellectual Digest, Orbis, Problems of Communism,* and other journals.

GARY W. WYNIA is professor of political science at the University of Minnesota. He has been a Fulbright fellow in Argentina and written *Argentina in the Postwar Era: Politics and Economic Policy Making in a Divided Society.* Also the author of *The Politics of Latin American Development* and *Politics and Planners: Economic Development Policy in Central America,* he received the Ph.D. from the University of Wisconsin in 1970.

Index

PITT LATIN AMERICAN SERIES

Cole Blasier, Editor